Discovering
English
Grammar

Contestant #3: Grammar for $300.

Alex: In *Discovering English Grammar*, Richard Veit says that it's okay to sometimes split these.

Contestant #1: What are infinitives?

Alex: That's it.

—*Jeopardy!*, December 22, 1994

Selected answers to exercises in *Discovering English Grammar* and other materials related to this book can be found at the following site on the World Wide Web:

www.uncwil.edu/people/veit/DEG

Discovering English Grammar

Second Edition

Richard Veit
University of North Carolina at Wilmington

Allyn and Bacon
Boston London Toronto Sydney Tokyo Singapore

This book is dedicated
to anyone who ever drew a tree diagram
and found that a little elf within the brain
was kicking up its heels and exclaiming,
"Hey, this is fun!"

Copyright © 1999 by Allyn & Bacon
A Pearson Education Company
160 Gould Street
Needham Heights, Massachusetts 02194-2130

Internet: www.abacon.com

Library of Congress Cataloging-in-Publication Data

Veit, Richard.
    Discovering English grammar / Richard Veit. -- 2nd ed.
        p.   cm.
    Includes bibliographical references and index.
    ISBN 0-205-28483-3
    1. English language--Grammar.   I. Title.
PE1112.V37 1998
428.2--dc21
                                            98-16612
                                            CIP

Printed in the United States of America

10 9 8 7 6 5 4 3 2 1   03 02 01 00 99 98

Contents

10 More Embedded Sentences: Adverbial Clauses and Relative Clauses

To the Instructor

Each semester, at the first meeting of my Structure of the English Language course, I make a non-financial "wager" with my students. I bet them that, when they fill out their anonymous evaluations at the end of the term, they will write that they found the course to be fun. I almost always see skepticism reflected in students' faces. But after the course has ended and the evaluations are returned, I learn in a large majority of cases that I have won my bet. The following response from a student is typical: "When you said this course would be fun, I thought you were crazy. I always hated grammar, and I only took the course because it was required. Now I have to admit you won your bet. Drawing trees was fun, and every exercise was like solving a puzzle."

I wrote *Discovering English Grammar* because I believe a textbook in syntax should reflect the joy and excitement that I feel for this fascinating subject. The many goals I had in mind as I wrote the book are as follows:

To teach a transformational approach to syntax   Transformational grammar is unquestionably the dominant school of modern linguistics. No other approach provides equivalent insights into the structure and workings of our language. What is more, I have found, no other approach lends itself so successfully to undergraduate teaching.

To provide broad coverage of the major constructions of the English language   Many textbooks, particularly those that teach transformational syntax, focus principally on the methodology of their approach, while examining a relatively few "interesting" constructions. In contrast, my purpose in this book is to offer a genuine survey of English grammatical structures. Methodological considerations have been made secondary to the goal of providing an understanding of the language itself. I want students who have used this book to feel confident that they "know English grammar."

To offer instruction that is clear to undergraduates in the liberal arts and in education
Many students who are not technically inclined have difficulty understanding advanced syntactic analysis, which can be quite complex and abstract. Accordingly, I have provided a "broad," rather than a "narrow," coverage of transformational syntax. When confronted with a conflict between complexity and clarity, I have always opted for clarity. I have eliminated many formalisms that are not necessary for students' understanding of the language, and I have generally chosen simpler, "classical" transformational analyses over more advanced but more difficult ones.

To teach grammar as a process of discovery   As its name implies, *Discovering English Grammar* does not teach grammatical information as received truth. Instead, it engages students as participants in an inductive search for the structure of the language. Students are asked to help discover the grammar of English by examining sentences and supplying hypotheses to account for them. In addition, the method of discovering grammar without relying on previous assumptions makes this book accessible to students who lack previous training in grammar.

To arrange material in a pedagogically useful way   Topics are not arranged according to a classification of constructions or parts of speech; instead, they are arranged in a practical teaching sequence. Simpler and more easily understood concepts precede more complicated ones. Concepts in later chapters build upon those in earlier chapters.

To offer frequent, useful exercises   Exercises are frequent and located throughout the text, not just at the ends of chapters. They provide experiences that reinforce lessons taught in preceding sections, and they challenge students to make their own discoveries about English grammar. Students are impelled not just to know grammar but to *do* grammar. Optional "discovery" exercises challenge students to think like grammarians as they solve syntactic problems on their own. Answers to selected exercises, posted on the book's website, allow students to monitor their progress.

To prepare future teachers of grammar   For those users of this book who will teach grammar in the schools, the best preparation is a thorough understanding of the English language. Although the approach of this book is transformational, readers will be prepared to teach with whatever materials and methods are mandated by their school systems. I have used widely accepted terminology throughout and include a chapter on teaching grammar in the schools.

To prepare students for more advanced syntactic study   For students who go on to more advanced work in linguistics, *Discovering English Grammar* offers the best preparation of all—a thorough familiarity with the structure of the language. Furthermore, the inductive method of this book instills a spirit of scientific inquiry that trains students to challenge hypotheses and to form new ones. Students who use this book will be well prepared to accommodate additional data and new theories and methods. Finally, Chapter 18 offers an introduction to advanced syntactic analysis.

And, as I said, **to stimulate students**   I have treated grammar with the same attitude of intellectual excitement that I feel for the subject. I have attempted to treat my readers with respect and to make my writing clear, straightforward, personal, and interesting.

New in the Second Edition

The second edition of *Discovering English Grammar* represents a thorough and painstaking revision. The aims and methodology have not changed, nor is the look of this edition strikingly different from the first. The difference is in the details. Having taught the book nearly every semester since its first publication, I have had constant opportunity to discover where students needed help with clearer explanations, less confusing formalisms, and additional or different exercises. To address those needs, I have added, modified, rearranged, and deleted, where appropriate. This edition also reflects the greater understanding of English syntax and grammar pedagogy that I have gained in the last decade. I have revised and class-tested the book repeatedly, and the result is the most teachable classroom text of which I am capable.

A few of the specific changes are the following:

- I have made the greatest revisions in areas where my students had the most difficulty, including the discussion of prepositional phrases, possessive determiners, and relative clauses.

- I have posted answers to selected exercises on the World Wide Web. Comparing their work with these answers allows students to monitor their success and learn from errors. I have not provided answers to all exercises, however, because students also need to be able to do grammar without a safety net.

- I have added a new chapter, Chapter 18: A Taste of Theoretical Syntax, to give interested students an introduction to advanced syntactic analysis.

A Note on the Text

This edition was printed from camera-ready copy that I provided, using two programs: WordPerfect for Windows for the text and RFFlow for the diagrams. Acting as my own typesetter gave me full control over the look and content of the book. It also means that any errors in the book are entirely my own.

Acknowledgments

I would like to thank those who helped me, directly and indirectly, with this book. First, I owe a debt to the nuns of St. Joseph School who taught me grammar with such energy and thoroughness, many years ago. They gave me my first love for the subject, and they prepared me well for my subsequent linguistic study. Thanks, too, to David Hacker and Larry Martin, who initiated me into the joys of transformational grammar at the University of Iowa. I would also like to thank the students and colleagues who gave invaluable advice and aid with this edition, including Rudy Troike, Cassie Schnatterly, and Eric Roller of the University of Arizona; and Kymberly Campbell, Mika Elovaara, Sandra Harris, Kristen Holmes, and Stan Pollard of the University of North Carolina at Wilmington. I am also grateful to language aficionado Eben Ludlow, my editor at Allyn & Bacon, who made this edition possible. To them all, my abiding thanks.

And with that sentence fragment, let the book begin.

Richard Veit

1 Introduction

*A writer's greatest pleasure is revealing to people
things they knew but did not know they knew.*
—*Andy Rooney*

The purpose of this book is to reveal to you something you already know. In fact, you not only know the subject, but you are an expert in it. If these sound like preposterous statements, I will give you one that will sound even more so: You, the reader of this book, know the grammar of English better than I know it—better, even, than any English teacher or professor of linguistics knows the grammar of English.

Those seemingly impossible statements are nevertheless completely true. Let me explain.

The word *grammar* is used in many different senses. Most people are familiar with *grammar* both as a subject they studied in grammar school ("A noun is the name of a person, place, or thing") and as a kind of language etiquette ("Don't say *ain't;* it's bad grammar"). Linguists use the word in a somewhat different sense, and that is the sense in which you are a grammar expert.

Grammar as we mean it is simply your language knowledge. Whatever your brain knows that allows you to use language we will call your grammar. Your grammar is what enables you to understand the very words you are now reading as well as to speak and write words and sentences of your own. You have had a grammar of English for as long as you have known English. This collected language knowledge is not a physical organ exactly. No surgeon can cut open the brain and say, "Aha! There's the grammar!" Nevertheless, we sometimes find it helpful to think of a grammar as if it were a thing, perhaps a compartment in the mind where language knowledge is stored, or even, if we want to compare the brain to a computer, as a program that runs language for us.

Your English grammar is certainly well developed. Most likely you have been using English for many years. Every day you produce and understand thousands of English sentences, and you do so effortlessly. You understand what others say to you, and they understand you. Clearly, you are an expert in English grammar.

Just as *grammar* is used in several senses, the word *know* can be used in different ways as well, and that is what allowed me to say that you "know" grammar better than I "know" it. Our brains have both conscious and unconscious knowledge, and I meant that you know grammar *unconsciously* better than I, or any other linguistics or English professor, know it *consciously.* Discovering consciously what we already know unconsciously about language is, in fact, the goal of this book and of all linguistic study.

Conscious and Unconscious Knowledge

English grammar is just one of many things you know unconsciously far better than you know consciously. When you walk up a flight of stairs, for example, you can do so without having to think about how to do it. You can climb stairs while carrying on a conversation, while composing a love sonnet, even while walking in your sleep. Although many hundreds of muscles are finely coordinated in the task of climbing stairs, you perform it errorlessly and even gracefully and without any apparent mental effort. Yet if you or I were asked to describe how we climb stairs we would do it very inaccurately at best: "Let's see," we might say. "First you bring the right leg up and bend the knee. You point the toe up, shift your weight forward, and bring the sole down on the next step. Then . . . ." Of course you would not have begun to describe which muscles you use when you bend the knee. Your description is a long way from capturing the directions your brain gives to your body as you move. The fact is that unless you are a highly trained physiologist, you do not "know" much about how you climb stairs. And yet in another sense you "know" how to do it quite well, because you do it all the time. Your conscious knowledge of the task cannot come close to matching what you know unconsciously.

Unfortunately no easy way has been discovered to move knowledge from the unconscious to the conscious part of the mind. If we want to know consciously how we climb stairs or regulate our heartbeats or create language or do any of a thousand other things we know unconsciously how to do, we have to work hard to discover them from the outside. If, for example, we wanted to know about stair-climbing, we would have to conduct meticulous studies of people climbing stairs. We would study slow-motion videos of the action, examine and perhaps dissect the human leg, and perform tests—and even then we would need to make guesses about how stair climbing is accomplished.

Learning about language is even more difficult because there are no language muscles to examine. We cannot simply look within the brain to see how it works. We can't see the insides of the mind at all. What we have to go on in our study is almost entirely on the outside. The best we can do is examine the language that we produce and then try to draw conclusions about how we produced it. Of course we can consult our intuitions and gut feelings about our language use, but intuitions are not always reliable guides to language, and we are wise to regard them skeptically.

Another obstacle to learning about language is that language is so much more complex than stairclimbing. Trying to describe just the structure of English (ignoring such other aspects of language as speech sounds and the creation of meaning) will take up this entire book, and even that will only introduce us to the subject. Linguists agree that we are just beginning to discover what language is about and that we will be learning more and more for centuries to come. Because we can gain conscious knowledge about our grammars only by examining what they produce (since we can't examine the grammars in our minds directly), it is at best a kind of enlightened speculation. Not all linguists make the same speculations, and there is much disagreement about what it is that we "know." You can easily see why you and I are far more expert in the unconscious knowledge of grammar than anyone is in the conscious knowledge of it.

How Does the Grammar Work?

Among the things that people disagree on is what the study of English grammar can show us. Surely it can examine the sentences we produce and classify their parts, calling this a noun, that a verb, and so on. But most modern linguists have a more ambitious goal than just describing the language we produce. They hope also to describe the *way* we produce it. In addition to showing you how the English language is constructed, this book will also consider how we *do* the constructing. It will try to gain some insights into what goes on in the mind when we create and understand English sentences. What is it that we know when we know language?

You can make a start at discovering what it is you know by considering your answers to some questions. Begin with this one:

> How many English words do you know?

Although no one can give an exact answer, that is still a reasonable question. The words you either use or can recognize probably number in the tens of thousands. But what about this question:

> How many English sentences do you know?

This one seems much less reasonable. You can't count the number of sentences you know because you hear and create new ones all the time. For example, there are many sentences on this page that you have never encountered before, and yet you have no difficulty understanding them. It may surprise you to learn that you frequently create entirely original sentences, sentences that are brand new to the English language. You could pause right now if you wanted and easily invent a perfectly clear English sentence that no human being living or dead has ever spoken or written or even thought of before. Even though there are a limited number of words that you know, you can put them together in an unlimited variety of ways.

The answer to the second question is that there is potentially an infinite number of sentences that we can know. Because our finite minds cannot store an infinite number of sentences, clearly we must have some means of creating sentences other than by pulling out the ones we want from a storage vault in the brain. We must have a way of creating them afresh by putting together their parts. The question this book is interested in is how we do it.

Clearly we don't throw words together at random. We would recognize only one of the following combinations of words as an English sentence:

> He who laughs last laughs best.
> Best laughs last laughs who he.
> Best he last laughs laughs who.
> Laughs who last best laughs he.

All but the first of these combinations are non-sentences. Because we are quite certain they are not products of our English grammar, we can label them as deviant or **ungrammatical**. The first sentence, on the other hand, is **grammatical**, and it surely didn't get that way by accident. How is it that we constantly create grammatical sentences like the first example and never produce gobbledygook like the other three?

The answer is that our unconscious knowledge must include some system, some set of principles for putting words together into sentences in a grammatical way. We can call these principles *grammatical rules* if we like, rules that we follow in order to create sentences, and these rules are an important component of our grammars. If our unconscious knowledge of English (which we are calling our English grammar) includes these rules, one goal in our quest for conscious knowledge about our language must be to discover what those rules might be.

This Book's Purpose

In this book we will try, then, to discover consciously the rules of our grammar, to create a model on paper of the grammar that exists in our minds. Although it is only a model of our grammar, we will use the term loosely enough to call it a *grammar* too. In that sense, this book aims to create a grammar of the English language.

How do we do it? Rather than guess what these rules are or accept on faith what others have said in the past, we can adopt a more scientific approach. A good start might be to try simply to describe some sentences that we produce. If we find some consistent feature in our descriptions, we can make a guess, or *hypothesis,* that the consistent feature represents a rule that speakers of English follow when they create sentences. We can then test the hypothesis on other sentences. If the rule works for them as well, we will say that our hypothesis is a good one, and we will keep the rule in our proposed grammar. If not, we will have to modify it or replace it with a better rule or abandon it altogether.

The procedure, then, that we will follow in this book is more like experimentation than the revelation of unquestioned facts. I intend the book to take you through a process of discovery. Rather than saying to you, "Behold the truth; accept and memorize it," I will say, "Let's see if this hypothesis accounts for what we do." This procedure will involve some trial and error. Each hypothesis we examine will be tentative, subject to later revision. Indeed, as we proceed in our investigation we will frequently revise some of the rules we proposed at an earlier stage.

You are invited to participate in this quest to understand the English language. Very likely you will think of some alternative explanations or better formulations of rules than I propose. Your instructor may provide additional hypotheses, and if you go on to take more advanced courses in syntax (the study of language structure), you will encounter still more alternatives for stating rules and still other theories about how language works.

Why Study Grammar?

The main reason we study grammar is that we human beings are curious and want to learn more about ourselves. Curiosity about what we are and what kind of world we inhabit has led humans to study such fields as psychology, biology, history, and linguistics. The study of how we create language can provide important insights into the nature of our minds and the way we think. It can help us understand better what it means to be human. In particular the discovery of how complex and yet elegant our grammars are will give us an appreciation of humanity's achievement in creating this marvelous instrument. We can also appreciate our own individual achievements (which we accomplished rather effortlessly as small children) in learning the English language.

Grammar study also has some more immediately practical benefits, but I would discourage you from spending time on the subject if practical gain is your only goal, because you may be disappointed. People who decide to study grammar because they want to be better writers or because they want to speak a more standard dialect or because they have trouble with punctuation will find some—but not complete—help here. Because our language knowledge is mostly unconscious, not conscious, the best way to become a good writer or speaker is to read widely and practice often. A writing or speech course is likely to be at least as important as a grammar course for these purposes.

On the other hand, grammar study is not without practical benefits. We use some conscious knowledge about language when we speak and write, and conscious grammatical knowledge can help us to understand what we are doing and allow us to make some enlightened choices. Knowledge of grammar can also give us a tool for analyzing our writing and a vocabulary for discussing it.

Another practical goal that at least some readers of this book will have is to gain a background for teaching grammar in the schools. Chapter 19 considers the goals and methods of teaching grammar to elementary and secondary students.

There is still one final reason for studying grammar, and that is that it can be a very exciting and even pleasurable activity. In each class I teach in the structure of the English language there are students (I hope a majority) who, like me, find it downright fun to study grammar. These include some students who had found grammar anything but fun in grade and high school where it was taught "the old way." I hope you are one of those who will share the joy this very exciting subject can bring.

Summary

To sum up these introductory remarks: A *grammar is* a person's unconscious language knowledge. You use your English grammar whenever you speak or write English or understand someone else's speech or writing. A grammar consists of principles or *rules* that allow you to create an infinite number of possible sentences out of a finite number of words. In this book the term *grammar* will also be used to describe the model on paper that we will construct of that mental grammar. That is the book's aim: to create a grammar or model of the rules we follow in using English. Actually, our investigation will be limited to one aspect of grammar, namely *syntax,* or the structure of language, the study of how words are put together in grammatical ways. Other aspects of language, such as how we form words or create sounds and meanings, are beyond the scope of this book.

2 Describing a Sentence

We humans are not the only species that engages in oral communication. Monkeys, like many other animals in the wild, communicate through a number of calls. A monkey community may have a dozen or more expressions for different communicative purposes—perhaps one call to signify danger on the ground (such as an approaching leopard), another to warn of danger from the air (a hawk), perhaps others to express anger or to attract a mate. One of many differences between their system of communication and ours, however, is that theirs consists of a limited set of fixed calls, while we can speak a limitless number of meaningful sentences. Monkeys cannot invent new expressions to suit their purposes the way we can.

Our language has this enormous range because it consists of parts that can be arranged in unlimited ways. The sentence you are now reading is made up of two dozen familiar parts, or words, arranged in what is presumably a novel way. In the following list, four words are variously arranged to produce many different sentences:

1   No monkeys have words.
     Monkeys have no words.
     Have monkeys no words?
     Have no monkeys words?
     No words have monkeys.
     Have no words, monkeys!

Some of these combinations are unusual, some are mildly ridiculous, but they are all grammatical sentences, nonetheless. You can probably think of still more combinations of these four words that would constitute English sentences, but not every possible combination is grammatical. The following, for example, is clearly not English:

2   * Words monkeys have no.

Notice the asterisk (*) in the example. We will adopt this commonly used symbol to designate combinations of words that are **ungrammatical**. *That is, we do not recognize them as English sentences. Notice too that I have numbered the examples and other data in this and subsequent chapters. This will give us a handy way to refer to them in our discussion.*

Our ability to arrange words in different ways allows us to produce a potentially infinite number of grammatical sentences, but because not all arrangements are grammatical, our grammar must consist of principles or rules for arranging them. Violations of the rules result in ungrammatical sentences. An important part of our study will be a search for these rules.

Discovering the Parts of Sentences

Our beginning plan of action will be to analyze sentences and see what conclusions we can draw from them. Notice that I am already making an assumption: that the sentence is the unit of language we should examine. That choice is arbitrary, in a sense. If we wished, we could start by examining larger units, such as paragraphs or longer verbal exchanges with one or more participants. But our intuitions tell us that sentences are units that are somehow basic—that have an integrity. They are the smallest communicative units that can stand alone (a complete verbal exchange might consist of a single sentence), and all the larger units are composed of sentences. No smaller unit of language can exist with the same independence (except perhaps for exclamations such as "Drat!" and abbreviated exchanges such as "You hungry?" "Not yet"—and even these might be called sentences too). So unless our experimenting shows us otherwise, we will assume that the sentence is the unit we should study first.

Let us begin with this one:

3   The monkey saw a leopard.

If you were asked to divide sentence 3 into its parts, you would of course identify the five words that comprise it. But what if you were asked about larger units? Are there any groupings of words in the sentence that seem to "go together"? Your intuitions would probably lead you to identify *the monkey* and *a leopard* as groupings in this sense. They seem to belong together in a way that *monkey saw* or *saw a* clearly do not. Furthermore, *the monkey* and *a leopard* seem very similar, as if they are groupings of the same type. In fact we can substitute one for the other and still have a grammatical (although different) sentence:

4   A leopard saw the monkey.

In contrast, if we switched *the monkey* with a different grouping such as *saw a*, the result would be ungrammatical:

5   * Saw a the monkey leopard.

This corroborates our intuition that *the monkey* and *a leopard* act as intuitive groupings in sentence 3.

How important is this discovery? If we determine that sentences are constructed out of such groupings, we will have gained an important insight into the structure of the English language. From now on we will call such intuitive groupings **phrases**. That is, we will consider a phrase to be one or more words that occur together in a sentence and that we recognize as somehow working together as a unit. Exactly how they "work together" remains for us to discover. Phrases can be said to function as **constituents** of sentences—that is, as parts that make up or *constitute* sentences. All subparts of sentences can be called constituents, from individual words like *monkey* to phrases like *the monkey* to the entire sentence itself.

I said in the first chapter that our intuitions, while important, are not always reliable guides to language analysis, and it is wise to subject them to independent tests. Another test of the reality of a phrase like *the monkey* is whether other such phrases can be found that can substitute for it in a grammatical sentence. Are there other groupings of words that can fill the blank in 6?

6   _____ saw a leopard.

In fact there is a limitless range of possible substitutes such as these:

7

           <u>The crocodile</u> saw a leopard.
           <u>A leopard</u> saw a leopard.
           <u>The wise, old, alert monkey</u> saw a leopard.
           <u>Anita</u> saw a leopard.
           <u>The man who had a scar above his right eye</u> saw a leopard.
           <u>We</u> saw a leopard.

Each of the underlined phrases works in our test, and each feels intuitively like a unit, a grouping of one or more words that "belong together." We will conclude that all of these phrases are constituents of the same type. For convenience, let us arbitrarily give this type of phrase a name. We will call it a **noun phrase**, or **NP** for short. Actually the name is not so arbitrary, but let us wait until the next chapter to consider why.

Not every intuitive grouping of words is a noun phrase, however. None of the groupings in 8 can successfully fill the blank in 6:

8

           *<u>Ate</u> saw a leopard.
           *<u>Ate a banana</u> saw a leopard.
           *<u>Very happy</u> saw a leopard.
           *<u>Fearfully</u> saw a leopard.
           *<u>Over the river and through the woods</u> saw a leopard.

According to our test procedure, none of the underlined groupings in 8 seems to be a noun phrase.

In addition to the two noun phrases, our sample sentence, *The monkey saw a leopard*, also contains the word *saw*, which, according to our test, is not a noun phrase. What can we discover about it? By performing the same substitution test that we conducted on noun phrases, we can find many other words that could take the place of *saw* in the sentence: *angers*, *tickled*, *resembles*, and *hypnotized*, to name a few. So *saw* belongs to another category of constituents; we will call it a **verb**, or **V** for short.

Our analysis of sentence 3 has shown us that it consists of a noun phrase (*the monkey*) followed by a verb (*saw*) and then another noun phrase (*a leopard*). We could restate that in shorthand form (with **S** standing for *sentence*, "=" standing for *consists of*, and "+" standing for *followed by*):

9   S = NP + V + NP

We can analyze sentence 3 further. Two of the constituents appear to have constituents of their own, because the noun phrases each consist of two words. The words *the* and *a* can be interchanged (*A monkey saw the leopard*), and we will call them **articles**, abbreviated **Art**. Likewise *monkey* and *leopard* belong to the category **noun** or **N**. Statement 10 can describe noun phrases such as *the monkey* and *a leopard*:

10   NP = Art + N

Statement 10 is a shorthand way of saying, for example, that the noun phrase *the monkey* consists of the article *the* followed by the noun *monkey*.

Finally, many people also have the intuitive feeling that, just as *a leopard* is a constituent of the sentence *The monkey saw a leopard*, so too is the longer phrase *saw a leopard*. That is, they sense that the sentence consists of two major parts, *the monkey* and *saw a leopard*. Or, to put it in terms of the sentence's meaning (something we have ignored until now in our analysis), the sentence consists of a "who-did-it?" part (*the monkey*) and a "did-what?" part (*saw a leopard*). Let us give the latter constituent the name **verb phrase**, or **VP**. We observe that it consists of a verb (*saw*) followed by a noun phrase (*a leopard*), or to put it in our shorthand:

11   VP = V + NP

We can revise 9, our original description of sentence 3, as follows:

12   S = NP + VP

That is, the sentence consists of two parts, a noun phrase (*the monkey*) and a verb phrase (*saw a leopard*). Both of those two constituents, in turn, have constituents of their own:

13   NP = Art + N

14   VP = V + NP

Note that statement 13 describes the noun phrase in 14 as well as the one in 12.

Exercises 2.1

Selected answers to these and other exercises in this book can be found at the Discovering English Grammar *website:* www.uncwil.edu/people/veit/DEG

Statement 12 claims that sentence 3 consists of two parts: a noun phrase, which we described as the "who-did-it?" part of the sentence, and a verb phrase, the "did-what?" part. Other sentences can also be divided into these two constituents, which are often called the sentence's **subject** and its **predicate**. Here are some examples:

NP (Subject) / VP (Predicate)

The monkey	/ saw a leopard.
The lima bean casserole	/ spoiled my appetite.
Jerry	/ fell asleep on the couch.
Knowing how to use a computer	/ got me a job as cashier in a movie theater.
The playhouse that Nell and Regis built in the back yard out of lawnchairs and blankets	/ collapsed.
They	/ never knew what hit them.

Perhaps we can form the hypothesis that *every* sentence consists of a subject (NP) and a predicate (VP). If this hypothesis is correct, then statement 12 is a description not just of 3 but of every English sentence.

Let us subject this hypothesis to some testing. See if you can divide the following sentences into subjects (noun phrases) and predicates (verb phrases). If you can, draw a slash (/) between those two constituents (the first one is done for you). Are there any uncertainties? If so, make note of them, and discuss them in class.

1. Vernon / sneezed.
2. Lucille's husband's uncle told an off-color joke.
3. A day-old bacon-lettuce-and-tomato sandwich on rye bread sat forlornly on the shelf.
4. You always hurt the ones you love.
5. The time it took me each morning to drive from home to my job at the park seemed relatively insignificant.
6. Our ability to arrange words allows us to produce a potentially infinite number of grammatical sentences.

Labeled Brackets and Boxes

Many people find it useful to put their analyses into a visual form. Just as a map helps a geographer comprehend a large territory or a blueprint helps an engineer, a *diagram* can help a student of grammar to visualize and better understand the makeup of a sentence.

One kind of diagram consists of **brackets** placed around constituents. Each bracket can be labeled with a subscript to show the type of constituent it is. The following is labeled as a sentence:

15   [$_S$ The monkey saw a leopard]

Because the sentence consists of two constituents, a noun phrase and a verb phrase, we can put labeled brackets around them as well:

16   [s [NP The monkey]   [VP saw a leopard]]

The verb phrase has a verb and a noun phrase as its constituents, as labeling can show:

17   [s [NP The monkey]   [VP [V saw]   [NP a leopard]]]

Finally, both noun phrases consist of two parts, an article and a noun:

18   [s [NP [Art The]   [N monkey]]   [VP [V saw]   [NP [Art a]   [N leopard]]]]

An evident limitation of labeled brackets is that after too many brackets are added they become confusing to look at—quite a drawback, because their purpose is to clarify the makeup of the sentence for us. Using *boxes* instead of brackets to show groupings of constituents can help somewhat:

19

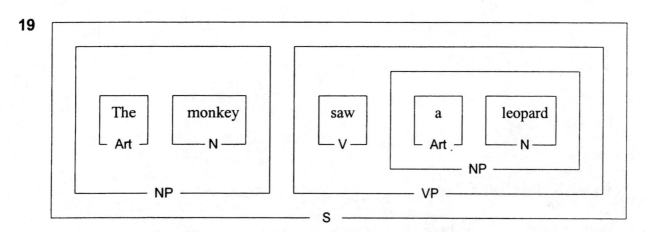

Exercises 2.2

1. Place labeled brackets around each of the constituents in these sentences, as in 18 above:

   a.   The   soldier   spied   an   enemy

   b.   A   downpour   spoiled   the   picnic

2. Draw labeled boxes around the constituents in these sentences, as in 19.

a.   The   ending   salvaged   the   movie

b.   An   amateur   won   the   championship

Reed-Kellog Diagrams

Both brackets and boxes have a limited usefulness, particularly with long, complex sentences. A better way of showing the structure and makeup of sentences is needed. In the late nineteenth century two grammarians named Alonzo Reed and Brainerd Kellog invented a type of diagram that became widely adopted for grammar study in American schools. Here is a ***Reed-Kellog diagram*** of sentence 3:

20

The longer vertical line separates the first noun phrase (the subject) from the verb phrase (the predicate), and the shorter one separates the two major constituents of the verb phrase. Articles are placed on diagonal lines below the nouns.

Reed-Kellog diagrams show us much about the sentence's structure, but they too have limitations. Constituents are not labeled as to category (noun, verb, and so on), the relationship of smaller constituents to larger ones is not always clear, and the diagrams do not always capture the sentence's word order.

Tree Diagrams

Since the 1950s, *tree diagrams* have become the most widely used way of displaying a sentence's makeup. In a tree diagram, the constituents of a sentence are shown branching out from it. For example, if a sentence such as sentence 3 has a noun phrase and a verb phrase as its constituents (that is, if we can describe it as S = NP + VP), then a tree diagram showing those constituents would look like this:

21

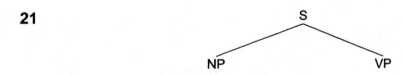

We can add to this tree by drawing in the constituents of the noun phrase, as in statement 13:

22

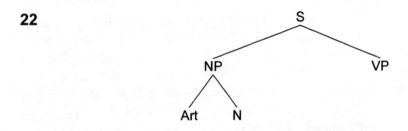

Next we can describe the verb phrase, as in 14:

23

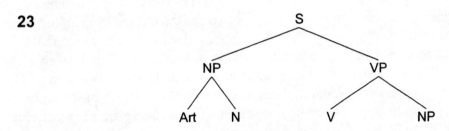

The only phrase still to be described is the noun phrase that follows the verb:

24

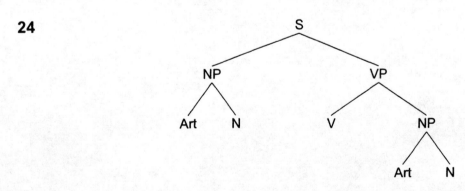

Finally, we can complete the tree by attaching the words to the appropriate labels:

25

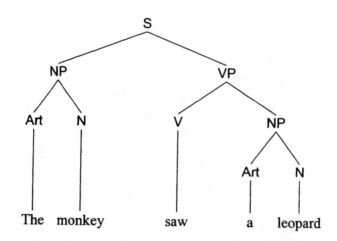

Look carefully at 25, our completed tree diagram of the sentence. It is important that you use tree diagrams to help you *see* the structure of sentences. Otherwise, drawing them becomes a useless exercise. Spend a few moments examining 25, trying to make its visual display meaningful to you. Notice that the tree is shaped somewhat like a triangle, with its apex on top at the sentence label S, and its base on the bottom made up of the words that comprise the sentence, arranged in left-to-right order. You will want to be able to look at any tree diagram and read the sentence across the bottom.

Look at what 25 shows about how the sentence is constructed. Notice that it shows that the article *a* and the noun *leopard* constitute a noun phrase. Notice too that this noun phrase (*a leopard*) combined with the verb *saw* make up a verb phrase. And this verb phrase combined with the noun phrase *the monkey* constitute the whole sentence. You can use a tree diagram as an aid to your understanding if you can look at it and actually *see* the sentence and the way it is put together.

Practice this important skill by skipping ahead a chapter or two and examining some of the trees you find. Can you look at the tree, read the sentence it diagrams, and see how it is structured?

You will notice that when we drew tree 25, we began with the sentence label S and ended with the sentence's words. We could just as easily have proceeded in the other direction, beginning with the words, then labeling them, and finally grouping them as constituents. The result would have been an upside-down tree (or actually a right-side-up one, because the trees we are used to seeing in nature have a single trunk at the bottom and many branches at the top):

26

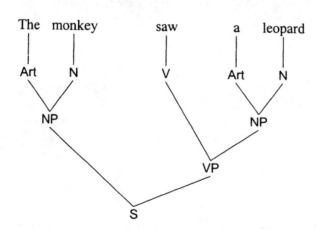

It is usual, however, to draw trees with the S on top, as in 25, and that is how we will draw them from now on in this book. You can practice drawing tree diagrams of sentences in the following exercises.

Exercises 2.3

1. Draw tree diagrams of the two sentences in question 1 of Exercises 2.2 on page 11. Your trees will have the same structure as tree 25. Draw a new tree for each sentence. Here are some pointers:

> *Unlike Olympic figure skating or platform diving, no style points are awarded in tree-drawing. Nevertheless, a well-drawn tree "works" a lot better than a sloppy or cramped tree. After all, the purpose of a tree is to enable you to see what the parts of the sentence are and how they are put together. Obviously, a clearly drawn visual aid works much better than one that is badly drawn. Here are some hints for effective tree drawing:*

- *Allow plenty of room. All your life, you have probably been told not to waste paper. Ignore that advice when you draw trees. Spread the constituents apart (left to right) and skip ample space between labels and their constituents (top to bottom). That is, do this:*   *and not this:*

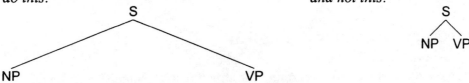

- *Connect the lines that radiate out underneath the category label. It is much easier to see the tree as the structure of a sentence rather than a bunch of lines and letters if you connect the lines,*
like this: *and not like this:*

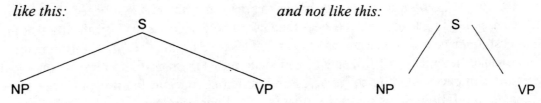

- *Don't forget to attach each word to its category label with a line. That is, do this:*   *and not this:*

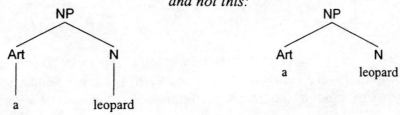

- *Start from the top (the S label) and work down to the words, rather than from the words and work up. The latter might seem a simpler way of drawing a tree, but I have observed that my students have the best success in the long run if they train themselves to think in terms of the larger constituents of the sentence first and then work down to progressively smaller units.*

- *Do not include punctuation marks such as periods and commas in your trees. These are conventions of our writing system, not inherent features of our mental grammars. Beginning the first word in your tree with a capital letter is entirely optional.*

- *And finally: Practice, practice! No matter how much sense your reading about grammar makes to you, you won't <u>know</u> grammar until you <u>do</u> grammar. My experience is that the best way for students to learn the structure of sentences is to draw many trees—and to learn from their mistakes. Even if no one but you sees them, it is to your advantage to do the exercises in this book religiously.*

2. Draw trees for the following sentences:

   a. The arsonist started a fire.
   b. A couple danced the tango.

An Elementary Grammar of English

So far we have looked at ways of describing the structure of a sentence, and we might rate the results as mildly interesting but not terribly significant. After all, we have not addressed our real goal—discovering how a sentence like 3 came to exist in the first place. We still want to know what goes on in our heads to allow us to construct such sentences in the first place. What, in other words, does our mental grammar look like?

   Because we cannot look into our brains to see the grammar, we will need to make some guesses if we are going to get anywhere. Let us then take a bold step. Let us hypothesize that the statements that best *describe* a sentence are also the principles used to *construct* it. If this hypothesis is correct, we can take statements 12, 13, and 14 and try to recast them as directions that the mind follows in creating sentences. Doing so involves only slight changes to the notation we have been using. Consider the following as principles (that is, directions or rules) for constructing a sentence:

27   S → NP VP

   NP → Art N

   VP → V NP

The three principles in 27 can be interpreted as follows: "To create a sentence, let it consist of two parts, a noun phrase and a verb phrase (in that order). For every noun phrase, let it consist of an article followed by a noun. For every verb phrase, let it consist of a verb followed by a noun phrase."

In our shorthand, the equal sign in our earlier descriptions has been replaced with an *arrow* (→), which can be read as "will have the following constituents" or simply as "consists of." The plus sign between constituents has been removed; instead, read the space between constituents as meaning "followed by." Principles or rules such as those in 27 are called *phrase-structure rules*, or *PS rules*, because they show how phrases, or groups of words, are structured. That is, a phrase-structure rule shows what constituents make up the phrase in question.

If we are to create a model English grammar (a model of our actual mental grammars), we might consider basing it on the cooking-recipe model. Just as a recipe consists of a set of directions ("Separate eggs and beat egg whites until stiff") and a list of ingredients ("3 eggs, 2 tbsp butter, . . ."), let us create a grammar that consists of directions, or phrase-structure rules, and ingredients, called a *lexicon*, a kind of vocabulary list or dictionary. The following grammar will allow us to produce our sample sentence 3:

28

AN ELEMENTARY GRAMMAR	
PS RULES	**LEXICON**
S → NP VP	Art: the, a
NP → Art N	N: monkey, leopard
VP → V NP	V: saw

By following the phrase-structure rules in 28 and then inserting words from the lexicon, we can produce tree 25. Actually, because there are two articles and two nouns in our lexicon, there is nothing to require us to insert words as we did. By making different choices about which articles and nouns to use, we could also have produced a slightly different sentence:

29

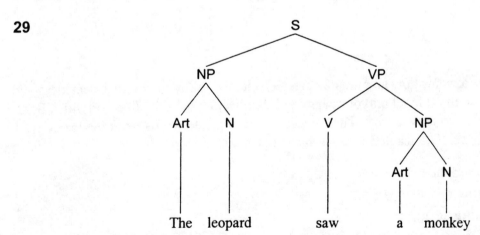

In fact, our grammar can produce sixteen different sentences, including these:

30   The monkey saw a leopard.

A leopard saw the monkey.

The monkey saw a monkey.

The leopard saw the leopard.

The grammar's ability to produce multiple sentences is an advantage, because our long-term goal is to construct a grammar that will be able to produce all possible sentences of English. Grammar 28 has another valuable quality, in that it will not produce any ungrammatical combinations of the words in its lexicon such as this:

31   * Monkey leopard a saw monkey the the.

The phrase-structure rules of 28 simply do not allow it to produce non-sentences like 31.

There isn't much variety in the sentences that grammar 29 will produce, but we are only beginning. By adding to its lexicon, we can allow our grammar to produce many more grammatical English sentences. Consider this expanded grammar:

32

PS RULES	LEXICON
S → NP VP	Art: the, a
NP → Art N	N: monkey, leopard, hunter, missionary
VP → V NP	V: saw, befriended, ate, amused, captured

Grammar 32 will produce dozens of sentences such as this one:

33   A monkey amused the missionary.

Another way of saying that the grammar's rules produce sentences such as 33 is to say that the grammar **generates** them. For that reason, grammars such as 28 and 32 are called **generative grammars**.

Exercises 2.4

1. Draw tree diagrams to show how grammar 32 can generate the following English sentences. For each sentence, place the S label on your paper and then follow the directions provided by the phrase-structure rules to draw a tree. Then select the appropriate words from the lexicon, and attach them to the tree. Draw a new tree for each sentence.

   a. A monkey amused the missionary.
   b. The hunter befriended a leopard.
   c. A monkey captured a hunter.

2. Use the grammar to generate three additional sentences. For each, draw the tree (as directed by the phrase-structure rules) and insert vocabulary from the lexicon.

Grammar 32, while it can generate many different sentences, still cannot produce all the grammatical sentences of English. To do that, it will need to be expanded considerably. Our goal,

I said, is to create a grammar on paper that does everything our mental grammars can do. That is, it should be capable of generating all of the grammatical sentences of English but incapable of generating any combinations of words that are ungrammatical.

Our goal is ambitious—so ambitious that we will not accomplish it fully. Linguists still have much to learn about what our mental grammars "know." But we can discover a great deal. The next chapter will extend our process of discovery.

3 Nouns, Verbs, and Adjectives

In the previous chapter, we decided that if we wanted to learn about English grammar, the sentence was the proper unit of language for us to investigate. Using a sample sentence, *The monkey saw a leopard*, we proceeded to do so, and we were able to construct a grammar capable of generating that and a number of other English sentences. If you look carefully at what we did, however, you will notice that our investigation was based on at least one unexplained assumption.

Our assumption for investigating sentences was that we already knew what sentences were. Was this assumption valid? All of us create sentences whenever we talk or write, but in identifying them, our conscious knowledge does not always match what we know unconsciously. How do we know what a sentence is? When we read, it is easy to spot a sentence as a group of words that begins with a capital letter and ends with a period or question mark. But how do we know where to put the capital letters and final punctuation when we write?

The traditional school-grammar definition of a sentence is not very much help: *A sentence is a group of words that expresses a complete thought.* This definition captures our understanding about a sentence's independence, but one person's idea of a complete thought may not be another's.

Some assumptions are unavoidable in scientific investigation, and one that will be basic to our study is that certain word groups that we believe to be sentences are indeed sentences. In this instance we must trust our intuitions, at least to start. Based on this assumption, we can try to construct a model of grammar, and if the model proves to be consistent with our intuitive feelings about sentences and if it proves capable of consistently generating groups of words that we recognize as grammatical English sentences, then we can be satisfied that our assumption is a valid one.

Starting with this and other assumptions, we have already provided a syntactic definition of a sentence, which took the form of a phrase-structure rule:

1   S → NP VP

In addition to giving directions for creating a sentence, the rule also explains what a sentence is. To recast this definition in words:

2   A **sentence** is a group of words that consists of a noun phrase followed by a verb phrase.

This, we will assume for now, is what a sentence is. Our continuing investigation of sentences will tell us if this assumption is a good one.

Proper and Common Nouns

Definition 2 says that a sentence consists of two kinds of phrases. A **phrase** is any grouping of words that acts as a constituent. In addition to noun phrases and verb phrases, we will also encounter other kinds of phrases in upcoming chapters.

A noun phrase, we discovered, is a group of words that can fill a slot like the one in 3:

3 _____ saw a leopard.
　　　　　(NP)

The monkey is a noun phrase, and so are *a leopard, a missionary,* and *the hunter.* These noun phrases all consist of an article and a noun, and so we described a phrase-structure rule for noun phrases:

4 NP → Art N

As you probably have guessed, it is the noun that gives its name to the phrase. The noun, it seems clear, is the more important constituent of the noun phrase.

Following rule 4, we identified *monkey* and *leopard* as nouns. That is, our classification was based on a word's ability to fill a slot like this one:

5 the _____
　　　　　(N)

Words like *headache, ocean, spinach,* and *romance* can also fill the slot and so are nouns. Meaning, you will notice, did not enter into our method of classifying nouns. Instead we have used the purely structural method of slot-filling. The study of grammar cannot ignore meaning, however, and we will have occasion to consider meaning as our inquiry continues. In traditional school grammar, a noun is usually defined in terms of meaning: *A noun is the name of a person, place, or thing.*

Rule 4 described a noun phrase as an article-noun combination, but a little investigating will show us that not all noun phrases have the same constituents. In some cases, a single word can fill the slot in 3.

6 Tarzan saw a leopard.
　　 Rover saw a leopard.

The names *Tarzan* and *Rover* must also be noun phrases, even though they do not consist of the two elements Art and N. Rule 4, then, is apparently inadequate because it does not describe all possible noun phrases. Let's try to improve it.

We will call all names like *Tarzan* and *Rover* **proper nouns** (abbreviated N_P; that is, N, followed by a subscript uppercase P). Specific names of persons, places, objects, and institutions, such as *Elizabeth, Tennessee, Oldsmobile, Microsoft,* and *Harvard,* are proper nouns. In writing, a convention has been adopted of beginning a proper noun with an upper-case letter. In the examples of 6, the underlined proper nouns act as noun phrases all by themselves, without any articles in front of them. We would need an additional noun-phrase rule to describe them:

7   NP → N$_P$

If *Tarzan* and *Tennessee* are proper nouns, let us call the more generalized nouns, the ones that are not used as proper names and are not usually begun with upper-case letters, **common nouns** (abbreviated **N$_c$**). Examples of common nouns are *sophomore, state, car, company,* and *college.* We can revise 4 accordingly:

8   NP → Art N$_c$

Notice that we now have two different noun-phrase rules, 7 and 8. With these rules, our model grammar is now expanded:

9

PS RULES	LEXICON
S → NP VP	Art: the, a, an
NP → Art N$_c$	N$_c$: engineer, car, city, company, detective, . . .
NP → N$_P$	N$_P$: Sidney, Constance, Chicago, Sony, . . .
VP → V NP	V: startled, bought, loves, hired, fired, . . .

When we construct a model of our grammar, we can include in the lexicon only a sample of the words available to us. Clearly we do not have room here to list all the nouns and verbs that speakers of English know.

Because there are now two noun-phrase rules, the grammar provides choices for generating sentences. In drawing trees based on these phrase-structure rules, you can use either rule whenever you encounter a noun-phrase label. Here are two of the trees that grammar 9 can generate:

10   **a.**   **b.**

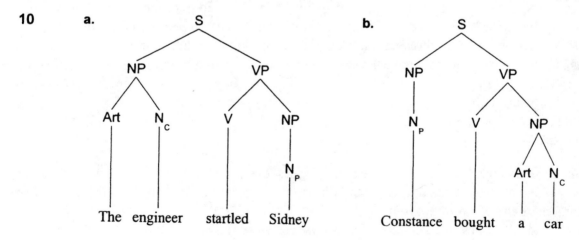

Until now all of the sentences we have examined have had precisely the same structure, with each phrase having exactly two constituents. Now, however, the choices available in grammar 9 result in trees with different structures. In trees 10a and 10b, some of the NP labels branch into a single N$_P$. Categories, as we will continue to discover, can have one, two, three, or more constituents.

Exercises 3.1

1. Draw trees to show how grammar 9 can generate the following sentences. For each tree, use the appropriate phrase-structure rules and insert the appropriate words from the lexicon.

   a. Sony hired a detective.
   b. Constance loves Chicago.
   c. The company fired Sidney.

2. Draw trees for two additional sentences that the grammar can generate. Include both proper and common nouns in your trees. Use only words from the grammar's lexicon.

Transitive and Intransitive Verbs

Earlier we defined verb phrases as phrases that can fill a slot like this one:

11   The monkey _____.
                        (VP)

According to this definition, possible verb phrases include *saw a leopard, imitated Francine, plays the cello,* and *attended Purdue.* We used the following phrase-structure rule to describe verb phrases:

12   VP → V NP

   The slot in 11, however, can also be filled by other verb phrases that do not meet the description of 12:

13   The monkey _wheezed_.
        The monkey _laughs_ .
        The monkey _died_ .

Here the verb phrase seems to consist of a single word. Lone words that can fill the slot in 11 will be called *intransitive verbs* (abbreviated V_I). *Wheezed, laughs,* and *died* are all intransitive verbs. Another way of describing them is to say that an intransitive verb is a verb that is not followed by a noun phrase. In contrast, verbs like *saw, imitated,* and *resembles* are all *transitive verbs* (V_T), because each is followed by a noun phrase. Some verbs can be used in either category:

14 a. The game *ended.*   —*Ended* is an intransitive verb, not followed by an NP.
   b. A riot *ended* the game. —*Ended* is a transitive verb, followed by an NP.

We already noted that the first noun phrase in a sentence such as 14a or 14b is often referred to as the *subject* of the sentence. Similarly the noun phrase that follows a verb is often called the ***direct object***. A transitive verb is said to take a direct object, while an intransitive verb does not. In intransitive sentence 14a, *the game* is the subject, but there is no direct object. In transitive sentence 14b, *a riot* is the subject, and *the game* is the direct object.

The similarity between transitive and intransitive verbs leads us to classify them in the same general category: ***verbs***. We have considered verbs from a purely structural point of view. In traditional grammar, however, they are defined in terms of meaning: *A verb is a word that expresses action or being.*

We can revise our verb-phrase rule 12 to account for the existence of both intransitive and transitive verbs. Two rules will now be needed instead of one:

15 $VP \rightarrow V_I$

$VP \rightarrow V_T \ NP$

We can incorporate these revisions into our grammar:

16

PS RULES	LEXICON
$S \rightarrow NP \ VP$	Art: the, a, an
$NP \rightarrow Art \ N_C$	N_P: Paul, Lucy, Pierre, Bermuda, Canada, . . .
$NP \rightarrow N_P$	N_C: rain, sailor, librarian, reptile, movie, . . .
$VP \rightarrow V_I$	V_I: continued, wept, sneezed, objected, triumphed, . . .
$VP \rightarrow V_T \ NP$	V_T: annoyed, threatened, dated, amused, admired, visited, . . .

Grammar 16 can generate sentences with both intransitive (17a) and transitive (17b) verbs:

17

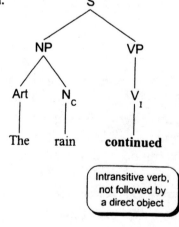

a.

Intransitive verb, not followed by a direct object

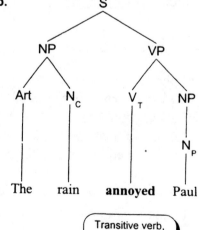

b.

Transitive verb, followed by a direct object

Exercises 3.2

1. Draw trees to show how grammar 16 can generate the following sentences. For each tree, use the appropriate phrase-structure rules and insert words from the lexicon.

    a. A sailor sneezed.
    b. Lucy threatened the librarian.
    c. Pierre wept.

2. Draw trees for three additional sentences that the grammar can generate. Include both transitive and intransitive verbs. If you wish, you may add additional words to the lexicon of 16.

Simplifying the Phrase-Structure Rules

Even with these revisions, our phrase-structure rules are still not adequate. Consider our rules for the noun-phrase category:

18   NP → Art N_C
      NP → N_P

These rules can generate the noun phrases in 19:

19   Chevrolet hired Ralph.
      Ramona ordered a pizza.

But sometimes proper nouns are preceded by an article, and sometimes common nouns are not. Consider the italicized NPs in 20:

20   Ralph owns *a Chevrolet*.
      Ramona loves *pizza*.

It would seem, then, that at least four different rules are needed for describing noun phrases:

21	a.	NP → N_C	c.	NP → N_P
	b.	NP → Art N_C	d.	NP → Art N_P

The grammar is now getting unpleasantly complicated. Is there anything we can do about it? Fortunately, there is.

Because rules 21a and 21b are so similar to 21c and 21d, we can simplify the way we write rules for noun phrases. Let us replace the four rules 21a–d with two general rules:

22   NP → N

NP → Art N

Although a distinction can be made between proper and common nouns, we will no longer bother to note it in our rules. Henceforth we will ignore the $_c$ and $_p$ subscripts and classify every noun (whether common or proper) simply as N.

Of course not every noun can take an article (*Mimi contracted *a tuberculosis, Albert attended *the Princeton*), nor can every noun exist without one (*Arnold got *hernia, Cindy visited *Bronx*). This knowledge about restrictions on the use of articles with nouns is part of our lexical knowledge (knowledge about words), and we will not aim for a full account of it here.

Even the two rules of 22 provide some unnecessary clutter, because the two of them can be summarized in a single statement: A noun phrase contains a noun, which may or may not be preceded by an article. In the writing of phrase-structure rules, *parentheses* ( ) allow us to express *optional* elements. By placing parentheses around the element Art, we can compress the two rules into one:

23   NP → (Art) N

We can read rule 23 as follows: A noun phrase consists of an optional article and an obligatory noun. Or, in other words, when you wish to create a noun phrase, you must have a noun, but whether an article precedes that noun is an optional matter. Rule 23 allows us to draw two different trees:

24

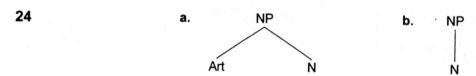

In the same manner, we will no longer note the distinction between transitive and intransitive verbs. From now on, we will write one rule, 25, that is equivalent to the two rules of 15:

25   VP → V (NP)

That is, a verb phrase contains a verb, which may or may not be followed by a noun phrase. Our grammar can be revised as follows:

26

PS RULES	LEXICON
S → NP VP	Art: the, a, an
NP → (Art) N	N: students, pizza, Paris, Louvre, . . .
VP → V (NP)	V: wanted, visited, smiled, . . .

Although grammar 26 appears simpler than grammar 16, it is actually more "powerful" in that it can generate more sentences. For example, it can generate all of the sentences in 27.

27 a. The students wanted a pizza.

   b. The students wanted pizza.

   c. The students visited Paris.

   d. The students visited the Louvre.

   e. The students smiled.

Adjectives

Articles are not the only optional elements that can occur in noun phrases. Consider the italicized noun phrases in these sentences:

28   *The tiresome monkey* saw a leopard.

         Severe storms battered Florida.

         An unscrupulous jeweler sold *defective watches.*

The words *tiresome, severe, unscrupulous,* and *defective* are all ***adjectives*** (abbreviated **Adj**). In traditional grammar this category is defined as follows: *An adjective is a word that describes (or "modifies") a noun.* All the following combinations of articles, adjectives, and nouns can occur in English noun phrases:

29   NP → N   *[Florida]*

      NP → Art N   *[a leopard]*

      NP → Adj N   *[defective watches, severe storms]*

      NP → Art Adj N   *[the tiresome monkey, an unscrupulous jeweler]*

By using parentheses, we can write a single rule for noun phrases that will account for all four structures in 29:

30   NP → (Art) (Adj) N

Rule 30 allows our grammar to generate sentences such as the following:

31

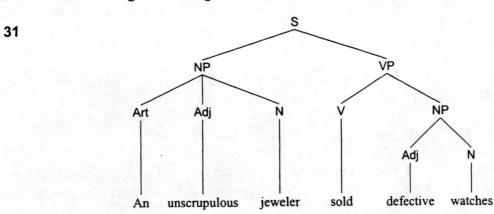

Nouns, Verbs, and Adjectives

Exercises 3.3

1. Note that in rule 30 the categories Art and Adj are placed in separate pairs of parentheses. Is the following rule equivalent to 30?

    NP → (Art Adj) N

    Are there any noun phrases in 29 that this rule would not be able to generate?

2. a. Imagine that in a grammar, all four of the following trees can exist. (Letters are used here in place of grammatical categories.)

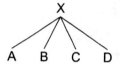

    Which one of the following rules can generate all four of these trees?

    i.   X → A B C D

    ii.   X → (A) B (C) D

    iii.   X → A (B) C (D)

    b. Is the rule you selected able to generate any other trees besides these four? How could you revise the rule so that it could also generate the following two trees?

    Rule 30 is still not perfect, because sometimes more than one adjective can occur in a noun phrase:

32   the old gray mare
        expensive new red sneakers

One solution would be to add additional optional adjectives to our NP rule. The following would allow one, two, or three adjectives in a noun phrase:

33   NP → (Art) (Adj) (Adj) (Adj) N

However, you can easily think of a noun phrase with more than three adjectives (for example, *the old, old, old, old, old philosopher*). Theoretically, there is no limit to the number of adjectives that

---

can modify a single noun. Because we can't write "(Adj)" an unlimited number of times, we need a better way of writing the rule. Let us place a ***raised plus sign*** (+) following an element in a phrase-structure rule to indicate that it may be repeated more than once. Our revised NP rule becomes:

33   NP → (Art) (Adj)⁺ N

That is, a noun phrase contains a noun, which may (but need not) be preceded by an article and may (but need not) also be preceded by one or more adjectives. Both the article and adjectives are optional. Notice how we have added to the power of our grammar. Even though the following grammar contains only three rules, it is capable of generating many more kinds of sentences than the earlier grammars we constructed.

34

PS RULES	LEXICON
S → NP VP	Art: the, a, an
NP → (Art) (Adj)⁺ N	Adj: adventurous, gaudy, purple, old, jaunty, sleepy, ugly, unreliable, . . .
VP → V (NP)	N: officer, soldier, shirt, actor, Amanda, Louis, professor, thieves, car, . . .
	V: rewarded, embarrassed, performed, owns, insulted, charmed, . . .

Linguists often use a raised asterisk (*) instead of a plus sign to mark a repeatable element. I will use a plus sign to avoid confusion with the sign for an ungrammatical element or for a footnote.

Grammar 34 can now generate sentences such as these:

35 a.

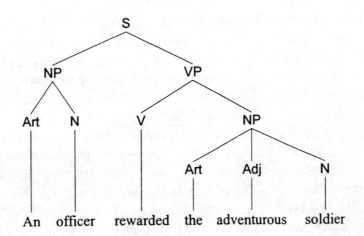

b.

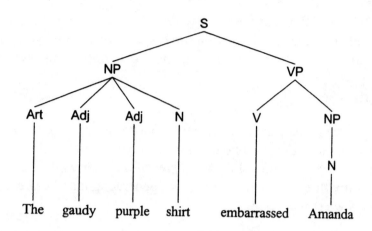

Exercises 3.4

1. Using grammar 34, draw trees for these sentences. Be sure to use a separate Adj label for each adjective.

   a. The jaunty actor performed.
   b. Louis owns an ugly unreliable old car.
   c. Ugly old thieves charmed the actor.

2. Draw two additional trees for sentences with adjectives that can be generated by grammar 34.

A Further Note on Meaning

To this point we have been examining the English language from a largely structural viewpoint, attempting to construct a model of grammar with little concern for meaning. Clearly, however, meaning is essential to language, because the very purpose of language is to communicate our meaning. Any attempt to construct a grammar that ignores meaning will fail. Grammar 34, for example, while it can generate many fine sentences, can also produce sentences that are certainly very odd, such as *The shirt insulted Louis* and *The sleepy car owns a purple soldier*. While these sentences may not strictly be ungrammatical—if we exercise our imaginations, we might conceive of situations in which they could actually be spoken—they do violate our usual conceptions of appropriate meaning. Our grammatical knowledge surely includes certain notions of appropriateness that tell us, for example, that verbs like *insulted* and *owns* can occur with "animate" subjects like *actor* or *professor*, but not with "inanimate" subjects like *shirt* and *car*. This knowledge about appropriate meaning (sometimes called **selectional restrictions** on the lexicon) is a part of our mental grammar. We will not aim for a full account of it here, but if you take more advanced courses in syntax, you will encounter attempts to account more fully for meaning in the grammatical models you create.

Linking Verbs

According to the traditional definition of a verb ("a word that expresses action or being"), not all verbs are action words. The others, verbs that "express being," are mostly forms of the verb *be*. These forms of *be* (such as *am, is, are, was,* and *were*), act as the verbal equivalents of an equal sign: They tell us that one thing is equivalent to another:

36 a. Brutus *is* an honorable man.
  b. The Titans *were* the winners.
  c. Millie *was* persistent.

Such verbs are distinguished from both transitive and intransitive verbs. They are usually called *linking verbs* (abbreviated **V$_L$**). They are also known as *copulative verbs* or *copulas*. Like a transitive verb, a linking verb can be followed by a noun phrase, as in 36a and 36b. Unlike other verbs, however, a linking verb can also be followed by an adjective, as in 36c. We can add these rules to our grammar:

37 VP → V$_L$ NP
  VP → V$_L$ Adj

The rules of 37 allow the grammar to generate sentences like these:

38

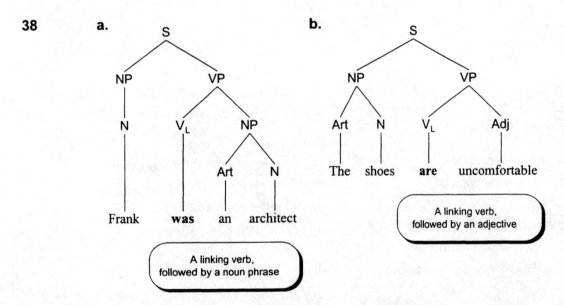

Recall that a noun phrase that follows a transitive verb is called the direct object. In traditional grammar, a noun phrase that follows a linking verb, such as *an architect* in 38a, is sometimes called a *predicate nominative*. An adjective that follows a linking verb, such as *uncomfortable* in 38b, is sometimes called a *predicate adjective*. Together, predicate nominatives and predicate adjectives are called *subjective complements* in traditional grammar, because they are said to complete or explain the subject.

In addition to forms of the verb *be*, a few other verbs are also linking verbs, as 39 shows.

Nouns, Verbs, and Adjectives

39   An unknown lawyer *became* the next governor.
          Ferdinand *seems* intelligent.

Both *became* and *seems* are linking verbs because they also function much like verbal equal signs. Notice that you can substitute a form of *be* for these verbs and get roughly equivalent sentences (*An unknown lawyer <u>was</u> the next governor, Ferdinand <u>is</u> intelligent*). Several verbs related to the five senses (*look, appear, sound, smell, taste, feel*) and a handful of other verbs (*remain, grow, get, act*) sometimes act as linking verbs and sometimes act as transitive or intransitive verbs, depending on how they are used.

40 a. Caroljane *felt* the sandpaper.   —transitive: *felt* is an action
   b. Caroljane *felt* angry.   —linking: she *was* angry

41 a. Marcus *smelled* the flowers.   —transitive: *smelled* is an action
   b. The flowers *smelled* sweet.   —linking: they *were* sweet

42 a. Others left. Darlene *remained*.   —intransitive: *remained* is something she did
   b. Darlene *remained* the treasurer.   —linking: she *was* the treasurer

A test for whether a verb is a linking verb is whether a form of *be* can be substituted for it without substantially altering meaning: *Caroljane was angry* is roughly equivalent to 40b, but **Caroljane was the sandpaper* completely changes the meaning of 40a.

Exercises 3.5

1. Underline the verb in each of the following sentences, and identify it as a transitive verb, an intransitive verb, or a linking verb. For each linking verb, state whether it is followed by a noun phrase or by an adjective.

    a. Mom <u>grew</u> impatient.   g. Lawrence tasted the casserole.
    b. Dad grew a moustache.   h. The casserole tasted fishy.
    c. The baby grew.   i. Conrad appeared healthy.
    d. Hortense sounded the alarm.   j. Hepzibah looks marvelous.
    e. Lavinia sounded confident.   k. Wayne got a headache.
    f. Honesty seemed the best policy.   l. Wayne got fidgety.

2. Draw trees for sentences 1a, 1b, and 1c.

In 37, we wrote two rules to describe verb phrases with linking verbs. We always value simplicity in our grammar, and it would be better if those two possibilities could be stated in a single rule. A single rule seems appropriate, because we can recast the rules of 37 in a single statement: "A verb phrase can consist of a linking verb that is followed by either a noun phrase or an adjective."

Fortunately a convenient rule-writing device allows us to express an either/or relation. Items that can be chosen as alternatives can be placed, one above the other, within **braces** { }. Using braces, we can now restate the rules of 37 as a single rule:

43

$$VP \rightarrow V_L \left\{ \begin{array}{c} NP \\ Adj \end{array} \right\}$$

In following this rule to generate a verb phrase, the grammar first selects a linking verb, and then it must select either a noun phrase or an adjective. Notice how braces differ from parentheses. When two items are in braces, the grammar must select one or the other of them. It may not select both options, and it may not select neither option.

Our grammar now looks like this:

44

⊕ *can have any # of them*

PS RULES	LEXICON
S → NP VP	Art: an, the, a
	Adj: enthusiastic, impatient, heavenly, skillful,
NP → (Art) (Adj)$^\oplus$ N	nonprofit, classical, silky, decadent,
VP → V (NP)	former, long, cold, spectacular, ...
	N: Sarah, skier, customers, casserole,
VP → V$_L$ { NP / Adj }	Eben, draftsman, bellyache, nuisance,
	station, music, pajamas, professor,
	class, winters, expedition, views, ...
	V: played, lacks, demoralized, ...
	V$_L$: was, are, smells, became, is, felt, were, ...

Exercises 3.6

1. Use grammar 44 to draw trees for the following sentences with linking verbs:

   a. Sarah was an enthusiastic skier.
   b. The new customers are impatient.
   c. The casserole smells heavenly.
   d. Eben became a skillful draftsman.
   e. A bellyache is a nuisance.

2. Grammar 44 is capable of generating a variety of English sentences. Draw tree diagrams of the following sentences:

   a. The nonprofit station played classical music.
   b. The silky pajamas felt decadent.

c. The former professor lacks class.

     [Is the verb *lacks* a linking verb? Compare: **The former professor is class.*]

d. Long, cold winters demoralized the expedition.

e. The views were spectacular.

3. The following three trees are among the structures that grammar 44 can generate. Complete the trees by supplying appropriate words. You are welcome and encouraged to add words to the lexicon of 44.

a.

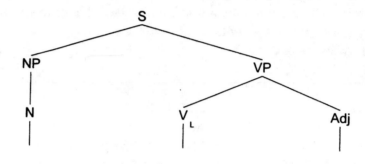

b.

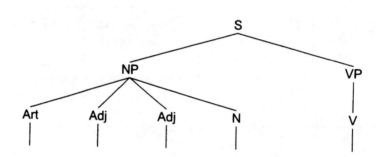

c.

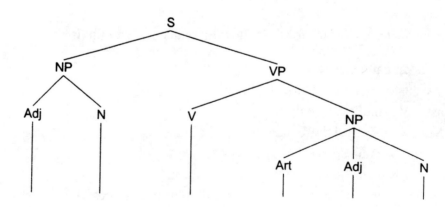

4. The trees in exercises 3a–3c immediately preceding show just three of the sentence structures that can be generated by grammar 44. Using that grammar, draw two additional tree structures that are different from those. Then insert words to create sentences. You may add words to the lexicon of 44 as needed. Be certain that the rules of 44 permit the trees you have drawn.

The Parts of Speech

Each of the word categories that we have seen so far (Art, Adj, N, and V) can be called a **part of speech**. In traditional grammar, eight parts of speech are usually identified: *noun, pronoun, adjective, verb, adverb, preposition, conjunction,* and *interjection*. We will encounter and explore these categories in upcoming chapters, but our classification will identify some additional parts of speech as well.

As one example of ways in which modern scientific grammar differs from traditional grammar, we have already introduced the *article* as an independent part of speech. In traditional grammar, however, *article* is classified as a subtype of *adjective* because, like adjectives, articles usually precede (or "modify") nouns. Nevertheless, there is good reason for separating the two categories. Besides serving different purposes, articles and adjectives fill different syntactic slots. They are not interchangeable. When both occur within the same noun phrase, the article precedes the adjective. We can have *a miserable time* but not **miserable a time*. And whereas a noun phrase can have multiple adjectives (*happy, happy olden days*), it can have no more than one article (**the the an owl*). In order for our grammar to generate grammatical sentences, it is necessary for it to distinguish between these two parts of speech.

Exercises 3.7

The article *the* is called a **definite article**, whereas *a* and *an* are called **indefinite articles**. Speculate on why they were given those names. Under what circumstances do we choose to use one or the other—or no article at all? For example what are the differences in meaning or implication among these four different noun phrases?

$$
\text{He admired} \left\{ \begin{array}{l} \text{the woman.} \\ \text{a woman.} \\ \text{women.} \\ \text{the women.} \end{array} \right.
$$

If I say to you, "He admired the woman," what do I assume you know? If instead I say, "He admired a woman," what do I assume you know (or do not know)?

4 Prepositions and Personal Pronouns

Our grammar-making is moving along nicely, and the model grammar that we have discovered can now generate many different kinds of sentences. Still, it cannot generate all of them, and you have probably spotted some of its inadequacies. You may already have your own suggestions for augmenting the grammar. Perhaps you have thought of better alternatives to some of our existing proposals. If so, by all means offer them in class. Remember that what we are engaged in is cooperative speculation about our unconscious knowledge. The more minds that participate in the speculation, the more successful our search for conscious knowledge will be.

Prepositions

One deficiency in our grammar is the ability to account for the italicized phrases in the following:

1.   a.   Mort scrambled *over the barricade*.
     b.   The smugglers sneaked the contraband *past the guards*.
     c.   The genetic researchers crossed a tiger *with a lion*.

Each of these phrases has the intuitive feel of a unit, and each consists of a noun phrase preceded by a word such as *over, past,* or *with*. We will call words of this kind ***prepositions*** (abbreviated **P**), because they are placed before (or "pre-positioned" in relation to) noun phrases. The word *over* is a preposition, and the entire constituent *over the barricade* can be called a ***prepositional phrase*** or **PP**. A prepositional phrase consists of a preposition followed by a noun phrase. We can state our analysis as a phrase-structure rule:

2   PP → P NP

In sentences 1a–1c, the prepositional phrases occur at the end of sentences. But is the prepositional phrase part of the verb phrase, or is it a separate major constituent of the sentence? These two options for writing phrase-structure rules involving prepositional phrases are shown in 3 and 4, along with different trees they can generate. Examine them and see if you can decide which option is preferable. Either:

3 a. S → NP VP
      VP → V (NP) (PP)

b.

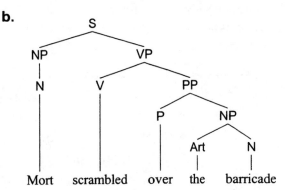

Or else:

4 a. S → NP VP (PP)
      VP → V (NP)

b.

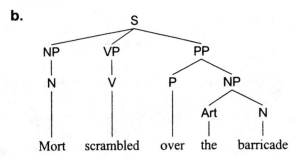

Both options "work" in the sense that both can generate the desired sentence, but does one tree better reflect our intuitions about the structure of the sentence? One reason to prefer option 3, which has the prepositional phrase as a constituent of the verb phrase, has to do with meaning: *Over the barricade* should be considered part of the verb phrase, because it "modifies" or "completes" the verb *scrambled*. That is, it describes where the scrambling took place. Most people have the intuitive sense that, in sample sentences 1a–1c, *scrambled over the barricade, sneaked the contraband past the guards,* and *crossed a tiger with a lion* are constituents. Accordingly, we will adopt analysis 3 and reject analysis 4.

When I was in the fifth grade, my class was assigned to memorize a list of the most common prepositions. The teacher said we would never forget them, and strangely enough she was right, at least in my case. Here is the list:

5

COMMON PREPOSITIONS				
about	behind	except	off	to
above	below	for	on	toward
across	beneath	from	out	under
after	beside	in	outside	until
against	between	inside	over	up
among	beyond	into	past	upon
around	by	like	since	with
at	down	near	through	without
before	during	of	throughout	

It probably isn't necessary for you to memorize the list too, but you should be able to recognize a preposition when you see one. With the adoption of rules 2 and 3a, our grammar now contains provisions for generating prepositional phrases:

6

PS RULES	LEXICON
S → NP VP	Art: the, a, an
NP → (Art) (Adj)⁺ N	Adj: hapless, interminable, . . .
VP → V (NP) (PP)	N: Beth, trapeze, Larry, oyster, shoehorn, wastrel, bar, Milo, grease, axle, colonel, corporal, private, Jones, Tibet, Wanda, smile, ceremony, . . .
VP → V_L { NP / Adj }	V: jumped, opened, stumbled, cleaned, demoted, flew, maintained, . . .
PP → P NP	P: from, with, into, to, across, throughout, . . .

Grammar 6 generates sentences like the following:

7

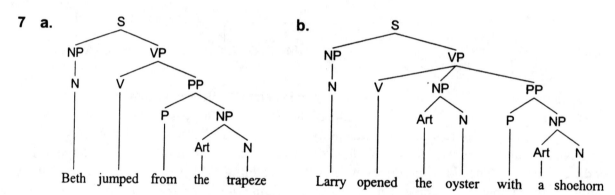

Notice that the prepositional phrase in 7a follows an intransitive verb (*jumped*), while the prepositional phrase in 7b follows a transitive verb (*opened*) and a noun phrase (*the oyster*).

Exercises 4.1

1. Use grammar 6 to draw trees for these sentences:

   a. The wastrel stumbled into a bar.
   b. Milo cleaned the grease from the axle.
   c. A colonel demoted the hapless corporal to private.
   d. Jones flew across Tibet.
   e. Wanda maintained a smile throughout the interminable ceremony.

2. Grammar 6 allows a prepositional phrase to occur following an intransitive verb (as in exercise sentence 1a above) and following a transitive verb (as in 1b), but it does not allow a prepositional phrase to occur following a linking verb. Yet sentences such as the following do occur in English:

a. Chauncey was absent during the exams.
b. The brothers are big heroes since the dramatic rescue.
c. Becky became a success after college.

How can you revise grammar 6 to allow it to generate sentences such as these? Write the revised rule, and use it to draw trees for those three sentences.

Prepositional Phrases within Noun Phrases

Each of the prepositional phrases we have so far considered has occurred within a verb phrase. These prepositional phrases can be said to "modify" the verbs they follow in that they provide information telling when, where, how, or why the action took place. In 7a, for example, *from the trapeze* modifies *jumped* because it tells us *where* Beth did the jumping. In 7b, *with a shoehorn* modifies *opened* because it tells us *how* Larry opened the oyster.

Consider, however, the following sentences:

8 a. The house *on the hill* overlooked the valley.
   b. The cover *of the book* attracted attention.
   c. The old man *with the harmonica* knew the words *to the songs*.

None of these italicized prepositional phrases seems to be modifying a verb. Instead, each identifies the noun that it follows and so can be said to modify that noun. For example, in 8a, *on the hill* tells us which house overlooked the valley. In 8b, *of the book* tells us which cover we are talking about. Likewise, in 8c, *with the harmonica* identifies which old man is meant, and *to the songs* tells us which words the man knew. Each of these prepositional phrases seems to be a constituent of a noun phrase. We can revise our noun-phrase rule accordingly:

9   NP → (Art) (Adj)$^+$ N (PP)

Just as the VP rule in 3a says that some prepositional phrases can be constituents of verb phrases, rule 9 says that other prepositional phrases can be constituents of noun phrases. Rule 9 allows the grammar to generate sentences such as 10:

10

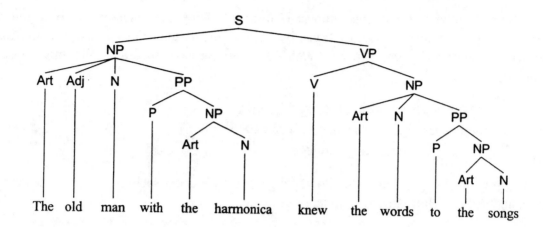

Our grammar can now be updated to allow not only prepositional phrases that modify verbs, as in 7, but also prepositional phrases that modify nouns, as in 10.

11

PS RULES	LEXICON
S → NP VP	Art: . . .
NP → (Art) (Adj)⁺ N (PP)	Adj: . . .
VP → V (NP) (PP)	N: . . .
VP → V_L $\left\{ \begin{array}{c} NP \\ Adj \end{array} \right\}$ (PP)	V: . . .
	V_L: . . .
PP → P NP	P: of, against, about, on, . . .

Exercises 4.2

Draw trees to show how grammar 11 can generate the following sentences, which include prepositional phrases that modify nouns. Except for the prepositions, I have left it to you to supply the lexicon in 11.

1. The contents of the box puzzled Cassandra.
2. The fight against pollution continued.
3. Sandra enjoys funny stories about lawyers.
4. A high grade on the exam was the result of long hard work.

We have now seen prepositional phrases that modify verbs (such as those in 1) and others that modify nouns (such as in 8). You may wonder if there is a way to determine which is which. The phrase's position in the sentence isn't necessarily an indication, as the following seemingly similar sentences demonstrate:

12 a. Joe hit the ball *with the bat*. —constituent of the VP; modifies *hit*

    b. Joe admired the woman *with the hat*. —constituent of the NP; modifies *woman*

It is necessary to consider the meaning of a prepositional phrase and the purpose it serves in the sentence in order to identify which element it modifies. For example, in **12a**, *with the bat* tells us *how* Joe did the hitting. Consequently, it modifies the verb *hit* and is a constituent of a verb phrase. In **12b**, however, *with the hat* does not tell us how Joe did the admiring (he didn't admire her with a hat). Instead it tell us *which* woman we are talking about. It modifies the noun *woman* and is a constituent of a noun phrase. The different purposes these prepositional phrases serve are reflected in the different structures of the sentences:

13

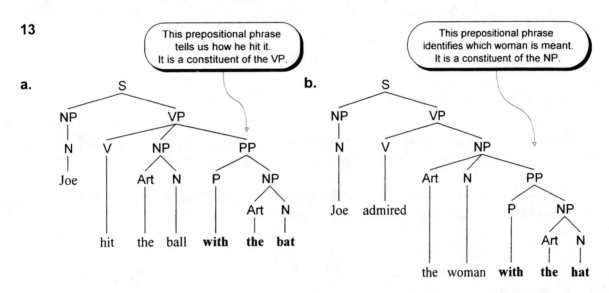

Look carefully at these two trees. In **13a**, *with the bat* modifies *hit* and so is a constituent of the VP. In **13b**, *with the hat* modifies *woman* and so is a constituent of the NP.

Exercises 4.3

1. Underline the prepositional phrases in the following sentences. For each prepositional phrase, state whether it is a constituent of a verb phrase or of a noun phrase.

    a. Ahab steered the boat <u>through rough seas</u>.   [constituent of the verb phrase]

If you have difficulty, you can use several tests to help you determine whether a prepositional phrase such as "through rough seas" modifies a noun or a verb.

- *Ask, "What kind of boat?" If "boat through rough seas" answers that question (it doesn't), the prepositional phrase modifies "boat" and is a constituent of the NP.*
- *Ask, "Steered it where (or when, how, or why)?" If "steered it through rough seas" answers that question (it does), the prepositional phrase modifies "steered" and is a constituent of the VP.*

- *See if you can move the prepositional phrase to the beginning of the sentence without changing meaning. If "Through rough seas, Ahab steered the boat" keeps the same meaning (it does), the prepositional phrase is a constituent of the VP.*

    b. Lulu met a woman from Lithuania.

                     [Hint: Is she a *"woman* from Lithuania," or did Lulu *"meet* her from Lithuania"?]

    c. Orville launched the plane from the beach.

                     [Hint: Is it a *"plane* from the beach," or did Orville *"launch* it from the beach"?]

    d. The detective recognized the man in the photograph.

    e. The detective identified the woman from the photograph.

    f. The trainer threw the old socks into the garbage.

    g. The leader of the gang buried the loot under the front porch.

    h. The menu features potatoes with sour cream.

2. Draw trees for exercise sentences 1a–1h.

3. Can you have constituents of both kinds together in the same sentence? Consider the following sentences and draw trees to show how grammar 11 can generate them.

    a. Phyllis photographed the bridge over the river with an old camera.

    b. Bret hid the keys to the car under the front seat.

A Case of Ambiguity

We have no trouble understanding what the sentences of 1 or 8 mean, but not all sentences are so clear. Consider sentence 14, for example. Is it possible to interpret it in more than one way?

14   Miranda saw the boy with a telescope.

Depending on your interpretation, sentence 14 could be equivalent to either of the following two sentences:

15 a. Miranda saw the boy by looking through the telescope.   [Miranda had the telescope.]

    b. Miranda saw the boy who had a telescope.   [The boy had the telescope.]

A sentence like 14 with two or more possible interpretations or "readings" is said to be **ambiguous**. In conversation or writing, the intended interpretation of such a sentence is usually clear from the context in which it occurs. But when it occurs in isolation, as 14 does, there is no way to decide whether the meaning of 15a or of 15b is intended.

    Sentence 14 is ambiguous because of the uncertain role of the prepositional phrase *with a telescope*. Because a prepositional phrase can occur either within a verb phrase or within a noun phrase, sentence 14 could have either of the following tree structures. Study them, and notice which phrase-structure rules are used to construct them.

16

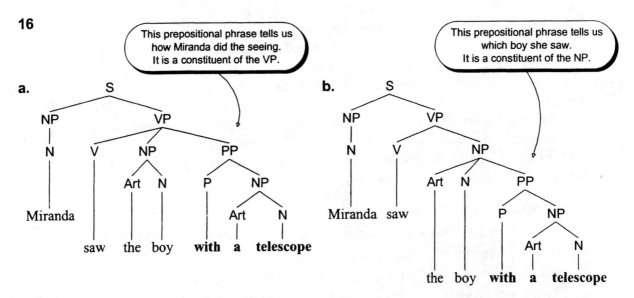

In 16a, the prepositional phrase *with a telescope* is a constituent of the verb phrase. As such, it modifies the verb *saw* and describes how Miranda did the seeing. It corresponds in meaning with 15a. In 16b, on the other hand, the prepositional phrase is a constituent of the noun phrase. It modifies the noun *boy* and tells which boy Miranda saw. It corresponds in meaning with 15b.

Let us review what our examination of sentence 14 has shown us. While 14 is ambiguous, the two trees 16a and 16b are not. The application of different phrase-structure rules has resulted in two trees with different internal structure. When words are inserted from the lexicon, however, it so happens that the wording of the two different sentences is identical. We will see that whenever two different trees can diagram the same sentence (actually two different sentences with the same words), the result is a case of ambiguity. The fact that our grammar can explain and account for such ambiguity is a gratifying indication that our model is a successful reflection of the internal grammar in our minds.

It is essential that you understand the difference in structure between 16a and 16b and can see why these trees correspond with 15a and 15b respectively. The purpose of a tree diagram, as I said earlier, is to display a sentence's internal makeup. By looking at a tree, you should be able to see what the constituents are and how they relate to each other. If you still have trouble, reread this chapter and ask your instructor for help. Do not allow yourself to remain confused, or you will have increasing difficulty as additional concepts are introduced.

Exercises 4.4

1. For each of the following ambiguous sentences, explain what two different interpretations it can have. Then draw trees to show the structure of each of those interpretations.

    a. The artist painted the picture in the museum.

    b. Cubby bought a bracelet with gold.

    c. The astronaut greeted the ambassador from the moon.

2. Linguists identify two types of ambiguity, structural ambiguity and lexical ambiguity. Two identically worded sentences such as 16a and 16b that are created using different phrase-structure rules and so have different internal structures are said to be ***structurally ambiguous***. Two identically worded sentences that have the same tree structure but contain an ambiguous word (more properly, two words with the identical sound) are said to be ***lexically ambiguous***. For example, the sentence *The rabbi married my sister* is lexically ambiguous because the word *married* can mean either "became the spouse of" or "performed a wedding ceremony for." For each of the following sentences, state whether it is structurally or lexically ambiguous, and discuss what accounts for the ambiguity.

    a. Veronica cannot bear children.
    b. W.C. Fields disliked small children and dogs.   [Hint: Did he like St. Bernards?]
    c. Actual newspaper headline: "Complaints about NBA Referees Growing Ugly"
    d. Actual newspaper headline: "Bill Would Permit Ads on Eyeglasses"
    e. Do you smoke after jogging?   ["No, but I perspire a little."]
    f. Oscar ate the baloney sandwich with relish.
    g. Sipping whisky can be costly.

Later chapters of this book will account for the different types of structural ambiguity presented in this exercise.

Recursive Prepositional Phrases

One interesting feature of rules 2 and 9 is that a prepositional phrase can contain a noun phrase, and a noun phrase can contain a prepositional phrase. This allows us to have one prepositional phrase within another, as in sentence 17:

17

The prepositional phrase *of the Declaration* modifies *author* because its purpose is to identify which author is meant, and the phrase *of Independence* modifies *Declaration* because its purpose is to identify which Declaration is meant. In fact, there is no reason why we would have to stop at two prepositional phrases. You could have any number of them, one inside the other. You could easily speak *about the size of the lettering on the top of the cover of the book about the writing of the Declaration of Independence*, to give an example of a series with eight prepositional phrases nested one within the other. This property of a grammar that allows it to generate constituents that recur again and again (as often as we choose) is called *recursion*.

Exercises 4.5

The following sentences contain recursive prepositional phrases (with one prepositional phrase nested inside another one). Draw trees to show their structure.

1. The name of the cat in the story is Felix.
2. Predictions of a large snowfall caused a big increase in the sale of shovels.
3. Fresh mint is the prime ingredient in the recipe for a sauce for the rack of lamb.

Don't be tricked by the following sentence. Consider which prepositional phrases modify the nouns that precede them and which ones modify the verb:

4. The grocer displayed a basket of the succulent peaches from Georgia in the front of the store.

Personal Pronouns

Our revised noun-phrase rule 9 allows our grammar to generate noun phrases with a great variety of structures, such as the underlined subjects of these sentences:

18 a. _____ George amazed Evelyn.
   b. _____ The acrobats amazed Evelyn.
   c. ___The zany, spontaneous exuberance___
      ___of the chimpanzees in the circus___ amazed Evelyn.

Another class of words can also act as noun phrases. In fact, these words can take the place of the noun phrases in 18:

19 a. _____ He amazed Evelyn.
   b. _____ They amazed Evelyn.
   c. _____ It amazed Evelyn.

The words *he, they,* and *it* in 19a–19c are called ***personal pronouns*** (abbreviated **Pro_P**). In traditional grammar, a pronoun is defined as a word that is used as a substitute for a noun. That is not quite accurate, because a pronoun substitutes for all the words in a noun phrase. In the sentences of 19, the pronouns are equivalent to the entire underlined noun phrases in 18. For example, the pronoun *it* in 19c is used in place of (and with the same meaning as) *the zany, spontaneous exuberance of the chimpanzees in the circus* in 18c.

Because a noun phrase can consist simply of a personal pronoun, our phrase-structure rule needs to be expanded:

20

$$NP \rightarrow \left\{ \begin{array}{c} (Art) \ (Adj)^+ \ N \ (PP) \\ Pro_P \end{array} \right\}$$

Rule 20 states that a noun phrase can be one of two things: either (1) a phrase consisting of a noun with or without the optional modifiers or else (2) a simple personal pronoun. This rule allows the grammar to generate sentence such as the following:

21

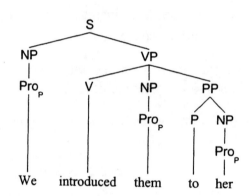

The following chart lists the personal pronouns in our language:

22

PERSONAL PRONOUNS		
	Singular	*Plural*
1st person = *speaker(s):*	I / me	we / us
2nd person = *hearer(s):*	you / you	you / you
3rd person = *person(s) or thing(s) spoken about:*	she / her he / him it / it	they / them

Of the three "persons" in the chart, ***first person*** refers to the speaker; ***second person*** refers to the hearer, the person spoken to; and ***third person*** refers to the person or thing being spoken about. A ***singular*** pronoun refers, of course, to a single person or thing, while a ***plural*** pronoun refers to more than one. Notice that for the second person, *you* is used for both singular and plural. Several centuries ago, English had the distinct second-person singular forms *thou/thee*, but those forms have become obsolete. In casual conversation, however, it is sometimes useful to make a distinction between singular and plural pronouns to make it clear to a hearer if the speaker is addressing that person alone (*you*-singular) or a group that includes that person (*you*-plural). Language always adapts to fill a perceived need, and regional dialects have created special plural forms to use in informal situations. These include *you guys, y'all, y'uns,* and *yuz.* Is one or more of these forms in use in your locale?

The difference between *I* and *me* (and between *we/us, she/her,* and the other pairs in the chart) is that the former (*I, we, she,* and so on) are said to be in the **nominative** (or **subjective**) **case**, while the latter (*me, us, her,* and so on) are said to be in the **objective case**. The nominative form is used for a sentence's **subject** (the noun phrase that precedes the verb, such as *we* in tree 21), while the objective form is used for a **direct object** (the noun phrase that follows a transitive verb, such as *them* in 21) or for an **object of a preposition** (the noun phrase that follows a preposition, such as *her* in 21). These cases are labeled in tree 23:

23

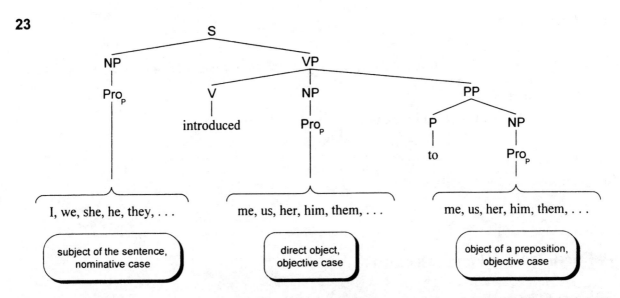

Whether or not you are familiar with the names of these cases, you certainly know about them unconsciously, and you use the right forms in the right situations. No speaker of English is likely to mistake them as in 24:

24   * Us introduced they to she.

Although we will not try to formulate them, we will assume that our grammar has rules that assign the proper number, person, and case to personal pronouns.

With the revised noun-phrase rule 20, our updated grammar contains the rules listed in 25. Notice that the two verb-phrase rules that were listed separately in our previous version (grammar 11) are here rewritten as a single verb-phrase rule. This is only a notational variation; notice how the one VP rule in 25 is identical in function to the two VP rules of 11.

25

```
                        PS RULES

              S  →  NP  VP

                      ⎧ (Art)  (Adj)⁺  N  (PP) ⎫
              NP  →  ⎨                          ⎬
                      ⎩        Proₚ              ⎭

                      ⎧  V  (NP)          ⎫
              VP  →  ⎨      ⎧ NP  ⎫        ⎬  (PP)
                      ⎩  Vₗ ⎨ Adj ⎬        ⎭

              PP  →  P  NP
```

Exercises 4.6

Using the rules in 25 and the appropriate lexical items, draw trees for the following sentences:

1. We warned her.
2. A present for them arrived in the mail.
3. She maintained a fast pace until the middle of the last lap.
4. The collision broke it into pieces.
5. You took me for a fool!

A Further Word on Inflections

Because different forms of personal pronouns are used for singular and plural number and for nominative and objective cases, we can say that the pronouns are **inflected** for number and case. **Inflections** are the different forms or endings a word takes to communicate different grammatical information. In addition to pronouns, other inflected parts of speech include nouns (which, for example, usually take -s for the plural: *monkeys*), verbs (which often take -ed for the past tense: *admired*), and adjectives (which often take -er and -est for the comparative and superlative forms: *smarter, smartest*).

Compared to many other languages (such as German, Greek, or Russian), English is not highly inflected. For example, nouns and articles in English, unlike pronouns, do not take different inflections for the nominative and objective cases. Consider the noun phrases in sentence 26.

26   The boy teased the girl.

In many other languages, different forms of the nouns (*boy* and *girl*) or of the article (*the*) would be used to show that *the boy* is the subject of the sentence and *the girl* is the direct object. In English, however, none of these words is inflected to show case information. Nevertheless, we have no doubt that it is the boy who is doing the teasing and the girl who is being teased. We are given this information by the sentence's word order. A noun phrase that comes before the verb is generally the subject in an English sentence. A noun phrase that comes afterward is generally the direct object. A language like English that relies largely on word order rather than inflections to convey case information is called a **word-order language**. A language that relies largely on inflections rather than word order is called an **inflected language**.

Languages are constantly changing, and English has changed greatly in the past thousand years. The English of a thousand years ago (called Old English or Anglo-Saxon) was a highly inflected language, and it placed less importance than does modern English on word order. In more recent centuries, however, word order has become increasingly important in our language, and we have gradually lost most of the inflections that no longer serve a useful purpose. The nonessential distinction between *who* and *whom* is one that is being lost within our own lifetimes. Of all the parts of speech, personal pronouns retain the most inflected forms. It is not inconceivable that a century or two from now, either the nominative or the objective pronouns will have died out, and it will be standard for our descendants to speak sentences such as *Me introduced them to her*.

Varieties of English

When scholars engage in any quest for knowledge, their inquiry is inevitably based on certain assumptions, and it is important for them to be aware of what those assumptions are and, if necessary, to question them. From time to time in our quest to discover the structure of the English language, we have paused to examine our assumptions. The most basic assumption of all—one that we have left unexamined until now—has been that there really is such a thing as "*the* English language." In fact, that is hardly the case. The English spoken by an English aristocrat differs markedly from that spoken by a teenager in a California suburb or that spoken by an Australian sheep rancher.

Even the very same person will use several different "Englishes." For example, there are noticeable differences between the language used by a government leader when delivering a prepared speech to a large audience and when answering questions at a press conference. And that same person may sound quite different still when talking informally with family members. You too sound different—you use a different variety of the language—when you talk comfortably with friends and when you speak on the telephone to an elderly great aunt. And the varieties of language you use in speaking are different from those you use in writing. The latter tend to employ longer sentences, a wider vocabulary, and a greater variety of syntactic constructions. (If, instead of writing, I were talking privately to you, I probably would not have spoken a sentence as long as the previous one nor have used such a "literary" word as *employ*).

Because English is so varied, what is the grammarian to do? How can we describe the structure of English when no single entity called "English" exists?

The answer is that our task is to describe an **idealized language**, if not in all respects an actual one. It is English as *generally* used by educated native speakers. It is, in short, a consensus of what most people agree is the English language. Each of us is different, of course, and there are unique and distinctive features to our individual speech and writing, but the general features and rules that we are attempting to describe are those about which there is general agreement.

Another characteristic of our grammar study is that it is *descriptive*, not *prescriptive*. Although of necessity it is based on an idealized language, our inquiry must be grounded securely in actual usage. Our goal is not to *prescribe* what English would be like if everyone spoke the way we decided they should speak. Instead our goal is to discover and *describe* the English that the majority of educated speakers actually produce. For example, because many literate users of the language routinely begin sentences with conjunctions or end them with prepositions, we have no choice but to accept those practices as "good English."

Written English, I have said, differs from *spoken English* in several ways. The sentences that we have been analyzing in this book would, for the most part, be considered grammatical both in speech and in writing. But because there is much less variation in written than in spoken English (people from different regions, for example, who sound very different in speech produce a very similar style of language when they write), the idealized language that we examine is much like written language. We will have occasion, however, to look at some distinctly oral constructions as well.

There are many other varieties of English that we could mention before we return to our idealized variety. Different groups of people speak different variations, or dialects, of English. These include *regional dialects* (the English spoken in the American South, for example, differs in some respects from the English spoken in New England), *class dialects* (a working-class Londoner speaks differently from an aristocratic Londoner), and *ethnic dialects* (the language spoken by many African Americans in Chicago is different in certain ways from that spoken by many Polish Americans in Chicago). Dialects are characterized by differences in accents, lexicons, and even phrase-structure rules, and each dialect could be analyzed and described in the same way in which we are here describing our idealized "standard" English. Indeed, it is important to see that what distinguishes one dialect from another is not an *absence* of rules but simply a *different set* of rules.

In addition, all sophisticated speakers and writers of English employ a range of *formal* and *informal* varieties of the language. For example, when you invite someone to join you for a meal, your language can range from the extreme formality of an engraved invitation (". . . requests the pleasure of your company at . . .") to an extremely casual and informal spoken invitation ("J'eat yet?").

There are also specialized aspects of language shared by interest groups. These include *slang*, the informal fad language used by teenagers, musicians, or similar in-groups. Slang words constantly enter the language and often quickly disappear. What was "solid" in the 1940s, "groovy" in the 1960s, and "bad" in the 1980s might now be "phat" or "da bomb"—at least for the moment among high school students in the city where I live. Groups that share a special interest may also have their own private lexicon, or *jargon*. Brain surgeons have their own jargon, and so do flight attendants, skiers, and Internet enthusiasts. Terms of linguistics jargon that are now familiar to you (but not to the general public) include *phrase-structure rule* and *trees*.

As we continue our exploration of the structure of an idealized version of the English language, you may also wish to think about the rules behind other varieties with which you are familiar.

5 Coordinate Phrases and Complement Clauses

Coordination

Coordinate Noun Phrases

Our rules seem to be getting more and more complex. To the simple noun-phrase rule that we started with in Chapter 2, we have added provisions for optional adjectives, prepositional phrases, and pronouns:

1

$$NP \rightarrow \left\{ \begin{array}{c} (Art) \ (Adj)^{+} \ N \ (PP) \\ Pro_{P} \end{array} \right\}$$

And we aren't finished yet! At times a noun phrase can have a kind of collective membership:

2 a. *The man and the woman* greeted Donald.

   b. The workers demanded *higher pay and better benefits*.

   c. They struggled without *food or a reliable source of water*.

Sentence 2a has only one verb phrase (*greeted Donald*), but two noun phrases seem to constitute its subject (*the man* and *the woman*, joined by the word *and*). In sentence 2b, two noun phrases joined by *and* constitute the sentence's direct object. And in 2c, two noun phrases joined by *or* act as the object of the preposition *without*. The words *and* and *or*, which connect the noun phrases, are called *coordinating conjunctions* (abbreviated C_{Co}).

To account for sentence 2a, we will say that the subject noun phrase (*the man and the woman*) has as its constituents two different noun phrases joined by a conjunction. The subject of 2a will have the following structure:

3

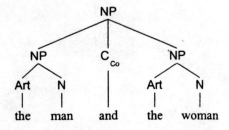

That is, one overall noun phrase (*the man and the woman*) consists of two smaller individual noun phrases (*the man*, *the woman*) linked together by a coordinating conjunction. Such a noun phrase is known as a ***coordinate noun phrase***. The rule that would allow noun phrases with this structure is the following:

4   NP → NP C_{Co} NP

The two rules 1 and 4 allow us to generate sentences like these:

5 a.

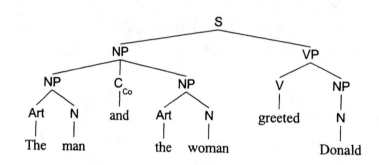

b.

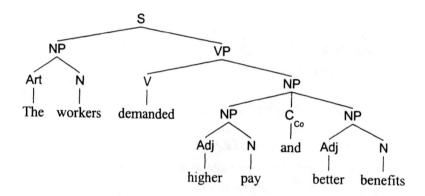

c.

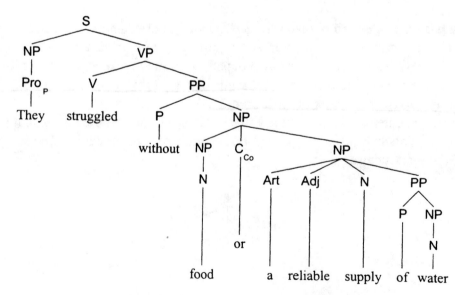

Look carefully at the coordinate noun phrases in 5a–5c. Notice that in each of these a noun phrase "splits" into two noun phrases, each of which behaves like an ordinary noun phrase.

Our updated grammar contains the phrase-structure rules in 6. Use these rules to practice generating coordinate noun phrases in the exercises that follows.

6

PS RULES	LEXICON
S → NP VP	. . .
	C_{Co}: and, or, . . .
NP → $\begin{Bmatrix} NP \ C_{Co} \ NP \\ (Art) \ (Adj)^+ \ N \ (PP) \\ Pro_P \end{Bmatrix}$	. . .
VP → $\begin{Bmatrix} V \ (NP) \\ V_L \begin{Bmatrix} NP \\ Adj \end{Bmatrix} \end{Bmatrix}$ (PP)	
PP → P NP	

Exercises 5.1

Use grammar 6 to draw trees for the following sentences with coordinate noun phrases:

1. The rain and the insects spoiled the party.
2. Loren cooked sweet potatoes and gravy.
   [Hint: Don't forget both the NP and N labels above *Loren* and *gravy*.]
3. Frank chose Myron or Stella.
4. Leonora worked with a hammer and a saw.
5. The explorer and the wolves lived in peace and harmony.
6. Algernon left the keys to the car and an umbrella in the room.
   [Hint: Pay attention to whether prepositional phrases modify nouns or verbs.]
7. The detective and I solved the mystery through simple logic and a month of tedious labor.

Another Case of Ambiguity

The following sentence is ambiguous. Can you see its two different interpretations?

7   Pat ate pancakes and sausages or fried eggs.

The different readings may become more evident when brackets are put around different groupings of noun phrases:

8 **a.** Pat ate [pancakes and sausages] or [fried eggs].
    b. Pat ate [pancakes] and [sausages or fried eggs].

Sentences 8a and 8b correspond in meaning, respectively, to the following two sentences:

9 **a.** Pat ate pancakes and sausages, or else Pat ate fried eggs.
    b. Pat ate pancakes, and Pat also ate either sausages or fried eggs.

By applying rule 4 twice (but in different ways), we can generate sentences that correspond with the two readings of 9:

10 a.

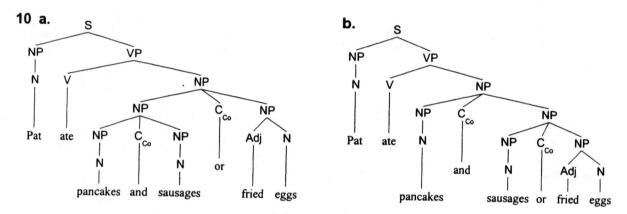

Notice how each element in these trees is generated by one of the phrase-structure rules in grammar 6. Once again our model has proved capable of accounting for and explaining an ambiguity.

Exercises 5.2

1. Which tree, 10a or 10b, represents the sentence with the same meaning as 9a?

2. The following sentence is ambiguous:

    The tour visits Italy or France and Spain.

    a. Draw the tree for that sentence when it means that either the tour visits Italy, or else it visits both France and Spain.
    b. Draw the tree for the sentence when it means that the tour visits either Italy or France, and it also visits Spain.

Other Conjoined Phrases

Noun phrases are not the only phrases that can be joined by conjunctions. In the following sentence, a single person performs two different actions.

11   James *dated Susan but married Phyllis*.

The sentence has one subject noun phrase (*James*) but two verb phrases (*dated Susan* and *married Phyllis*) joined by a conjunction (*but*). A rule is needed to account for coordinate verb phrases, equivalent to rule 4 for noun phrases:

12   VP → VP C$_{Co}$ VP

Adding rule 12 allows the grammar to generate trees such as 13:

13

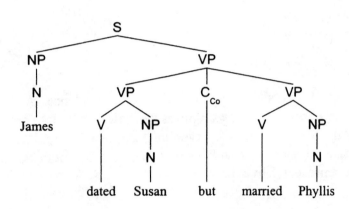

Exercises 5.3

Draw trees for the following sentences with coordinate verb phrases:

1. Norm did the work but failed the oral exam.
2. The children in the audience looked at the monster and screamed.
3. Stan and Dixie visit the beach or relax at home.

We can have coordinate noun phrases and coordinate verb phrases. Can any other phrases be linked by conjunctions? Consider the following sentence:

14   Stephanie stepped *off the pier and into the lake*.

Here the coordinating conjunction *and* connects two prepositional phrases, *off the pier* and *into the lake*. Let us add the following rule to our grammar:

15   PP → PP C$_{Co}$ PP

Rule 15 allows us to draw a tree diagram for sentence 14:

16

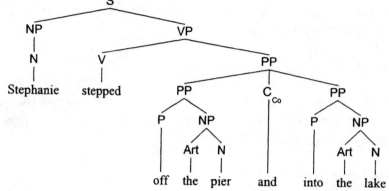

Notice that we now have three quite similar rules for coordinate phrases:

17 NP → NP C$_{Co}$ NP
VP → VP C$_{Co}$ VP
PP → PP C$_{Co}$ PP

The similarity of these rules does not appear to be mere coincidence. A pattern seems at work here. Because we want our grammar to be as simple as possible, we look to capture generalizations. Let us hypothesize that *all* phrases of the same type can be joined by coordinating conjunctions. We can replace the three separate rules of 17 with a single rule 18 that captures this generalization. We will use the label **XP** to represent "any type of phrase."

18 XP → XP C$_{Co}$ XP

That is, any two phrases of the same type may be joined together to form a larger phrase of that type. Two noun phrases can be conjoined to form a single noun phrase, and the same is true of verb phrases, prepositional phrases, and, we will assume, other types of phrases as well. With this simplification, our grammar now looks like the following:

19

PS RULES	LEXICON
S → NP VP	. . .
NP → { (Art) (Adj)$^+$ N (PP) / Pro$_P$ }	C$_{Co}$: and, or, but, yet, nor . . .
VP → { V (NP) / V$_L$ { NP / Adj } } (PP)	. . .
PP → P NP	
XP → XP C$_{Co}$ XP	

Exercises 5.4

1. Use grammar 19 to draw trees for the following sentences with coordinate prepositional phrases:

   a. Celeste left in sadness but without anger.
   b. People from Austria and from Germany speak the same language.
   c. Grandma rode the sleigh over the river and through the woods.

2. Double underline the conjunctions in each of the following sentences. Then underline the phrases on both sides of each conjunction, and label each of them as NP, VP, or PP. Remember: You will have the same type of phrase on both sides of the conjunction. Finally, use grammar 19 to draw the tree for each sentence:

   a. Kit admired <u>Lucy</u> <u><u>and</u></u> <u>Alex</u>.
                     NP   NP
   b. The boxes of foodstuffs and of supplies filled the warehouse.
   c. A half-empty glass of Scotch and soda lay beside the victim of the crime.
   > [Hint: Is there a prepositional phrase on both sides of the conjunction? If not, what kind of phrase occurs on both sides of the conjunction? When in doubt, it often helps to look at the phrase immediately to the right of the conjunction.]
   d. The waiter heard the order yet brought the wrong appetizer.
   e. The child and an elderly woman entered the station and bought tickets.

   Check your trees to be certain you have followed the phrase-structure rules carefully. Note that whenever you have a coordinating conjunction, it will be surrounded by a trio of identical phrase labels, like these:

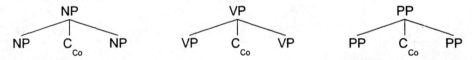

   If ever you draw a coordinate phrase that does not have the triangular structure shown above, you have made a mistake. Check especially to see if the label at the top of the triangle is missing.

(3.) Optional discovery exercises: These exercises call for you to make original contributions in syntax.

   a. In addition to the coordinate phrases we have examined so far, some coordinate phrases have more than two members. Sometimes they are all joined by conjunctions (*Bob and Ted and Carol and Alice*), and sometimes all conjunctions but the last are omitted (*Barb, Ned, Carl, and Alison*). Consider what the trees for these phrases might look like, and hypothesize how the grammar might be revised to account for these phrases.

---

b. Consider the following sentence:

> Dad washes the car and mows the lawn on weekends.

Assume the sentence means that Dad does both activities on weekends. If so, the prepositional phrase *on weekends* does not just modify the verb *mows*. What problems does this create for our model? How might the grammar be revised to account for sentences like this?

Coordinate Sentences

Like phrases, entire sentences can also be joined by a conjunction:

20 Albert cooked the dinner, and Dominique brought a dessert.

A complete sentence occurs on either side of the conjunction. We can add a new rule, 21, to our grammar and use it to generate trees such as 22.

21 S → S C_{Co} S

22

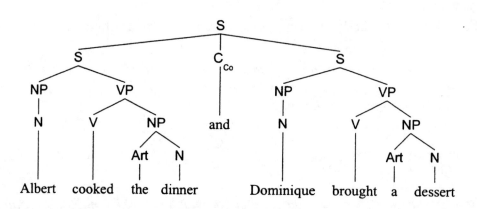

Rule 21 tells us that a larger sentence can be constructed out of two smaller sentences by joining them with a conjunction. Note that each of the lower S-groupings in 22 could stand by itself as an independent sentence. A sentence that contains only a single S-grouping (such as *The monkey saw a leopard*) is called a **simple sentence**. A sentence such as 20 that has two S-groupings joined by a coordinating conjunction is called a **compound sentence**. ~2 that can standalone as phrases- not complete though

Although we proposed rule 21 to account for compound sentences, its addition to our grammar is not really necessary, because sentence coordination can be covered by our general coordination rule 18, which allows the conjoining of any two phrases of the same type. We defined a phrase as any group of words that acts as a constituent, so an S is also a type of phrase—just like an NP, a VP, or a PP.

Although S-groupings are indeed phrases, in common speech the term *phrase* usually refers to a grouping smaller than a sentence, such as a noun phrase or verb phrase. An S-grouping (on a tree, the words that branch out beneath an S-label) is usually called a **clause**. Sentence 22 consists of two clauses joined by the coordinating conjunction *and*. Although a distinction is often made between phrases and clauses, it should be remembered that a clause is a particular type of phrase, and any rule such as 18 that applies to phrases can also apply to clauses.

Exercises 5.5

Draw trees to show how grammar 19 can generate the following sentences with coordinate clauses and phrases. Because some of them are long, your trees may fit better on the page if you turn your paper sideways. Always leave plenty of room for your trees. If you do not, the trees will be cramped and will lose their effectiveness as clear diagrams of the sentences' structures.

1. A nail caused the puncture, and Shirley changed the tire.
2. Victor and Constance dreamed glorious dreams, yet they lived mundane lives.
3. Caesar invaded Britain, but Britain withstood Napoleon and Hitler.
4. Julio rescued the crew and won a promotion.   [Don't be tricked by this one.]

Now that you have gotten this far, you may be ready for a final challenge, a sentence that has everything:

5. The holy man and I climbed the steps and entered the lost temple, but the priestesses captured us and threatened us with torture or with a slow death by starvation.

Exercise sentence 5, you may be relieved to learn, is the longest sentence you will be asked to diagram in this book. If you overcame that challenge, you are certainly on top of the subject, and you have demonstrated considerable aptitude as a grammarian. As a true grammarian, you no doubt consider the tree you drew for that sentence to be not just an object of pride but a thing of beauty as well.

A note on usage: In writing, a comma is usually placed before a conjunction when it joins two clauses (as in exercise sentences 1 through 3) but not when it joins two simple phrases (as in sentence 4).

Complement Clauses

Sentential-Complement Clauses

At the beginning of this chapter, we observed that noun phrases can take various forms. For example, the direct-object slot in the following tree can be filled by many different kinds of constituents, including one that we have not previously seen:

23

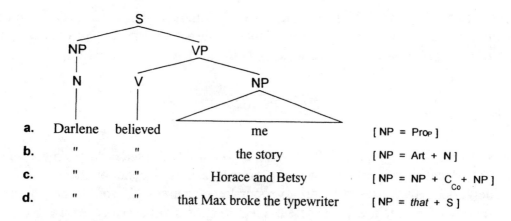

a.	Darlene	believed	me	[NP = Pro$_P$]
b.	"	"	the story	[NP = Art + N]
c.	"	"	Horace and Betsy	[NP = NP + C$_{Co}$ + NP]
d.	"	"	that Max broke the typewriter	[NP = *that* + S]

Tree 23 actually represents four different trees, each with a different direct object. It also introduces a new shorthand device, a triangle used to represent missing elements in the tree. Note that I did not fully analyze the constituents of the direct object NP. A complete analysis of tree 23a would have the Pro$_P$ label above the word "me," and a complete analysis of 23b would have the Art and N labels above "the" and "story, and so on. Whenever we draw a triangle, it means that, for the sake of simplicity, constituents are omitted that we could easily supply if we chose to.

In sentence 23d, the object noun phrase, the thing that Darlene believed, is an entire clause. Such clauses are called **complement clauses** (more specifically, **sentential-complement clauses**), because they are clauses that complement (or complete) the main clause. They are also called **nominal clauses** because they function as noun phrases. Sentential-complement clauses can occur either as subjects or as objects of sentences:

24 a. *That Tom remembered the appointment* amazed the doctor. —clause as subject

    b. The doctor warned *that nicotine causes cancer.* —clause as object

The word *that*, which introduces the complement clauses in the two sentences, is called a **complementizer** or **complementizing conjunction** (abbreviated **C$_{Cj}$**). Notice that the word *that* in these sentences has no meaning by itself, but rather it acts as a kind of verbal signpost, alerting the listener or reader that a complement clause (and not the main clause) is about to follow. Notice how confusing sentence 24a would be if the "meaningless" complementizer *that* were omitted. Parts of speech such as complementizers that have no independent meaning but that instead express a relationship between other words in a sentence are called **grammatical** or **structural words**. In addition to complementizers, other grammatical words include articles, prepositions, and coordinating conjunctions. Words that have an independent meaning, such as nouns, verbs, and adjectives, are called **lexical** or **content words**. Note that if you consider a lexical word in isolation (for example, *happiness, write, small*), you can envision a concept. In contrast a grammatical word (*that, but, of*) needs to occur in connection with other words for it to conjure up an image.

We will represent complement clauses by the abbreviation **CompP**. The "P" in the abbreviation stands for "phrase"; we could use the abbreviation "CompC" if we chose, but later on we will discover that complements can include phrases as well as clauses. Consequently we will find CompP a useful abbreviation to stand for *all* complements, both clauses and phrases.

The following additional NP rule expresses our discovery that a noun phrase can be an entire complement clause:

25   NP → CompP

Sentences 24a and 24b will have this general structure:

26 a.

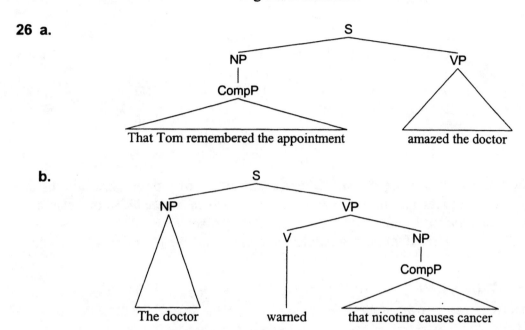

b.

Notice that in 26a, something amazed the doctor. That something could have been a simple noun phrase (such as *the trick*), but instead what amazed the doctor is expressed in a complete sentence, namely, *that Tom remembered the appointment*. We can observe, then, that each of the two complement clauses consists of the complementizer *that* and an S-clause. We can state this observation in the following rule:

27   CompP → C$_{Cl}$ S

With rules 25 and 27, we can now draw the complete trees for 24a and 24b:

28 a.

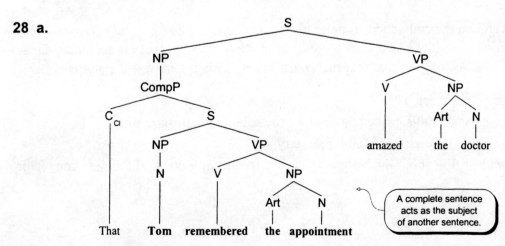

b.

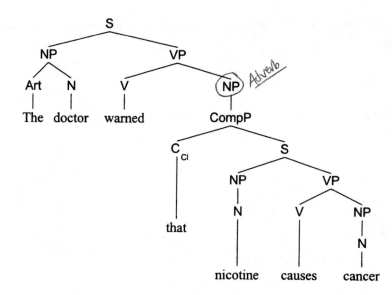

Each of the lower S-clauses in 28a and 28b is a constituent of a noun phrase in the upper S-clause. When one clause is a constituent of another, it is said to be *embedded* in that clause. The clause *nicotine causes cancer* is embedded in the main clause of sentence 28b.

When rule 27 is incorporated into the grammar, the comprehensive NP rule looks like this:

29

$$NP \rightarrow \left\{ \begin{array}{c} (Art)\ (Adj)^+\ N\ (PP) \\ Pro_P \\ CompP \end{array} \right\}$$

It should be clear that when a rule such as 29 provides options, any one of the options may be chosen whenever a noun phrase occurs. There is no significance to the order in which the three options are listed in 29. For example, the rule would have had exactly the same effect if the pronoun or the complement-clause option had been placed first.

Exercises 5.6

1. Place brackets around the embedded complement clauses in the following sentences, and decide whether each complement clause acts as the subject or the direct object of the sentence. Finally, draw trees to show how a grammar that incorporates rule 29 can generate the sentences:

   a. Roscoe knew [that roses have thorns].   — direct object
   b. That a computer had bugs caused anxiety for the squeamish programmer.
   c. Willie doubts that babies understand geometry.
   d. That Margot testified about the burglary resulted in the conviction of the notorious felon.

Sometimes a sentence can have more than one complement clause:

e. That the sun shone meant that the groundhog saw a shadow.

And sometimes one complement clause can be embedded in another:

f. Pedro heard that Pierre believed that Olga loves Hans.

2. *That* is not the only word that can introduce a complement clause. Other complementizers include *if* and *whether*. Draw trees for the following sentences:

    a. I doubt whether you remember me.
    b. A thoughtful homeowner asked if the gardener wanted a cold drink.

3. All the complement clauses we have seen so far have been either subjects or direct objects, but none has been the object of a preposition. Draw trees for the following sentences:

    a. Carson overheard an argument about whether angels have navels.
    b. The suspect denied everything except that he was a friend of the victim.   [N: *everything*]

4. Note the coordinating conjunctions in the following sentences. Draw trees to show their structure.

    a. Whether we win or whether we lose is immaterial.
    b. She asked if we won or lost.

(5.) Optional discovery exercise: Sometimes the complementizer *that* can be omitted before a complement clause. Compare these two sentences:

    We heard that Murray was a gambler.
    We heard Murray was a gambler.

But at other times it cannot be omitted:

    That Perry ran for public office amazes me.
    * Perry ran for public office amazes me.

Of the sentences in exercise 1, in which can the complementizer be omitted? Can you discover a general principle for when a complementizer is optional? Is there a practical reason for this principle?

Nominal-Complement Clauses

In a sentence with a sentential-complement clause, the complement clause acts as a noun phrase:

30   *That the neighbors threw a wild party* angered Randolph.

In the following sentences, however, complement clauses follow (and complement) nouns:

31 a. The fact *that the neighbors threw a wild party* angered Randolph.
   b. He conceived the idea *that insomnia prolongs life.*
   c. We laughed at the ridiculous notion *that Martians inhabit Vermont.*

The italicized complement clauses in 31 are called ***nominal-complement clauses*** because they complement or complete the meaning of the nouns that they follow. In 31a, for example, the complement clause *that the neighbors threw a wild party* complements the noun *fact*; that is, it completes its meaning by explaining what the fact is. We can introduce another option to our basic NP rule:

32   NP → (Art) (Adj)⁺ N (PP) **(CompP)**

In addition to its other constituents, a noun phrase can include a nominal-complement clause. This rule allows us to generate the sentences of 31. Here are trees for 31a and 31c:

33 a.

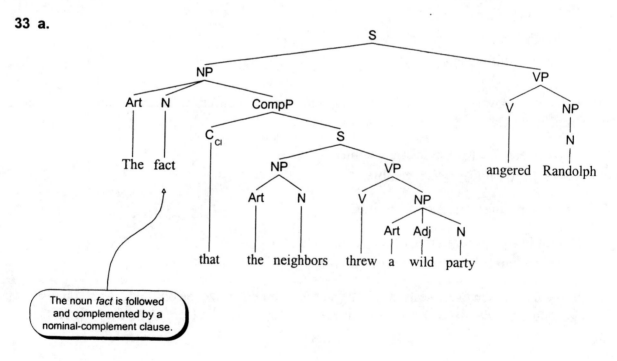

The noun *fact* is followed and complemented by a nominal-complement clause.

b.

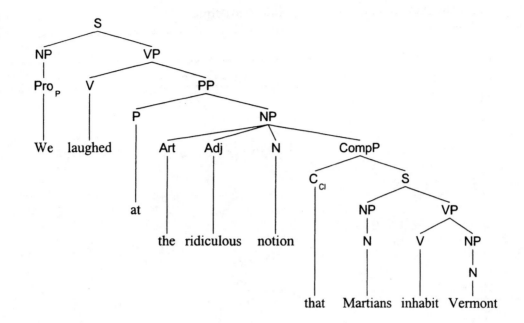

The following, then, represents the difference between sentential complements and nominal complements:

34 a.

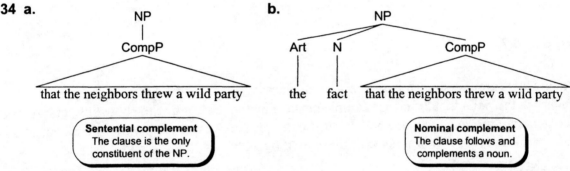

Our grammar now includes the following phrase-structure rules:

35

```
                          PS RULES

            S  →  NP  VP

                       ⎧ (Art) (Adj)⁺ N (PP) (CompP) ⎫
            NP  →     ⎨          Pro_P              ⎬
                       ⎩          CompP              ⎭

         CompP  →  C_Cl  S

                       ⎧  V  (NP)        ⎫
            VP  →     ⎨        ⎧ NP ⎫    ⎬  (PP)
                       ⎩   V_L ⎨ Adj ⎬   ⎭

            PP  →  P  NP

            XP  →  XP  C_Co  XP
```

Exercises 5.7

1. Put brackets around the nominal-complement clauses in each of the following sentences. Then underline the noun that the clause complements. Finally, draw a tree to show how grammar 35 can generate the sentence. If you have difficulty, be sure you are applying rule 32 accurately. Compare each NP in your trees with those in 33a and 33b.

   a. The <u>fact</u> [that Brandi has a bad knee] excused her from PE.
   b. The arbitrator released a statement that the negotiators reached an agreement.
   c. The news that the forecasters predict rain delighted the farmers.
   d. The defendant denied the allegation that he committed perjury.
   e. The lawyer convinced me of the necessity that I write a will.
   f. The strong wish of the voters that the parties in Congress cooperate swayed the election.
      > [Hint: Which noun is being complemented? In other words, is it "the *voters* that they cooperate" or "the *wish* that they cooperate"? Be certain that the complement clause is attached to the correct NP label.]

2. The following sentences contain both sentential and nominal complements. Place brackets around each complement clause. Underline each noun that is modified by a nominal complement. Finally, draw the tree for each sentence.

a. The proposal by the commission that students wear suits and dresses to class shows that they desire a return to the past.

b. That Paula and Marc married confirmed the theory that opposites attract.

3. Nouns such as *fact, theory,* and *statement* can take a nominal complement, and so they can fill the slot in the following noun phrase:

the _____ that the earth is round

Many other nouns, however, cannot take a complement, such as *bride, school, personality,* and *geometry.* List a dozen nouns that can fill the slot in that phrase. Examine the data you have gathered, and make a general statement about which kinds of nouns can take nominal complements.

Adjectival-Complement Clauses

In sentences 31a–31c, a nominal-complement clause follows a noun and completes the noun's meaning. In the following sentences, a complement clause follows an adjective and completes its meaning:

36 a. Randolph was angry *that the neighbors threw a wild party.*

 b. Lana is confident *that she knows the correct answer.*

In 36a, the italicized clause complements (explains) the adjective *angry.* In 36b, the clause complements the adjective *confident.* As you have probably guessed, clauses that complement adjectives are called ***adjectival-complement clauses***. Together, the adjective and the complement clause constitute a phrase, which we will call an ***adjectival phrase*** (abbreviated **AdjP**). The general structure of adjectival-complement clauses, along with those of sentential and nominal-complement clauses, is shown in 37:

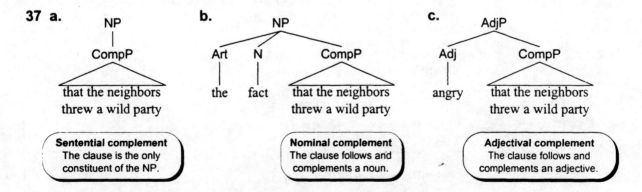

We can assume, then, that the tree for 36a should be the following:

38

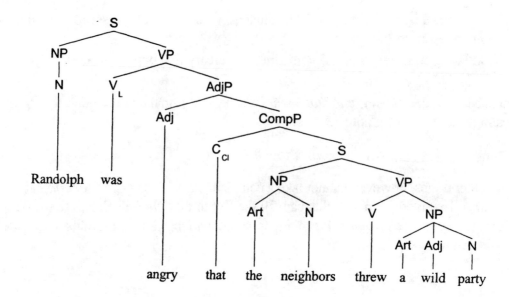

We need to revise our phrase-structure rules in order to account for this tree. In our earlier grammar, a linking verb could be followed either by a noun phrase or by an adjective. Now we see that we must change the latter to an adjectival phrase. Here are new rules:

39

$$VP \rightarrow V_L \left\{ \begin{array}{c} NP \\ AdjP \end{array} \right\}$$

$$AdjP \rightarrow Adj \; (CompP)$$

With these changes, our complete grammar is as follows:

40

<u>PS RULES</u>

$$S \rightarrow NP \; VP$$

$$NP \rightarrow \left\{ \begin{array}{c} (Art) \; (Adj)^+ \; N \; (PP) \; (CompP) \\ Pro_P \\ CompP \end{array} \right\}$$

$$CompP \rightarrow C_{Cl} \; S$$

$$VP \rightarrow \left\{ \begin{array}{c} V \; (NP) \\ V_L \left\{ \begin{array}{c} NP \\ AdjP \end{array} \right\} \end{array} \right\} (PP)$$

$$AdjP \rightarrow Adj \; (CompP)$$

$$PP \rightarrow P \; NP$$

$$XP \rightarrow XP \; C_{Co} \; XP$$

Exercises 5.8

1. For each of the following sentences, place brackets around the adjectival-complement clause, and underline the adjective it complements. Then use grammar 39 to draw the tree for each sentence.

    a. The players were <u>certain</u> [that victory was inevitable]. *adj*
    b. The miners are angry [that the company broke the agreement] *adj*
    c. Vincent seemed happy [that the vacation started] *why* *adj*

2. Place brackets around the complement clauses in the following sentences, and identify each as a sentential, a nominal, or an adjectival complement. Draw a tree for each sentence.

    a. The minister observed [that the organist slept during the sermon] *D.O.*
    b. [That they made a donation] is an indication [that they care] *nominal*
    c. The fact [that she smiles is a sign [that she is glad [that she is alive]
    d. The idea [that Marsha believed [that Charles was furious [that Mona divorced Brad] surprised Vanessa] *nom.* *sent* *adj.*

3. Adjectives such as *happy, perplexed,* and *angry* can take an adjectival complement, and they can fill the slot in the following adjectival phrase:

    _____ that the rained stopped

    On the other hand, many other adjectives, such as *tall, dry,* and *mischievous*, cannot take a complement. List a dozen adjectives that can fill the slot in that phrase. Examine the data, and make a general statement about which kinds of adjectives can take adjectival complements.

4. We have used the label CompP to represent complement clauses. Is there also such a thing as a complement *phrase*? In the following sentences, adjectives are complemented by prepositional phrases, in the same way that adjectives are complemented by clauses in exercise sentences 1a–1c:

    a. The players were certain *of victory*.
    b. The miners are angry *at the company*.
    c. Vincent seemed happy *with the schedule*.

    The italicized adjectival phrases constitute complement phrases. Let us revise the CompP rule to allow for both types of complements:

    $$\text{CompP} \rightarrow \left\{ \begin{array}{c} C_{Cl} \ S \\ PP \end{array} \right\}$$

Use this revised rule to draw trees for sentences *a*, *b*, and *c* with adjectival complement phrases.

(5.) Optional discovery exercise: In sentences 36a and 36b, adjectives are followed by complement clauses. Consider now the following data:

The student is happy.
The student is happy that the rain stopped.

the happy student
* the happy-that-the-rain-stopped student

An adjective such as *happy* can follow a linking verb (*the student is happy*), and it can also precede a noun (*the happy student*). What restrictions do there appear to be about when adjectival complements can occur in English?

Classification of Clauses

In this chapter, we have examined sentences with coordinate clauses, such as 41a, and sentences with complement clauses, such as 41b:

41 a. *Albert cooked the dinner*, and *Dominique brought a dessert*.   —coordinate clauses
b. Darlene said *that Max broke the computer*.   —complement clause

The structure of these sentences falls into the following two general patterns, respectively:

42

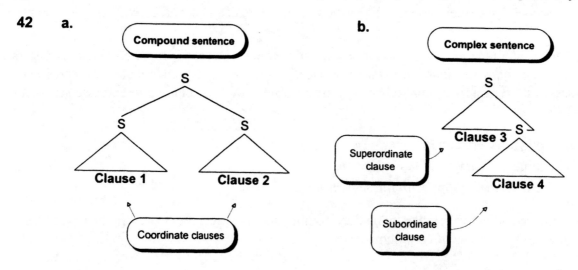

Tree 42a represents a sentence like 41a with two coordinate clauses, and tree 42b represents a sentence like 41b with a complement clause. In traditional grammar, a sentence with coordinate clauses, such as 42a, is called a *compound sentence*. A sentence that has one clause embedded in another, such as 42b, is called a *complex sentence*.

Also in traditional grammar, clauses are usually classified as ***independent clauses*** (also called ***main clauses***) and ***dependent clauses*** (also called ***subordinate clauses***). An independent or main clause is a clause that "can stand on its own" and "is not embedded in another clause." In 42, clauses 1, 2, and 3 are traditionally classified as independent or main clauses. Embedded clauses, such as clause 4, are traditionally classified as dependent or subordinate clauses.

An argument can be made that the traditional terms for clauses are not entirely appropriate. While the two coordinate clauses in 42a are certainly "independent" in the sense that each can function as a sentence on its own (for example, *Albert cooked the dinner* in 41a), they are not necessarily "main" in that they are both embedded under a higher S-label. On the other hand, clause 3 in 42b is certainly "main" because it is the uppermost clause in the tree, but whether a clause like *Darlene said . . .* in 41b is "independent" (able to stand on its own) is questionable.

While it is useful for a grammarian to be familiar with the traditional terms, we might adopt somewhat different terminology. We can refer to clauses 1 and 2 simply as ***coordinate clauses***, which we will define as "two clauses joined on the same level in a tree." We can refer to clause 3 as a ***superordinate clause***, which we will define as "one clause located above another clause in a tree," and to clause 4 as a ***subordinate clause***, which we will define as "one clause located below another in a tree." More simply, we can also refer to clauses like 3 and 4 as ***upper clauses*** and ***lower clauses***, respectively.

A complement clause is one type of subordinate clause. In later chapters, we will encounter several other types of subordinate clauses as well.

6 Determiners, Adverbs, and Other Modifiers

After witnessing our grammar's NP rule grow ever more complicated, you may wonder if at last we have got it the way we want it—at the point where it can generate all the possible noun phrases in English. It cannot, at least not yet, but having come this far, you are well prepared to take any additional modifications in stride. Look at the positive side: With each change we have made, our grammar has become more and more powerful, able to produce ever more varied types of English sentences.

Our noun-phrase rule to date is as follows:

1

$$NP \rightarrow \left\{ \begin{array}{c} (Art) \ (Adj)^{+} \ N \ (PP) \ (CompP) \\ Pro_P \\ CompP \end{array} \right\}$$

Determiners

We will take another look at the top line of rule 1, which generates noun phrases such as this one:

2

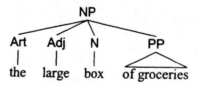

In particular, let us consider the slot occupied by the category Art in that phrase. In addition to the articles (*a*, *an*, and *the*), other words could also fill that slot in a grammatical phrase:

3

This
Each
My   } large box of groceries
John's

Each of these four words can occur in place of *the* in the sample noun phrase 2. A few more tests can help us decide if these words can be true replacements for the Art category. First, none of them can occur along with *the*:

4
$$\left. \begin{array}{l} \ast \ \text{The this} \\ \ast \ \text{This the} \\ \ast \ \text{The each} \\ \ast \ \text{John's the} \\ \ast \ \text{The my} \end{array} \right\} \ \text{large box of groceries}$$

Second, just as two articles cannot occur in a phrase (** the a box*), the four words also cannot occur with each other:

5
$$\left. \begin{array}{l} \ast \ \text{This each} \\ \ast \ \text{John's this} \\ \ast \ \text{Each my} \end{array} \right\} \ \text{large box of groceries}$$

Finally, like the article, each of the four substitutes must precede the adjective; none can follow it:

6
$$\left. \begin{array}{l} \ast \ \text{Large this} \\ \ast \ \text{Large each} \\ \ast \ \text{Large John's} \\ \ast \ \text{Large my} \end{array} \right\} \ \text{box of groceries}$$

The apparent exception, *Large John's*, has a different meaning. It is ungrammatical if it is to retain the meaning that the box is large.

From these tests, we conclude that the four words *this, each, John's,* and *my* do fill the same slot as the article in the noun phrase. A larger grammatical category is needed, one that will include articles as well as these four as-yet-unlabeled words. We will call all such words ***determiners*** (abbreviated **Det**). If we substitute "Det" for "Art," the first line of rule 1 now becomes:

7   NP → **(Det)** (Adj)⁺ N (PP) (CompP)

Determiners can be a variety of things, including articles as well as our four substitute words. Once we find categories for them, we can insert their names in place of the dotted lines in this rule:

8
$$\text{Det} \rightarrow \left\{ \begin{array}{l} \text{Art} \\ \ldots \\ \ldots \end{array} \right\}$$

Demonstratives and Quantifiers

The words *this, that, these,* and *those* are called **demonstrative modifiers** (abbreviated **Dem**), because they *demonstrate* (point out definitely) which particular box of groceries is being discussed. The word *each* is called a **quantifier** or **Quant** (also called an **indefinite modifier**). Other quantifiers include *all, any, enough, every, few, many, more, most, much, no, several,* and *some*. They are called quantifiers because they quantify (provide quantity information about) the nouns that follow them.

So far we have named three options to fill the missing categories in rule 8:

9

$$\text{Det} \rightarrow \left\{ \begin{array}{l} \text{Art} \\ \text{Dem} \\ \text{Quant} \\ \ldots \end{array} \right\}$$

Rules 7 and 9 allow us to generate trees such as the following:

10

Exercises 6.1

1. Underline each determiner in the following sentences, and label it as an article, a demonstrative modifier, or a quantifier. Then draw trees to show how a grammar with rules 7 and 9 can generate the sentences.

   a. That play had many funny scenes.
      Dem   Quant

      [Notice that the demonstrative *that* in sentence *a* is a different word from the complementizer *that* (such as the second word in this sentence).]

   b. They preferred all small towns over this city.

   c. The hikers packed enough supplies for any emergency.

   d. These people have no interest in any kind of culture.   [N: *interest, kind*]

2. All of the following nouns can be modified by the quantifiers *no* and *some*. However, some of them can be modified by *much* (but not by *many*), and the rest can be modified by *many* (but not by *much*). First, identify which nouns in the list can be modified by *much* and which by *many*.

water	gallons	love	embarrassment
sand	children	snowstorms	sheep
people	attempts	snow	wealth

When you speak, how do you know whether to use *much* or *many*? Can you think of a principle that would determine whether a noun would take one or the other of the two quantifiers? Would the same principle also apply to *little* and *few*?

(3.) Optional discovery exercise: Modifiers such as adjectives and determiners are said to have a **scope**, which consists of the word or words that they modify. In the sentence *Jane eats no rich, fatty foods*, the scope of the adjective *rich* is the noun *foods* because the sentence is talking about rich foods. The scope of the adjective *fatty* is also *foods*, for the same reason. However, the scope of the quantifier *no* is not just the noun *foods* but the three words *rich, fatty foods*. That is, the sentence is not saying that Jane eats no *foods* but no *rich, fatty foods*. Decide if our grammatical model adequately captures the scope of modifiers. Our NP rule 7 produces a tree like the following for the noun phrase *no rich, fatty foods* (I have deliberately omitted internal category labels such as Det and Adj from this "skeletal" tree):

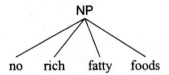

The tree gives no indication that *no* has a different scope from *rich* and *fatty*. To do so, the tree would have to have a structure something like this:

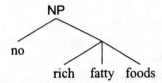

Draw skeletal trees for the following noun phrases in such a way as to capture the scope of the modifiers, and speculate about how our grammar might be adjusted to account for the scope of modifiers.

a. hot, sweaty palms
b. fresh cold cuts
c. every old miniature Schnauzer

Can these same adjustments for scope explain the ambiguity of *good sweet pickles*? Consider the following:

d. good, sweet pickles [meaning pickles that are both good and sweet; spoken with stress on *pickles*]
e. good sweet pickles [meaning good examples of the kind of pickles known as "sweet pickles"; spoken with stress on *sweet*]

Possessive Pronouns and Possessive Noun Phrases

The third new determiner that we saw in 3, *my*, is a **possessive pronoun** (more accurately, a possessive personal pronoun), which we will abbreviate as **Pro$_{P-S}$**, with the subscript *P* standing for "personal" and *S* for "possessive." For each of the personal pronouns, there is a corresponding possessive variant, as represented in chart 11:

11

PERSONAL AND POSSESSIVE PRONOUNS		
	Personal (Pro$_P$)	***Possessive*** (Pro$_{P-S}$)
1st person *(sing.):*	I / me	my
(pl.):	we / us	our
2nd person *(sing. & pl.):*	you / you	your
3rd person *(sing.):*	she / her	her
	he / him	his
	it / it	its
(pl.):	they / them	their

A note on usage: If you are unsure about the difference between "its" and "it's," you are not alone. "Its" is the possessive pronoun, and "it's" is the contraction for "it is." Just remember that possessive pronouns never take an apostrophe (my, his, its), but that contractions always do (don't, I'll, it's).

Whereas personal pronouns act as noun phrases, possessive pronouns act as determiners. With possessive pronouns, we now have four options for determiners:

12

$$\text{Det} \rightarrow \left\{ \begin{array}{l} \text{Art} \\ \text{Dem} \\ \text{Quant} \\ \text{Pro}_{P-S} \\ \ldots \end{array} \right\}$$

Notice the difference between possessive and personal pronouns in the following sentence:

13

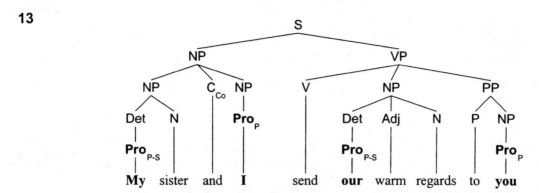

The final example of a determiner in 3, *John's*, is a ***possessive noun phrase***. Like a possessive pronoun, its purpose is to indicate ownership. Although *John's* is the possessive form of a single noun (*John*), multiword noun phrases can also have possessive forms, as the following indicates:

14

$$
\left.\begin{array}{r}
\text{John's} \\
\text{The boy's} \\
\text{A small family's} \\
\text{Those rambunctious twins'} \\
\text{My boss's} \\
\text{The man in the moon's}
\end{array}\right\} \text{large box of groceries}
$$

Each phrase to the left of the brace in 14 is a possessive noun phrase. Each acts as a determiner that modifies the noun *box*. Because possessive noun phrases can be so much longer and more complex than single-word determiners (articles, demonstratives, quantifiers, and possessive pronouns), they can be confusing at first and somewhat difficult to master. Do not be discouraged if the following is not clear initially. The concept will become clear after a little experience and practice.

In the simplest terms, you form a possessive noun phrase by taking a noun phrase (such as *John* or *the boy*) and adding *'s* to the end. When the final word of the noun phrase is plural and already takes an *s*-ending (such as *those rambunctious twins*), an apostrophe alone is added. We will abbreviate these ***possessive markers*** (*'s* and *'*) as **Poss**.

A possessive noun phrase, then, is formed by taking a noun phrase and adding a possessive marker, thus giving us the final option for determiners:

15

$$
\text{Det} \rightarrow \left\{\begin{array}{l}
\text{Art} \\
\text{Dem} \\
\text{Quant} \\
\text{Pro}_{P-S} \\
\text{NP Poss}
\end{array}\right\}
$$

Following rule 15, possessive noun phrases will have structures such as the following:

16

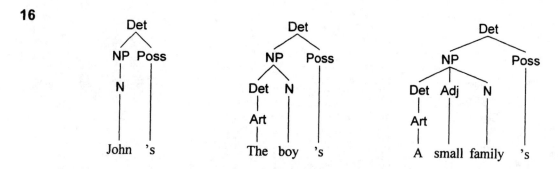

Like other determiners, these can then be used to modify nouns:

17

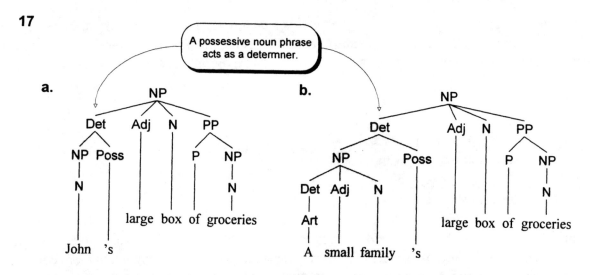

Because these structures are complex, it is worth your while to study these trees carefully to be sure you understand why they are constructed as they are. Notice how each of these noun phrases is created using rules 7 and 15, and that it consists of a determiner, an adjective, a noun, and a prepositional phrase. What makes them different from other noun phrases that we have seen is the complexity of the determiner, which here happens to be a possessive noun phrase—that is, a noun phrase followed by the possessive marker *'s*. The result is that we have structures with one noun phrase modifying (embedded within) another. Pay attention to why words are situated where they are. For example, in 17b, notice that there are two adjectives, *small* and *large*. *Large* is a constituent of the main NP because it modifies *box*, whereas *small* is a constituent of the lower NP because it modifies *family* rather than *box* (the box is large, but the family is small).

It is time to update our grammar, which now looks like the following:

```
                          PS RULES
                                                      LEXICON

            S  →  NP  VP
                                                Art:   the, a, an
                    ⎧ (Det) (Adj)⁺ N (PP) (CompP) ⎫   Dem:   this, that, these,
            NP  →  ⎨         Proₚ                 ⎬           those
                    ⎩         CompP               ⎭   Quant: all, any, each
                                                             enough, every, few,
                    ⎧   V  (NP)      ⎫                        many, more, most,
            VP  →  ⎨        ⎧ NP   ⎫ ⎬ (PP)                   much, no, several,
                    ⎩  V_L ⎨ AdjP ⎬ ⎭                        some, . . .
                            ⎩      ⎭
                                                     Pro_{P-S}: my, our, your, her,
                    ⎧ Art       ⎫                              his, its, their
                    ⎢ Dem       ⎥                    Poss:  's, '
            Det →  ⎨ Quant      ⎬                           . . .
                    ⎢ Pro_{P-S} ⎥
                    ⎩ NP  Poss  ⎭

           AdjP  →  Adj (CompP)

                        ⎧ C_{Cl}  S ⎫
           CompP  →    ⎨            ⎬
                        ⎩ PP        ⎭

            PP  →  P  NP

            XP  →  XP  C_{Co}  XP
```

Exercises 6.2

1. Use rules 7 and 15 to draw trees for the following noun phrases:

    a. a new Mustang
    b. her new Mustang
    c. Sandy's new Mustang
    d. a young lady's handkerchiefs
        [Notice that *a* and *young* modify *lady*, not *handkerchiefs*.]
    e. the violent criminal's contrite apology
        [Be sure your tree shows that the criminal, not the apology, is violent.]
    f. many weeks' worth of groceries   [The noun *worth* is the main noun in the noun phrase.]
    g. the Queen of England's horses

    It is even possible to have one possessive noun phrase embedded in another:

    h. Sandy's new Mustang's dirty carburetor

    *In drawing the tree for a complex noun phrase such as 1h, it often helps to do your
    analysis from right to left, rather than left to right. In any noun phrase, everything*

Determiners, Adverbs, and Other Modifiers   79 centers around the main noun. First ask, what is the thing we are talking about in 1h? The answer: a carburetor. Consequently, "carburetor" is the noun in the main noun phrase. As we move left from there, we find "dirty," which is an adjective modifying "carburetor." Immediately before "dirty" is an apostrophe-s, a signal that we have a possessive noun phrase (an NP-Poss determiner). Our analysis so far indicates that the tree for 1h will look like the following:

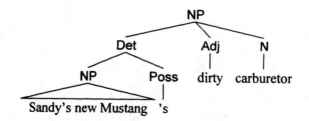

Now analyze the lower noun phrase, "Sandy's new Mustang," in the same way. Its main noun is "Mustang," and the words to its left will be modifiers of "Mustang." As it happens, the lower NP in the tree (represented by a triangle in our diagram) will be identical to the tree you drew for 1c above.

Finally, analyze the following noun phrase in the same way, and draw the tree:

   i.   my sister's best friend's strange behavior

2. Use grammar 18 to draw trees for the following sentences:

   a. Her happiness is Tom's fondest wish.
   b. My opinion of Sam's cousin was unfavorable.
   c. The elderly butler's favorite book of limericks disappeared.
   d. Those dirty rotten scoundrels impressed few people with their honesty.
   e. Peter followed a young wolf's tracks into the forest.
   f. The police talked to that nice woman's delinquent sons.
   g. My sister's announcement that she is a vegetarian stunned our parents.
         [Hint: Sentence 2g contains a nominal-complement clause.]

3. As lengthy as it seems, our list of determiners may not be complete. Decide whether the **cardinal numbers** (one, two, three, and so on) and the **ordinal numbers** (first, second, third, and so on) should be regarded as determiners or adjectives.

(4.) Optional discovery exercise: Our classification of determiners may still not be as neat as we would like. Here is a more difficult problem: How should we account in our grammar for such expressions as *a few pencils, the first six pens, many a fine eraser, all the king's men,* and *such an unusual crayon*? Do they cause us to revise the claim that a noun phrase can have no more than one determiner?

Adverbials

Adverbs

One major part of speech that we have not yet explored is the **adverb** (abbreviated **Adv**). Adverbs can modify verbs, because they tell how, when, where, or why the action occurred. Consider the italicized adverb in this sentence:

19   Winifred gazed at the sky *intently*.

Intently tells how Winifred did the gazing, and so it modifies the verb *gazed*. We can add an adverb option to our VP rule:

20

$$VP \rightarrow \left\{ \begin{matrix} V \ (NP) \\ V_L \left\{ \begin{matrix} NP \\ AdjP \end{matrix} \right\} \end{matrix} \right\} \ (PP) \ (\textbf{Adv})$$

Our tree for 19 looks like this:

21

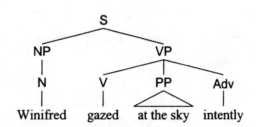

Most adverbs are easy to spot because they are formed by adding the suffix *-ly* to an adjective: *rapidly, angrily, happily*. Adverbs that do not end in *-ly* include *well, much, little, once, twice*, as well as many adverbs of time such as *often, soon, yesterday, now*, and *then* and many adverbs of place such as *here, there, eastward*, and *skyward*.

While it can generate sentence 21, rule 20 is still not satisfactory. It can generate an adverb following a prepositional phrase, but some grammatical sentences have the reverse order:

22   Winifred gazed intently at the sky.

Perhaps we also need a second verb-phrase rule to allow for adverbs that precede prepositional phrases. But the following sentences show still other possibilities as well:

23

Winifred gazed
$\left\{ \begin{matrix} \text{intently at the sky yesterday.} \\ \text{at the sky intently with binoculars.} \\ \text{intently yesterday at the sky with binoculars.} \end{matrix} \right.$

— Adv PP Adv
— PP Adv PP
— Adv Adv PP PP

Prepositional phrases and adverbs seem to occur interchangeably in a variety of combinations. We could try to write a separate rule for each of them, but clearly there are many other possibilities as well—in fact, a limitless number of them—and we cannot write rules for all of them.

Despite these problems, a solution is in sight. Because adverbs and prepositional phrases are interchangeable, we can hypothesize that they belong to the same general category, in the same way that articles and quantifiers belong to the general category *determiner*. Further evidence is the fact that some adverbs and prepositional phrases are equivalent in meaning, such as *enthusiastically* and *with enthusiasm*. We will call the general category that includes them both an **adverbial phrase** (abbreviated **AdvP**) or simply an **adverbial**. Any number of adverbial phrases can occur within a verb phrase. Until now our rule for a verb phrase allowed it to end with an optional prepositional phrase. Let us change that so that it can end with one or more adverbial phrases:

24

$$VP \rightarrow \left\{ \begin{array}{l} V \ (NP) \\ V_L \left\{ \begin{array}{l} NP \\ AdjP \end{array} \right\} \end{array} \right\} \ (AdvP)^+$$

These adverbial phrases can be either adverbs or prepositional phrases:

25

$$AdvP \rightarrow \left\{ \begin{array}{l} Adv \\ PP \end{array} \right\}$$

Rules 24 and 25 can generate verb phrases with adverbs and prepositional phrases, such as this one with four adverbial phrases:

26

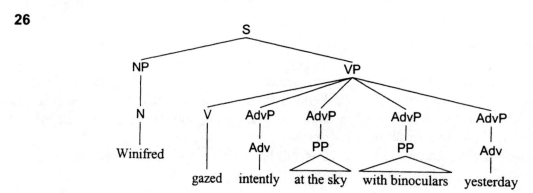

Notice that each adverbial in the tree is marked with its own AdvP label.

Consider now the sentence *The student from Greece spoke several languages without an accent.* Prepositional phrases that modify verbs (spoke *without an accent*) are now labeled as adverbial phrases. However, this does not apply to prepositional phrases that modify nouns (the student *from Greece*). Note the difference between the two prepositional phrases in tree 27.

27

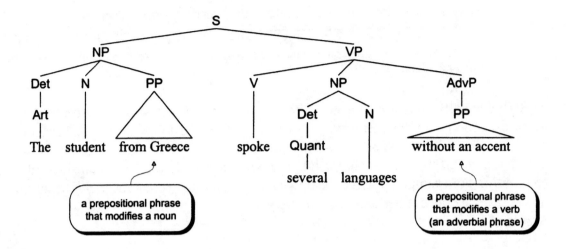

a prepositional phrase
that modifies a noun

a prepositional phrase
that modifies a verb
(an adverbial phrase)

Exercises 6.3

1. Underline the adverbials in the following sentences, and label each as an adverb or a prepositional phrase. Finally, draw trees for these sentences using rules 24 and 25.

   a. She gets headaches <u>lately</u>.
                               Adv

   b. The dancers glided <u>effortlessly</u> <u>across the patio</u>.
                                Adv   PP

   c. Alexis helped Carl gladly with his project recently.

   d. The fact that he glared fiercely at me for a solid minute discomforted me greatly.

   Remember the difference between prepositional phrases that modify nouns and those that modify verbs:

   e. George sat impassively for five minutes alone on the couch without any sign of life.

   f. Wade's errors in judgment hurt him during the competition.

   g. Luke rode in the front of the car on the trip to Mexico.

2. Our coordination rule (XP → XP C_Co XP) predicts that adverbial phrases can be joined by coordinating conjunctions. If a coordinating conjunction can join an adverb and a prepositional phrase, that would be strong confirmation of our claim that both are indeed the same kind of phrase. Draw trees for the following:

   a. The music stopped abruptly and with no warning.

   b. You worked on the weekend and today.   [Adv: *today*]

3. The following sentence is ambiguous because it is unclear whether the adverb *yesterday* modifies the verb *learned* or the verb *won*:

   We learned that he won the medal yesterday.

a. Draw a tree for the sentence when it means that yesterday was when he won it.

b. Draw a tree for the sentence when it means that yesterday was when we learned it.

[Note: An adverbial can come at the end of a verb phrase, even if that verb phrase contains an embedded clause.]

4. Most (but not all) adverbs end in *-ly*. Although most words that end in *-ly* are adverbs, there are some exceptions. What category (part of speech) do the following non-adverbs belong to: *friendly, comely, homely, stately,* and *timely*? We can add *-ly* to most adjectives to produce an adverb (*beautiful + -ly = beautifully*). But how do we adverbialize an adjective that already ends in *-ly*? For example, if Ashley's drawings are beautiful, we say she draws beautifully. How do we say she draws if her drawings are ugly?

Adverbials That Follow Linking Verbs

Earlier, we saw that a linking verb can be followed by a noun phrase (for example, *The plane is a jet*) or an adjectival phrase (*The plane is new*). An adverbial phrase can also follow a linking verb:

28 a. The plane is *here*.

   b. The plane is *on the runway*.

   c. The departure is *tomorrow*.

   d. The departure is *after the rainstorm*.

We can state this option as a phrase-structure rule:

29   VP → V_L AdvP

Unfortunately, however, rule 29 is a bit too powerful, meaning that it can generate some unwanted phrases. Only some—not all—adverbials can follow a linking verb. That is, a linking verb can be followed by a ***place adverbial*** such as *here* and *on the runway* (an adverbial that answers a question like "*Where* is the plane?") or by a ***time adverbial*** such as *tomorrow* and *after the rainstorm* (an adverbial that answers a question like "*When* is the departure?"). But a linking verb cannot usually be followed by a ***manner adverbial*** such as *beautifully* or *with enthusiasm* (an adverbial that answers a "*How?*" question). That is, we do not want 29 to generate sentences such as **The plane is beautifully*.

Fortunately, we can solve our problem if we differentiate between the standard unrestricted adverbials that modify a verb (which we can continue to label AdvP) and the time/place adverbials that follow a linking verb, which we might label **AdvP$_L$**. Rules for these two forms of adverbials are:

30 a.
$$AdvP \rightarrow \begin{Bmatrix} Adv \\ PP \end{Bmatrix}$$

    b.
$$AdvP_L \rightarrow \begin{Bmatrix} Adv_{(Time/Place)} \\ PP_{(Time/Place)} \end{Bmatrix}$$

With this distinction, we can update our rule for linking verbs as follows:

31

$$VP \rightarrow V_L \begin{Bmatrix} NP \\ AdjP \\ AdvP_L \end{Bmatrix}$$

Using these rules, we can diagram sentences 28b and 28c as follows:

32

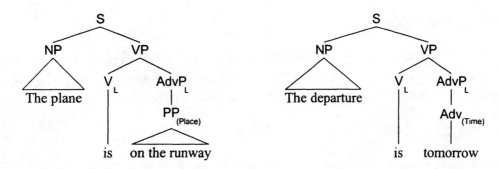

We can now recap all our discoveries about transitive, intransitive, and linking verbs with this comprehensive verb-phrase rule:

33

$$VP \rightarrow \begin{Bmatrix} V\ (NP) \\ V_L \begin{Bmatrix} NP \\ AdjP \\ AdvP_L \end{Bmatrix} \end{Bmatrix} (AdvP)^+$$

Exercises 6.4

1. Draw trees to show the derivations of the following sentences with adverbials that follow linking verbs:

    a. The boys were at the concert.
    b. Pandemonium is everywhere.
    c. The coach says that the future is now.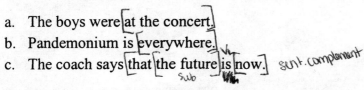

(2.) Optional discovery exercise: An oddity of rule 33 is that it can allow not only an adverbial that follows a linking verb (AdvP_L) but also *another* adverbial (AdvP) that modifies the verb. Draw trees for the following sentences in which both kinds of adverbials occur in the same sentence:

    a. The plane was in the air frequently
    b. The pilot was there for the convention.

The trees for these sentences show a possible limitations of our grammatical model in that both kinds of adverbials appear to modify the verb *was* in exactly the same way, even though they have quite different relationships to the verb. Speculate, if you can, about how we might modify our model to account for these different relationships.

Degree Modifiers

Modifiers of Adjectives

Our method of discovering English grammar has involved examining data and then devising hypotheses about what rules in our mental grammars might account for and explain the data. Following this method, let us consider the following noun phrase:

34   a very quick tempo

We recognize *tempo* as a noun, *a* as an article, and *quick* as an adjective. But what about *very*? Is it an adjective too? If so, noun phrase 34 would have this structure :

35

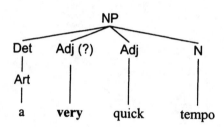

A problem with this analysis is that we can have "*a* tempo" and "*quick* tempo" but not "*very* tempo." That is, while *a* and *quick* seem to modify *tempo*, *very* does not. What *very* seems to be modifying is the adjective *quick*, not the noun *tempo*. In fact, its purpose is to tell us the degree of quickness. (How quick? *Very* quick.) Consequently, the analysis in 35 must be wrong. For the time being, let us omit category labels such as "Det" and "Adj" from the following "skeletal" trees.

36   a.   b.

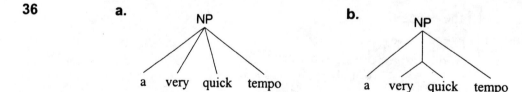

Our analysis has shown us that, rather than having a structure like 36a (where the other words in the phrase all modify *tempo*), the noun phrase will have to have a structure along the lines of 36b, where *very* is shown to modify *quick*, and the two words together (*very quick*) form a phrase. It is that entire phrase, *very quick*, that modifies *tempo*. Let us call a phrase like *very quick* an ***adjectival phrase*** (abbreviated **AdjP**), because the adjective *quick* is clearly the important element in the phrase.

of these words specifies a degree of quickness. Consequently, they are known as ***degree modifiers*** (abbreviated **Deg**). These modifiers are sometimes called ***degree adverbs*** because many of them end in *-ly*, but degree modifiers differ from other adverbs in that they modify other modifiers instead of verbs.

We will adjust our noun-phrase rule by replacing "Adj" with "AdjP":

37   NP → (Det) **(AdjP)⁺** N (PP) (CompP)

An adjective phrase will consist of an adjective with or without a preceding degree modifier:

38   AdjP → (Deg) Adj

Rules 37 and 38 allow the grammar to generate noun phrases whose nouns are modified by adjectival phrases, such as the following:

39   **a.**   **b.**

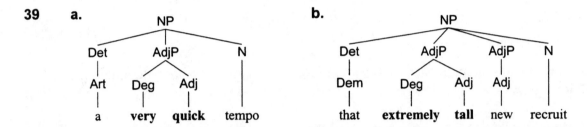

Note that all adjectives (including *new* in 39b) are now labeled as adjectival phrases.

You will remember from Chapter 5 that we have already used the term *adjectival phrase* for adjectives that follow linking verbs (as in a sentence like "The tempo was *quick*"). An adjectival phrase can take a degree modifier whether it precedes a noun ("the *very quick* tempo") or follows a linking verb ("The tempo was *very quick*"). But there is one difference between these two types of adjectival phrases: In Chapter 5, we discovered that an adjectival phrase that follows a linking verb can include an adjectival-complement clause ("The children are *happy that you came*"). However, adjectival-complement clauses occur only following a linking verb; they never occur before a noun (* "the *happy-that-you-came* children"). We need, then, to distinguish between these two types of adjectival clauses. As we did with adverbial clauses on page 84, let us make a distinction between an **AdjP** (which precedes a noun) and an **AdjP_L** (which follows a linking verb). The distinction is captured in the following rules:

40   **AdjP** → (Deg) Adj   —adjectival phrase that precedes a noun

      AdjP_L → (Deg) Adj (CompP)   —adjectival phrase that follows a linking verb

That is, only when an adjectival phrase follows a linking verb can it take an adjectival complement clause. The difference between the two types of adjectival phrases is reflected in the following sentence:

41

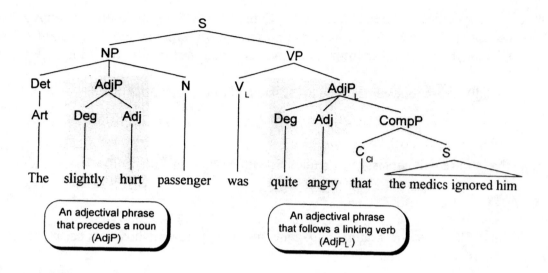

An adjectival phrase that precedes a noun (AdjP)

An adjectival phrase that follows a linking verb (AdjP$_L$)

Modifiers of Adverbials

We have examined sentences such as *The tempo was very quick.* Consider the following sentence as additional data:

42   The musicians played the piece *very quickly.*

Not only can the degree modifier *very* modify an adjective such as *quick*, but 42 shows that it can also modify an adverb such as *quickly*. Let us see what happens if we add an optional degree modifier to our rule for adverbial phrases:

43 $$\text{AdvP} \rightarrow \textbf{(Deg)} \left\{ \begin{array}{c} \text{Adv} \\ \text{PP} \end{array} \right\}$$

Rule 43 predicts that all adverbials (both adverbs and prepositional phrases) can be modified by degree modifiers. The sentences of 44 show that this prediction is correct:

44 a. The play ended *quite* suddenly.   —a degree modifier that modifies an adverb

  b. The senator spoke *entirely* without notes. —a degree modifier that modifies a prepositional phrase

In 44a, the degree modifier *quite* modifies the adverb *suddenly*. In 44b, the degree modifier *entirely* modifies the prepositional phrase *without notes*. Rule 43 allows us to draw trees for these sentences:

45 a.

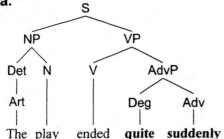

Det — Art — The
N — play
V — ended
AdvP — Deg — **quite**, Adv — **suddenly**

b.

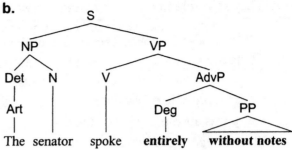

Det — Art — The
N — senator
V — spoke
AdvP — Deg — **entirely**, PP — **without notes**

In addition to modifying verbs (as in 44), adverbials can also follow linking verbs (as in 28). Let us add degree modifiers to the AdvP$_L$ rule as well:

46

$$AdvP_L \rightarrow (Deg) \begin{Bmatrix} Adv_{(Time/Place)} \\ PP_{(Time/Place)} \end{Bmatrix}$$

Rule 46 correctly predicts that degree modifiers can modify adverbials that follow linking verbs, as in 47:

47 a. Our guests are *almost here*.

    b. The outings were *exclusively during the summer*.

In 47a, *almost* is a degree modifier that modifies the place adverb *here*. In 47b, *exclusively* is a degree modifier that modifies the prepositional phrase *during the summer*. Rule 46 allows us to draw trees for these sentences:

48

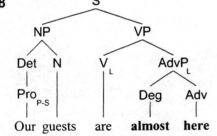

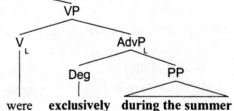

Exercises 6.5

1. Underline each degree modifier in the following sentences and decide if it modifies an adjective or an adverb. Then use the rules in this section to draw trees for these sentences.

    a. The <u>grossly</u> overweight athlete began his diet <u>almost</u> immediately.

    b. The fire had terribly sad consequences.

c. They schedule the most important classes too infrequently.

> [Note that the word "most" can be either a degree modifier ("the *most* important classes") or a quantifier ("*Most* people have jobs").]

d. Zelda flaunted her large, brand new, shiny BMW.

> [This tree's direct object should contain three separate AdjP labels.]

e. Cheesecake is highly caloric.
f. Ruby was absolutely furious that Arthur forgot his manners.
g. Stan arrived unfashionably early in an extraordinarily garish tuxedo.
h. Cosmo's stray dog wandered halfway into the next county.

> [Hint: To what degree into the next county?]

i. Urban sprawl is practically everywhere.

2. Adjectival phrases, like all other phrases, can be linked with a conjunction to form a coordinate phrase, according to the XP rule. Draw a tree for this sentence:

> The sadder but wiser champion won an exceptionally bloody but meaningless contest.

(3.) Optional discovery exercise: Degree modifiers modify adjectives and adverbs, but can they also modify other degree modifiers? What would trees for the following sentences look like, and how would the grammar have to be adjusted to account for them?

a. They played the music much too quickly.
b. You are ever so kind.

Nominal Modifiers

Nouns can be modified by adjectives, but consider the following noun phrases:

49 wool sweater   evening performance   graduation party
    football league   luggage compartment   sausage pizza

It appears that not only can nouns be modified by adjectives (*tasty* pizza), but they can also be modified by other nouns (*sausage* pizza). Let us consider the possibility that adjectival phrases can include noun modifiers as well as adjectives. If so, the phrase *a tasty sausage pizza* would have this structure:

50

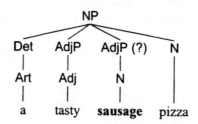

Both *tasty* and *sausage* modify *pizza*, but whereas *tasty* is a quality (and consequently an adjective), *sausage* is a thing (and consequently a noun).

We can observe some problems with the analysis in 50, however. If both *tasty* and *sausage* are adjectival phrases, then we would expect them to occur in either order, but they do not: That is, we can have *a tasty sausage pizza* but not ** a sausage tasty pizza*. (Notice that when a noun is modified by two adjectives they do occur in either order: That is, we can have either *a hot, tasty pizza* or *a tasty, hot pizza*.) Similarly, if both words are adjectival phrases, we should be able to join them with a conjunction, but we cannot: ** a tasty and sausage pizza*. (Notice that we can join two adjectives in this way: *a hot and tasty pizza*. We can also join two nouns: *a sausage and cheese pizza*.)

The conclusion must be that adjectives and noun modifiers are two different kinds of modifiers. Moreover, we have seen that when both modify the same noun, an adjective modifier comes before a noun modifier. For now, let us call a noun that acts as a modifier a ***nominal modifier*** and give it the label **Mod_NP**. We can revise rule 36 by adding an option for a nominal modifier:

51   NP → (Det) (AdjP)$^+$ (**Mod_NP**) N (PP) (CompP)

Rule 51 will generate noun phrases such as the following:

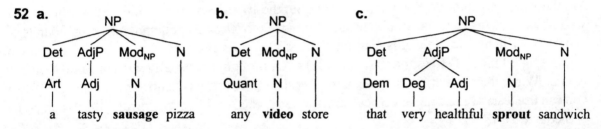

52 a.   **b.**   **c.**

Notice in 51 that *sausage, video,* and *sprout* are all nouns (things). In contrast, *tasty* and *healthy* are adjectives (qualities.)

If it is not clear to you if a modifier is an adjective or a noun, you might try some tests: If it can be modified by a degree modifier, it is an adjective ("very tasty" but not "very sausage"). If it can be modified by a determiner, it is a noun and not an adjective ("a sausage" but not "a tasty").

Exercises 6.6

1. Use the noun-phrase rule of 51 to draw trees for these noun phrases:

   a. the Stone Age
   b. a popular student hangout
   c. all rock videos
   d. designer jeans with leather cuffs
   e. thick, creamy milk shakes
   f. friendly purple people eater

2. Draw trees for these sentences:

    a. The child prodigy wrote a piano concerto.
    b. An overly enthusiastic sports fan demanded an autograph.
    c. Jake's obnoxiously loud CD player caused a riot in Farley Hall.

3. A word formed by joining two other words is called a **compound**. Examples of compounds are *homework, basketball, railroad,* and *bathroom*. In contrast, a phrase consisting of a nominal modifier and a noun (*sausage pizza, wool sweater*) is often called a **construct**. The main difference between compounds and constructs is that speakers tend of think of compounds as whole units but of constructs as having separate parts. Another difference is in pronunciation: Speakers generally put greater stress on the first word in a compound (*SHOElace, BATHroom*), but in a construct they often stress either the second word (*sausage PIZZA*) or both words almost equally (*SAUSAGE PIZZA*). Compounds usually began their existence as constructs, but with time the phrases became "frozen" into single word units. We can imagine, for example, that the cook who first made a cake using cheese called it a *cheese CAKE*, but, with repeated use, the designation soon changed to the one-word compound *CHEESEcake*. A compound can also be formed from an adjective + noun. For example, the British soldiers in the Revolutionary War who wore *red COATS* (a construct) became known as *REDcoats* (a compound). Compounds are generally written as single words, but not always: *Dog food* is clearly a compound (we think of it as a single unit and stress the first syllable) even though it is usually written as two separate words. While the distinction between compounds and constructs is not always absolute, see if you can use tests of meaning and vocal stress to label each of the following as either a compound or a construct:

    a. credit card   c. linguistics student   e. a white house   g. milk shake
    b. mutton sandwich   d. hockey puck   f. the White House   h. milk allergy

4. Sometimes the distinction between nominal modifiers and adjectives is not obvious. Consider the expressions "silver spoon" and "silver hair." Are these modifiers nouns or adjectives? Does it make a difference if *silver* is used as the name of a metal or as the name of a color? What about *orange* in "orange juice" and "orange wallpaper"?

So far we have seen that a modifier of a noun can be another noun (as in *book dealer* and *quiz show*). Why, you may ask, did we abbreviate these nominal modifiers in rule 51 as "Mod$_{NP}$" rather than simply as "Mod$_N$"? For an answer, consider the following noun phrases:

53 a. the rare book dealer
   b. a quiz show contestant

In 53a, the noun *book* modifies *dealer*, but what about the adjective *rare*? It seems to be modifying *book*, not *dealer* (the books are rare, not the dealer). Similarly in 53b, the noun *show* modifies *contestant*, but the noun *quiz* modifies *show*, not *contestant*. It appears that entire noun phrases (such as *rare book* or *quiz show*) can act as nominal modifiers, as the following trees demonstrate:

54   **a.**

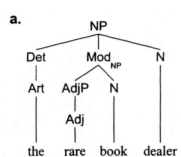

    b.

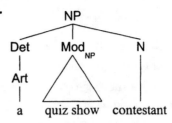

If we assume that the Mod_{NP} modifiers can have the same constituents as other noun phrases, we can complete our analysis of these phrases:

55   **a.**

    b.

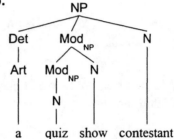

It does appear, however, that only some of the elements that can occur in other noun phrases (see rule 51) are possible in a nominal modifier. We have established that a Mod_{NP} can consist of a noun modified by an adjectival phrase (a *rare book* dealer) or by another nominal modifier (a *travel book* dealer) or even both (a retired *very rare travel book* dealer). But what about the other elements that rule 51 tells us can occur in a noun phrase?

Prepositional phrases in nominal modifiers are rare, but they also occur occasionally, as these bracketed nominal modifiers demonstrate:

56 a. the [Bay *of Pigs*] invasion

  b. an [end *of year*] report

On the other hand, determiners (see 57a) and nominal complements (57b) do not seem to be permitted in nominal modifiers:

57 a. the retired [** a* book] dealer

  b. a [theory ** that the earth is flat*] book

Based on these discoveries, let us conclude that our Mod_{NP} rule should be the following:

58   Mod_{NP} → (AdjP)⁺ (Mod_{NP}) N (PP)

Exercises 6.7

1. Use rules 51 and 58 to draw trees for the following noun phrases which contain nominal modifiers:

   a. the lonely hearts club
   b. a peanut butter sandwich
   c. a cost-of-living increase   [Ignore the hyphens in drawing your tree. N: *living*]
   d. the cheerful travel book author   [Assume that the author, not the book or the travel, is cheerful.]
   e. the very new old age home   [Note that the age is old but the home is new.]

2. Draw trees to show the structure of these noun phrases whose modifiers are joined by coordinating conjunctions:

   a. the peanut butter and jelly sandwich
   b. a life or death situation

3. Rule 51 claims that a noun phrase can contain as many as six different kinds of elements. Can all six occur within the same noun phrase? Use that rule to draw the tree for the following noun phrase:

   the defendant's futile last minute plea to the judge that he was innocent

4. Certain noun phrases are ambiguous. Can you spot two interpretations of each of these phrases?

   a. a wild horse trainer   d. a crusty pizza lover
   b. the German language teacher   e. the flaky pie dough maker
   c. a dirty book shelf

   It would be to the credit of our grammatical model if it could account for both interpretations of these phrases. See if our rules allow you to draw the tree for 4a so that it means that the horses are wild. Then draw the tree so that it means that the trainer is wild. Finally, draw trees for the two interpretations of 4b.

5. In written English, punctuation is sometimes used to eliminate ambiguity among modifiers, as in these examples:

   a. Anna is a hyperactive child psychologist.
   b. Anna is a hyperactive-child psychologist.

   How do these sentences differ in meaning? What is the result if you insert hyphens between the second and third words of the noun phrases in exercise 4? State the general principle for when you use hyphens in such phrases to avoid ambiguity.

(6.) Optional discovery exercise: In the discovery exercise on page 74, you were asked to consider the scope of modifiers—exactly what words they modify. As that exercise revealed, the model grammar presented in this chapter may not fully capture the scope of modifiers. Consider the following noun phrases with adjectival and nominal modifiers:

a.   the best sausage pizza   [interpretation: of all sausage pizzas, the one that is best]
b.   my favorite grammar book   [interpretation: of all grammar books, the one that is my favorite]

Decide if the nominal modifiers are included in the scope of the adjectives *best* and *favorite*. Draw skeletal trees that would capture the scope of the modifiers. Now consider the following noun phrases:

c.   a small town on the prairie
d.   the smallest town on the prairie

Is the prepositional phrase *on the prairie* included in the scope of the adjective *small* in sentence 6c? Is it included in the scope of *smallest* in sentence 6d? Draw skeletal trees for these noun phrases. Speculate further about how the grammar might be adjusted to account for the scope of modifiers.

(7.) Optional discovery exercise: In addition to the modifiers of nouns that we have identified, we can find instances in English where nouns are modified by all kinds of things. Hyphenated phrases that can precede and modify nouns include prepositional phrases (an *off-the-cuff* remark), verb phrases (*pay-as-you-go* financing, a *come-hither* stare), even entire sentences (her *I-don't-give-a-damn* attitude). Does this anything-goes anarchy (there's another one!) cause problems for our grammar?

Summary and Review: Chapters 1–6

We have reached a good point to sum up and review what we have discovered so far about English grammar. The current state of our grammatical model is shown in 59.

59

$$\underline{\textbf{PS RULES}}$$

$$S \rightarrow NP \ VP$$

$$NP \rightarrow \left\{ \begin{array}{c} (Det) \ (AdjP)^{+} \ (Mod_{NP}) \ N \ (PP) \ (CompP) \\ Pro_{P} \\ CompP \end{array} \right\}$$

$$VP \rightarrow \left\{ \begin{array}{c} V \ (NP) \\ V_{L} \left\{ \begin{array}{c} NP \\ AdjP_{L} \\ AdvP_{L} \end{array} \right\} \end{array} \right\} \ (AdvP)^{+}$$

$$Det \rightarrow \left\{ \begin{array}{c} Art \\ Dem \\ Quant \\ Pro_{P\text{-}S} \\ NP \ Poss \end{array} \right\}$$

$$Mod_{NP} \rightarrow (AdjP)^{+} \ (Mod_{NP}) \ N \ (PP)$$

$$AdjP \rightarrow (Deg) \ Adj$$

$$AdjP_{L} \rightarrow (Deg) \ Adj \ (CompP)$$

$$AdvP \rightarrow (Deg) \left\{ \begin{array}{c} Adv \\ PP \end{array} \right\}$$

$$AdvP_{L} \rightarrow (Deg) \left\{ \begin{array}{c} Adv_{(Time/Place)} \\ PP_{(Time/Place)} \end{array} \right\}$$

$$CompP \rightarrow \left\{ \begin{array}{c} C_{Cl} \ S \\ PP \end{array} \right\}$$

$$PP \rightarrow P \ NP$$

$$XP \rightarrow XP \ C_{Co} \ XP$$

Exercises 6.8

1. Use grammar 59 to draw trees for the following sentences. Review earlier sections and chapters as needed to draw these trees.

   a. He climbed to the top of the mountain without any oxygen.
   b. The circus performer on the trapeze flew merrily through the air.
   c. The fact that Muggsy escaped from the officer's custody outraged the commissioner and prompted an investigation.
   d. Those gullible, extremely foolish people believed that the magician knows all mysteries of the universe.
   e. Our friends lived in France very briefly, but they learned the language thoroughly and easily.
   f. The bitterly cold weather angered the golfers but pleased the skiers.
   g. We were certain that few people boarded the plane to Siberia.
   h. That helicopter pilot flew our package to Miami.
   i. The news that the mayor was very sick saddened the villagers.
   j. The old gypsy's tame monkeys danced comically for the children, and he rewarded each trick with a slice of banana.
   k. The police trapped the leader of the gang in the mob's hideout.
   l. The reason that Mark was late was that his car had a flat tire.
   m. Her hard luck story was quite sad.
   n. Those workers repaired the telephone lines diligently and with great courage.
   o. She traveled across the mountains on foot yesterday with Barbara and Connie.
   p. Some highly intelligent college students needed practice with their trees.

2. Write answers to the following questions:

   a. In drawing trees of exercise sentences 1a and 1b, you had to decide for each prepositional phrase whether to make it a constituent of a noun phrase or of a verb phrase. For each prepositional phrase in those two sentences, explain why you decided as you did.

   b. Does the word *that* perform the same function in sentences 1h and 1i? Explain.

   c. From sentences 1a–1p, identify a sentence with a sentential complement clause, a sentence with a nominal complement clause, and a sentence with an adjectival complement clause.

7 Transformational Rules: Altering Elements in a Sentence

Particles

In chapter 4, we saw that words like *in, off, on,* and *out* are prepositions, and that they precede noun phrases to form prepositional phrases. In sentence 1, for example, *in* is a preposition, and *in a circle* is a prepositional phrase:

1   Clyde turned in a circle.

In this sentence we intuitively recognize *in a circle* as a phrase. Taken together, these words tell us something about how Clyde did his turning. But now consider the following sentence:

2   Clyde turned in the money.

Our analysis of 2 is quite different. The word *in* does not seem to relate to *the money* in the same way that *in* and *a circle* are related in 1, nor does *in the money* seem like a prepositional phrase. Whereas in sentence 1 "in a circle" was how Clyde turned, in sentence 2 it makes no sense to say that "in the money" was how Clyde turned. In 2 *in* seems connected with the verb in front of it, *turned*, rather than with the noun phrase following it, *the money*. The two words *turned in* seem to be a phrase. The action that Clyde undertook was to "turn in" the money. In fact, neither *turned* nor *in* expresses meaning by itself in sentence 2: Clyde didn't "turn" the money, and he didn't "in" the money—he "turned in" the money. Only when taken together do the two words communicate the intended meaning. They constitute the action of the sentence: "Turning in" was what Clyde did.

In sentence 2, we can conclude, the word *in* isn't acting as a preposition at all. It is undertaking a very different role, pairing up with a verb to describe an action. We can find many other sentences with the same kind of construction:

3   **a.** Bonnie *shut off* the engine.
         b. The announcer *called out* the winner's name.
         c. Dave *put on* a warm sweater.
         d. Eliza *looked up* the address in the directory.

Apparently the very same words that can act as prepositions (*in, off, on, out, up,* and so on) can do double duty as a very different grammatical category. When they pair with a preceding verb (rather than with a following noun phrase), we call these words ***particles*** (abbreviated **Prt**). We can define a particle as a word that has no meaning by itself but that can pair with a verb to describe an action.

In sentence 1 (and in all the sentences we examined in previous chapters) a single word acts as the verb; in sentence 2 (and sentences 3a–3d) two words act together as the "verb." Our grammar needs to reflect this observation. Let us diagram verb constructions with particles as follows:

4

We can use the abbreviation V_P to represent a verb that is paired with a particle to state the sentence's action. The V label at the top of the tree shows that the two words act in concert to do exactly what a single verb does in other sentences (note that *turned in* could be replaced by a one-word verb such as *surrendered*). For that reason a verb-particle combination is sometimes called a ***phrasal verb***.

We can now show the differences between sentences 1 and 2:

83 **5a.**

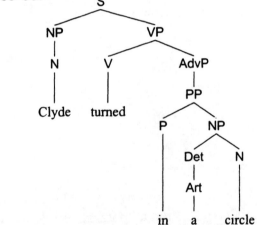

b.

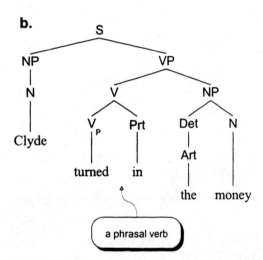

In sentence 5a, *turned* is the verb, *in* is a preposition, and *a circle* is the object of that preposition. In 5b, the phrase *turned in* constitutes the verb, *in* is a particle, and *the money* is the sentence's direct object.

We will need a phrase-structure rule to state that a verb can optionally consist of a V_P and a particle:

6 $(V \rightarrow V_P \ Prt)$

Rule 6 is different from previous rules we have seen in that we are putting it in parentheses to signify that the rule offers an optional alternative to a one-word verb. Why are parentheses needed? Consider the procedure for applying phrase-structure rules: To generate a sentence, we begin with the S rule and continue to apply rules until we cannot apply any more. Often the grammar allows us a choice between rules. For example, whenever the rules generate the category NP we must then apply one or another of the NP rules in order to generate that noun phrase. The tree cannot simply stop at the NP label. On the other hand, it can stop at the V label. Rule 6 is placed in parentheses to show that when we encounter the category V, we have the option either of applying rule 6 or of applying no further phrase-structure rules before inserting a verb from the lexicon.

Exercises 7.1

1. For each of these pairs of sentences, decide which sentence has a phrasal verb (a verb-particle combination) and which has a single-word verb. Underline each phrasal verb and double underline each prepositional phrase:

   a. Terry cried <u><u>on my shoulder</u></u>. intrans
      Terry <u>tried on</u> my sweater. trans

   b. He looked up the phone number. trans
      He walked up the street. intrans

   c. She thought over the offer. trans
      She jumped over the fence. intrans

   d. We took out the garbage. trans
      We stared out the window. intrans

   e. They strolled in the garden. intrans
      They took in the orphan. trans

   f. You drove off the road. intrans
      You turned off the radio. trans

2. Draw trees for these sentences:

   a. Belinda called up her friend.
   b. Knute's army drove out the barbarian invaders.
   c. Sigmund figured out the solution without any help from me.
   d. The vandals tipped over the statue.
   e. The vandals tripped over the statue.

(3.) Optional discovery exercise: We called a verb-particle combination a "phrasal verb," but we didn't use the P (for "phrase") abbreviation to label it. That is, we labeled *tried on* as a "V" rather than as a "V$_P$P" or something similar. An alternative hypothesis would be to claim that *all* verbs are phrases with some consisting of a one-word V and others consisting of a V$_P$ and a Prt. How would you rewrite the phrase-structure rules if you chose this hypothesis? Would your verb-particle rule (akin to rule 6) still need to be placed in parentheses? Are there reasons to prefer one hypothesis over the other?

Moving the Particles

Rule 6 says that a Prt comes immediately after a V$_P$, as it did in all our sample sentences. Of course we would expect a V$_P$ and a particle to occur next to each other, because together the two words state the sentence's action and because neither one by itself expresses much of anything. We have to put the two words together in our minds in order to know what the sentence's "verb" is.

Despite that logical observation, we find that a very curious thing happens in certain English sentences. In addition to sentences like 2 and 3a–3d in which a particle immediately follows a V_P, we also find sentences in which the two words are separated:

7 **a.** Clyde *turned* the money *in*.

     b. Bonnie *shut* the engine *off*.

     c. The announcer *called* the winner's name *out*.

     d. Dave *put* a warm sweater *on*.

     e. Eliza *looked* the address *up* in the directory.

These sentences seem odd indeed in that their "verbs" consist of two words separated from each other by an intervening direct object! Yet despite this structural oddity, the sentences of 7 not only are perfectly grammatical but are identical in meaning with those of 2 and 3.

The problem that now faces us is how we should capture the structure of sentences 7a–7e in our grammar. If we followed our usual procedure, we would add a new option to our VP rule:

8   (**?**)   VP → V_P (NP) Prt (AdvP)⁺

This solution is clearly unsatisfactory. For one thing, it doesn't capture our observation that the V_P and the Prt work together to constitute the sentence's "verb." For another, it doesn't capture our observation that sentences like the following are identical in meaning:

9 **a.** Clyde turned in the money.

     b. Clyde turned the money in.

In fact, we can even say that 9a and 9b are in a sense the *same* sentence with some words rearranged. Yet rule 8 makes the unsatisfactory claim that 9b is derived in a completely different way from 9a. For these reasons, let us reject rule 8.

One alternative solution might be to claim that 9b has a tree like the following:

10

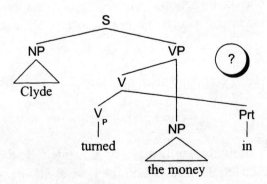

Tree 10 gets the phrases right. It shows that *turned* and *in* work together to constitute the sentence's "verb." It also correctly shows that the VP consists of the phrasal verb *turned in* and the direct object *the money*. Furthermore, it shows that *in* is separated from *turned* and follows the direct object. The problem is that the lines of the tree are crossed, and we have no explanation of how they might have gotten that way.

To find a more satisfactory solution to our problem, let us go back to our intuitive sense that sentences 9a and 9b are stylistic variants—that they are in some sense the *same* sentence, with the words arranged in different orders. At this point let us pose a radical hypothesis: Let's claim that sentence 9b is created using the very same phrase-structure rules that created 9a (including rule 6), but that, before the sentence is actually spoken, another kind of rule then allows the particle to *move* to a new position following the direct object. We will call this new kind of rule a *transformational rule* (or a *T-rule*, for short) because it allows us to transform a sentence created by the phrase-structure rules. Let us call the specific transformational rule we have in mind the *particle-movement transformational rule* (abbreviated **T-Prt**), which we can state as follows:

11   Particle-Movement Transformation (T-Prt): When a sentence with a phrasal verb (verb-particle combination) has been generated by the phrase-structure rules, the particle may then be moved to a position following the first noun phrase within the verb phrase.

Our hypothesis says that the creation of a sentence can be a two-part procedure: First generate a sentence using the PS-rules, and then transform it (if you wish) using a T-rule. So to generate *either* sentence 9a or 9b, we would first apply the PS-rules to produce tree 12:

12

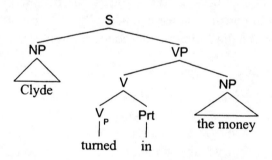

If we want to produce sentence 9a, we stop right there and speak the words "Clyde turned in the money." However, if we want to produce sentence 9b, we then perform the additional step of moving the particle to the end of the sentence (using transformational rule 11), and we speak the words "Clyde turned the money in." In the latter case, the T-Prt rule transforms the sentence, as shown in 13:

13

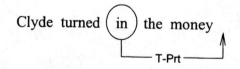

How can a tree diagram show the application of a T-rule? The best option for showing how sentence 9b is created would be to take tree 12 and then use a video clip to show the sentence being transformed, with the particle literally moving to the end of the sentence. Unfortunately, a book like this lacks the necessary technology. We will just have to make the best of our paper-and-ink medium. Because we can't show actual motion, let us examine three alternative ways of diagraming transformations on paper. The first is to take a tree like 12, circle the element to be moved, and draw an arrow to show its movement:

14

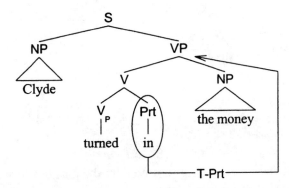

This method works well enough for this sentence, but later on we will encounter cases where diagrams drawn in this way would become too complex to be clear—and visual clarity is the whole point of a diagram.

An alternative method of showing a transformation is to take the tree generated by the PS-rules, draw a broken line beneath it to represent the transformational rule, and then draw arrows to show changes made by that rule below that line:

15

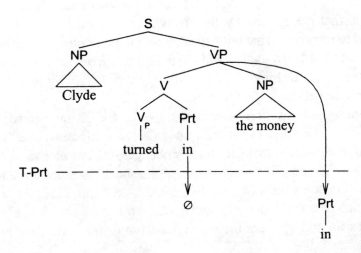

Arrows that extend down below the broken line can show an element being deleted, added, or replaced. The first arrow in 15 shows the particle *in* being deleted from its original position next to the V_P and replaced by ⌀ (⌀ is the ***null symbol***; it stands for "nothing" and in this case represents that the particle has been deleted). The arrow on the right shows the particle *in* being added to the end of the VP. In this form of diagraming, the movement of an element is shown by its being deleted from one position and added to another.

Still a third alternative is to draw a diagram that consists of before-and-after trees: one to show the structure *before* the T-rule has applied and another to show the structure *after* the transformation has taken place. To show that the transformation has occurred, we will draw an arrow between them labeled with the name of the transformation (in this case, T-Prt):

16

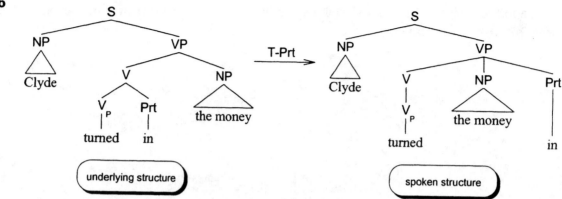

Diagram 16 shows the particle *in* being removed by the particle-movement rule from its original position as a partner of *turned* and moved to a new position at the end of the verb phrase. We will call the tree on the left, which is produced by the phrase-structure rules, the ***underlying structure*** of the sentence. (The term ***deep structure*** is also used for this tree.) We will call the tree on the right, representing the sentence as actually spoken or written, the ***spoken structure*** of the sentence. (The term ***surface structure*** is also used for the spoken sentence.)

Although the diagraming method used in 16 takes the longest to draw, it has one principal advantage over the other two methods: It clearly shows the difference between the underlying and spoken structures of the sentence, and both structures are important. Whereas the spoken structure represents the words that are *spoken* by the speaker and *heard* by the listener, the underlying structure may be said to represent what both speaker and listener *understand* the sentence to mean. Remember we said that in order to understand the action of *Clyde turned the money in*, we have to put *turned* and *in* together in our minds. That is another way of saying that we have to consult the underlying structure to understand what it is that Clyde did.

We can sum up our hypothesis for how sentences like 9a and 9b are created: A speaker conceives a meaning and applies the PS-rules to generate an underlying structure like 12 that represents that meaning. If the speaker decides to make no further changes, the speaker says, "Clyde turned in the money" (in which case the underlying structure and the spoken structure are identical). Or, if the speaker decides instead to apply the T-Prt rule to move *in* to the end, the speaker says, "Clyde turned the money in" (in which case the underlying and spoken structures are different). According to our hypothesis, sentences 9a and 9b have the same underlying structure; they merely differ in their spoken structures.

From the listener's point of view, the process is reversed. The listener who hears the spoken sentence "Clyde turned the money in" *undoes* the transformational rule to arrive at the underlying structure, which communicates the speaker's intended meaning.

You don't want to read too much into the model we are creating. Of course we are not claiming that when you or I talk we literally move words around or that we draw trees and arrows in our minds. Our model is simply a way of representing our observation that before a speaker can say, "Clyde turned the money in," the concept of "turned in" must first exist as a unit in that person's mind. And in order to comprehend the spoken sentence, the listener too must link *turned* and *in*. The concept that is understood by both speaker and listener is what we are calling the sentence's underlying structure.

Let us assume for now that this hypothetical model is the process by which all sentences are generated. In upcoming chapters we will see that many different kinds of transformational rules can be applied to alter a sentence's underlying structure. It is also important to understand that our model is a simplified one, and many linguists would have reservations about our claim that "underlying structure represents the meaning of the sentence." If you go on to take advanced courses in syntax, you will encounter different models and hypotheses about how sentences are generated. Nevertheless, this model is the simplest and clearest for our purposes.

Diagrams 14, 15, and 16 are equivalent methods of representing the ways sentences are produced according to our model. In upcoming chapters we will often draw before-and-after diagrams like 16 to show the operation of transformational rules, but we will sometimes find it useful to save time and space by drawing broken-line diagrams like 15 as well.

Finally, let us add one new term to our discussion. We will call a diagram that shows how a sentence is produced a **derivation** of that sentence. Diagram 12 (with one tree) is the derivation of the spoken sentence *Clyde turned in the money*, and diagram 16 (with two trees) is the derivation of *Clyde turned the money in*.

Exercises 7.2

1. The following are all spoken sentences (spoken structures). Draw trees to show the derivations of these sentences. For some of these sentences only one tree is required to show the derivation, while for others, two trees are required.

   a. Mavis whipped up a splendid dessert.

   Because the V$_P$ and Prt are together in this spoken structure, the T-Prt rule has not been applied. The underlying and spoken structures are the same, so only one tree is necessary to show the derivation. It is true that there is <u>another</u> perfectly good spoken sentence that could be derived from the same underlying structure ("Mavis whipped a splendid dessert up"), but in exercise 1a you are not being asked to show the derivation of that sentence.

   b. Mason brought the groceries in.

   Because the V$_P$ and Prt are separated in this spoken structure, the T-Prt rule has been applied. The underlying and spoken structures are different, so two trees are necessary to show the derivation. Your derivation will have the following structure:

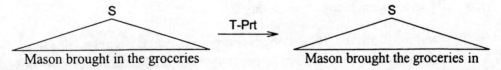

   In your diagram you should supply the missing elements represented by the triangles. Note that in all the sentences in this exercise you are given spoken structures to derive, and your task is to show how these sentences came to have that structure. When a derivation requires more than one tree, the sentence you are given will be

the final tree you draw, not the first tree (unless only one tree is needed, as in exercise 1a above). Remember that the verb and particle will always be together in the first (underlying) tree. If they are still together in the spoken structure, no transformation has occurred, and only one tree is required to show its derivation. If they are not together, a transformation has occurred, and two trees must be drawn to show the derivation.

    c. He put the project off repeatedly.
    d. The kids rounded up their friends.
    e. The tornado blew some buildings down.
    f. The wind blew the paper down the alley.   [Don't be tricked by this one.]

2.   Particles can be moved to follow a noun phrase, but prepositions cannot. A good test of whether a word such as *in* is acting as a particle or a preposition in a sentence is to see if can be moved. For example, regarding sentence 2, we can say either *Clyde turned in the money* or *Clyde turned the money in*, so *in* must be a particle in this sentence. On the other hand, regarding sentence 1, we can say *Clyde turned in a circle* but not **Clyde turned a circle in*, so *in* must be a preposition in this sentence. See if this test works with the sentences in Exercises 7.1 on page 100.

(3.) Optional discovery exercise: The sentences *The child turned the light on* and *The child turned the light off* are both grammatical. We can also join the particles with a coordinating conjunction:

    a. The child turned the light on and off.

The sentences *The obnoxious tenant put his neighbors off* and *The obnoxious tenant put his neighbors down* are also grammatical. But we cannot join these particles with a conjunction:

    b. * The obnoxious tenant put his neighbors off and down.

Speculate on why coordination is possible in 3a but not in 3b.

(4.) Exercise 2 claims that a particle can be moved by T-Prt to follow a direct object. Some phrasal verbs seem to be intransitive, and so they cannot be moved (*The plane took off for Aruba, Chico passed out at the sight of blood*). Others present more of a problem:

    a. McDuck came by his wealth honestly.
    b. Willy calls on a dozen accounts each day.

Decide if *by* and *on* in these two sentences are prepositions, particles, or something else. If particles, do they represent an exception to our statement that particles can be moved? Finally, consider these sentences:

    c. Gwen looked forward to lunchtime.
    d. The governor put forth her legislative agenda.

Looked forward and *put forth* seem to be phrasal verbs, but *forward* and *forth* are not words that can also act as prepositions, nor can they be moved. Speculate on how we might classify *forward* and *forth* in sentences *c* and *d*.

Optional and Obligatory Rules

A grammar with both phrase-structure rules and transformational rules is called a ***generative-transformational grammar***. So far we have introduced one T-rule, called the particle-movement rule or T-Prt. It is an ***optional rule*** because whenever a phrasal verb occurs we have a choice about whether to apply it. A grammatical sentence results whether or not T-Prt is applied.

But to be more accurate, I should say that the rule is not always optional. Consider the following sentences:

17 a. Ed took up golf.

   b. Ed took golf up.

   c. Ed took it up.

   d. *Ed took up it.

It appears from **17d** that a phrasal verb cannot be followed by a pronoun like *it*. Further tests confirm this observation: * *Clyde turned in it,* * *The announcer called out it*, and so on. A hypothesis we can make is that in English the T-Prt rule is optional when the direct object contains a noun, but it is ***obligatory*** when the direct object is a pronoun. In upcoming chapters we will encounter both optional and obligatory transformational rules.

Our Goals—A Review and Update

In the first chapter, I claimed that our goal in this book is to discover a grammar for English with two important qualities: First, it should be capable of generating the grammatical sentences of English. Second, and far more ambitiously, it should also be a model of our mental grammars, reflecting in some way the process our minds go through as we create sentences.

We have been successful so far in our first goal. Every time we have introduced new data in the form of additional sentences, we have been able to augment or modify our grammar to accommodate the data. We have made our rules as simple as we can yet still capable of producing grammatical sentences.

Success in our second goal is far less certain. We have no means of verifying it, because we cannot directly observe the workings of our minds in order to make the comparison. The best we can do is hope that if we have created a model that generates good sentences in the most efficient way possible and that captures most accurately our intuitive feelings about our language, then such a grammar comes close to doing what our mental grammars do.

Linguists continue to debate the nature of the ideal grammar model. Whether ours attains both of our goals is open to question, and we should keep an open mind as we continue to develop our model. Remember that we are constructing hypotheses about language and then testing them. We must always be willing to change or reject a hypothesis if it does not work or if a better explanation presents itself. The quest for understanding about our language continues, and we must remain active and honest participants in the quest.

For now, let us continue to hypothesize that in some way our grammar reflects what the mind does when it generates language. One consequence that follows from this hypothesis is the claim that, in producing sentences, our minds observe the equivalent of phrase-structure and transformational rules. This will not seem far-fetched if we consider what the "rules" really mean. We should not think of our minds as blindly and mechanically directed by a set of mathematical formulas. Rather, we should think of the rules as descriptions of what our minds must do (unconsciously) in order to produce sentences.

For example, the first PS-rule (S → NP VP) reflects our unconscious knowledge that when we begin a sentence with a noun phrase, we must keep track, no matter how complex that noun phrase may be, of the fact that a verb phrase must follow. Surely that is what happens whenever we speak. Similarly the NP and VP rules are statements of what options we have for those categories. The test of whether these and other PS-rules are accurate is whether we produce the sentences they describe, and, at least so far in our analysis, we seem to do just what the rules say.

Transformational rules raise other questions. You may ask whether derivation 16 is an accurate account of how your mind produces the sentence *Clyde turned the money in*. Again it is important to consider what the model is *not* saying. It does not mean that you first think the completed sentence *Clyde turned in the money* and then you create another sentence with the words switched around. What it is saying is that the mind generates a basic structure that it can then easily — and almost instantaneously — alter in a certain way if it decides to. In order to show the details of this change clearly on paper we may draw an entirely new tree, but that should not deceive us into thinking the change is more complicated than it is. Remember that the rules that we state and the trees that we draw are meant only as visual aids to our understanding.

8 Three More Transformational Rules

Moving Adverbial Phrases

Particles, we have seen, can be moved by a transformational rule. Regardless of whether particles come before or after the direct object in the spoken form of a sentence, they are always located next to the verb in the sentence's underlying structure. Are there any other elements beside particles that can be moved by a transformational rule?

Consider adverbial phrases, which can also occur in various places in spoken sentences:

1 **a.** The child opened the present *eagerly*.
   b. *Eagerly* the child opened the present.
   c. The child *eagerly* opened the present.

It would seem that an adverbial like *eagerly* can occur in several different places in a sentence, represented by the roman numerals in the following tree:

2

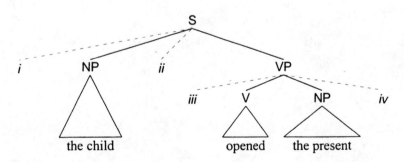

In sentence 1a the adverbial occurs in position *iv*. In Chapter 6, we accounted for this possibility with a phrase-structure rule that allows for adverbials at the end of a verb phrase:

3   VP → V (NP) **(AdvP)⁺**

It makes sense for an adverbial like *eagerly* to be a constituent of the verb phrase because *eagerly* modifies the verb *opened*, telling how the child did the opening.

How then do we account for 1b, where the adverbial occurs in position *i*? One possibility is to revise our S rule to allow adverbials to begin a sentence:

4   (?)   S → (AdvP)⁺ NP VP

We have reason to be uncomfortable with this analysis, because it makes *eagerly* a major constituent of the sentence, which is contrary to our intuitions, and it doesn't capture our sense that *eagerly* describes the verb *opened* in 1b, just as it does in 1a.

Sentence 1c is even more problematic. Is *eagerly* a direct constituent of S (position *ii*) or of VP (position *iii*)? If we decide it is a constituent of the sentence, we could make a further change to rule 3:

5   (?)   S → (AdvP)⁺ NP **(AdvP)⁺** VP

On the other hand, if we decide it is the first element in the verb phrase, we could add this possibility to our VP rule:

6   (?)   VP → **(AdvP)⁺** V (NP) (AdvP)⁺

Besides cluttering our grammar, these solutions are all unsatisfactory ways of accounting for the different positions in which an adverbial can occur. They do not capture our intuition that all three sentences in 1 say essentially the same thing. That is, 1a, 1b, and 1c are all in a fundamental sense the *same* sentence, with some words rearranged for reasons of style or emphasis. No matter where it is located, the adverb *eagerly* has the purpose of telling us how the child did the opening, and so in each case it modifies the verb *opened*. We should expect all three sentences to be derived in similar ways.

Fortunately, our notion of transformational rules can capture our intuitions nicely. We can claim that sentences 1a, 1b, and 1c all share the following underlying structure, which represents (in some sense) the meaning of the sentence:

7

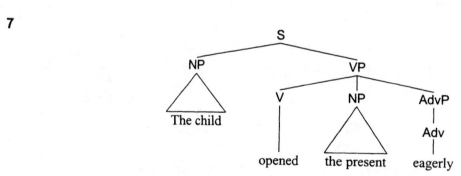

Having produced this underlying structure, a speaker is then free either to make no changes and so produce spoken sentence 1a or else to move the adverb and so produce either 1b or 1c. In other words, we can claim the existence of a second T-rule, which we will call the ***adverbial-movement transformational rule***:

8   **Adverbial-Movement Transformation (T-AdvP)**: An adverbial phrase may be moved out of the VP and made a constituent of S.

Rule 8 states that after underlying structure 7 has been generated, an adverbial can be moved if we choose. The rule gives us three options, represented in the following diagram:

9   **Underlying structure:**   The child   opened the present <u>eagerly</u>

Options: **(a)** T-AdvP is not applied;   **(b)**   **(c)** |⎯⎯⎯⎯ T-AdvP ⎯⎯⎯|
no change

|⎯⎯⎯⎯⎯⎯⎯⎯⎯⎯ T-AdvP ⎯⎯⎯⎯⎯⎯⎯⎯|

Option *a* corresponds to sentence 1a, in which the underlying and spoken structures are identical. Options *b* and *c* correspond to sentences 1b and 1c respectively, in which the spoken structure has resulted from a change made to the underlying structure.

If we want to show in detail how the grammar generates 1b, we first draw the underlying tree and then use T-AdvP to move the adverb to the front of the sentence. Here is the derivation of 1b:

10

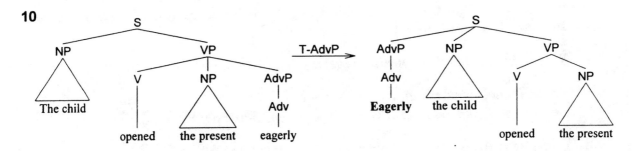

If we want to show the derivation of sentence 1c, we start with the same underlying structure but this time we show T-AdvP moving the adverb to a new location between the subject and the verb:

11

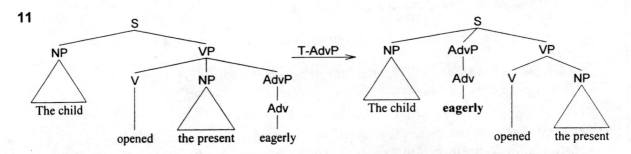

The derivation of sentence 1a, in which T-AdvP is not applied, is tree 7 by itself.

Exercises 8.1

1. Underline each adverbial in the following sentences, and draw trees to show its derivation. In each case you are given a spoken sentence and asked to derive it — that is, to show how it got that way. If your derivation requires more than one tree, the sentence you are given represents the *final* tree you will draw (the spoken structure), not the first (underlying) tree.

a. Jocelyn arrived <u>punctually</u> <u>for class</u> <u>at noon</u> <u>yesterday</u>.

Spoken sentence 1a has four separate adverbials (two adverbs, two prepositional phrases), but each occurs following the verb, just as it does in the underlying structure. That means that T-AdvP has not applied and nothing was moved in order to produce this spoken form, so only one tree is needed to show the derivation. You may have noticed that many <u>other</u> spoken sentences could also be derived from the same underlying structure ("Punctually, Jocelyn arrived . . . ," "Jocelyn punctually arrived . . . ," "At noon, Jocelyn arrived . . . ," and so on), but here you are <u>not</u> being asked to show derivations for <u>those</u> sentences.

b. Barnabas usually knew the correct answer.

In this spoken sentence, the adverb "usually" has been moved by T-AdvP from its underlying position at the end of the verb phrase, and your derivation will show two trees (Barnabas knew the correct answer usually → Barnabas usually knew the correct answer). Your derivation will resemble derivation 11.

c. With dramatic flair, the detective revealed the solution.

Prepositional phrases can also be moved by T-AdvP. This derivation will resemble derivation 10, but here the adverbial is a prepositional phrase instead of an adverb.

d. Comedians always deliver their monologues without notes.

Both adverbials in this sentence ("always" and "without notes") appear at the end of the verb phrase in the underlying structure. Here T-AdvP has moved "always" (but not "without notes") to result in this spoken sentence.

e. The man with the wooden leg without assistance climbed the ladder.

Assume that "with the wooden leg" identifies which man we are discussing, rather than how he did the climbing.

(2.) Optional discovery exercise: We speculated about whether the adverb *eagerly* in 1c is a constituent of S (position *ii* in tree 2) or of VP (position *iii* in 2). Rule 8 assumes that it is an S-constituent, but no justification was given for that assumption. Can you think of any reason to prefer one assumption over the other? If we assume instead that it is a VP-constituent, how would you have to rewrite rule 8? In the absence of any better reason to prefer one hypothesis over another, we always prefer the simpler hypothesis. Which assumption results in the less complicated T- rule?

Applying More Than One T-Rule in a Derivation

Consider the following spoken sentence, in which two adverbials have been moved:

12   *At the signal*, the police *quickly* stormed the building.

Here we need to apply T-AdvP twice, once to move the adverb *quickly* and once to move the prepositional phrase *at the signal*. Diagram 13 shows the derivation of sentence 12.

In this and the following trees in this book, let us allow ourselves a shortcut. We are now well aware that determiners can be articles (Art), demonstratives (Dem), and quantifiers (Quant), but let us agree to save time and space, if we like, by omitting those labels and identifying them simply as determiners (Det) in our trees. However, we will continue to provide labels for possessive pronouns (Pro_{P-S}) and possessive noun phrases (NP Poss) when we encounter them.

13

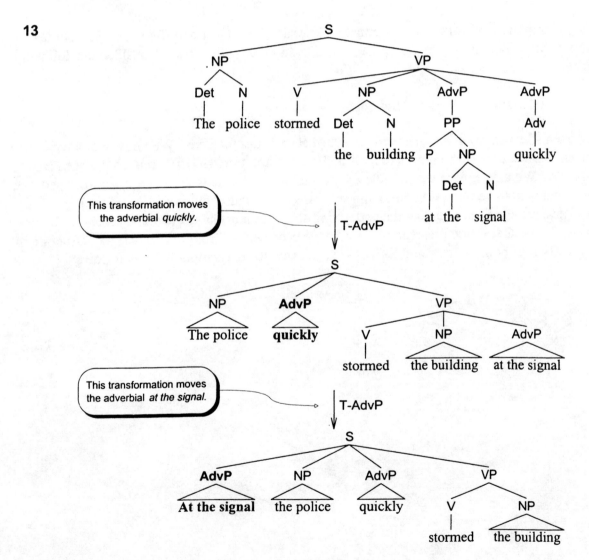

When applied the first time in derivation 13, T-AdvP moves *quickly* so it follows *the police*. When applied the second time, it moves *at the signal* to the front of the sentence.

The first tree in the derivation represents the underlying structure, and the final tree represents the spoken structure. We will call any middle trees in a derivation *intermediate structures*.

A couple of observations should be made about how we drew this derivation. First, we drew an underlying structure in which *at the signal* preceded *quickly*. However, this was an arbitrary decision, because we have no way of deciding which of these adverbials should come first in the underlying structure; they could just as easily have been drawn in the opposite order. Second, there is no significance to the order in which the two adverbials were moved; the effect would have been the same if the movement of *at the signal* had been shown first. In fact, we have no reason to assume the transformations occurred one-after-another rather than simultaneously. We could have drawn just the first and last trees, linked by an arrow labeled as follows:

$$\frac{\text{T-AdvP}}{\text{(twice)}}\longrightarrow$$

Our grammar now contains two transformational rules, T-Prt and T-AdvP. Sometimes the derivation of a spoken sentence requires the operation of both rules. Consider the following sentence:

14   The pitcher easily struck Casey out.

This spoken structure contains an adverb, *easily*, that precedes the verb. We know that adverbs are generated at the end of verb phrases in their underlying structure, so *easily* must have been moved by T-AdvP. We also notice the particle *out* at the end of the sentence. We know that particles always occur next to verbs in the underlying structure, so *out* must have been moved by T-Prt. From this analysis, we can figure out that the underlying structure must have been *The pitcher struck out Casey easily* and that spoken sentence 14 must have been derived from this underlying structure by the application of both T-AdvP and T-Prt. We can show the derivation of 14 as follows:

15

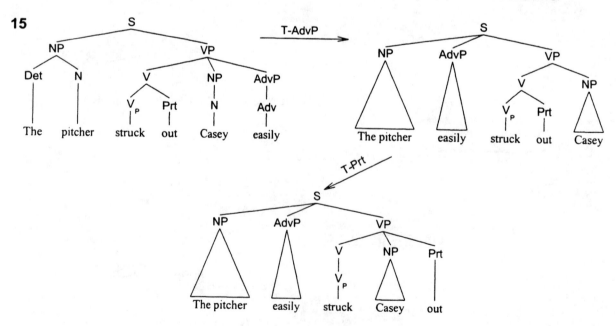

Remember that the underlying structure is generated by the phrase-structure rules. Transformational rules can then make alterations to this structure. The resulting spoken sentence may have a structure that the phrase-structure rules would be incapable of generating directly.

Exercises 8.2

For each of the following spoken sentences, determine the underlying structure of the sentence and decide what transformations were needed to derive this sentence. Then draw trees to show the derivation. Show the result of each transformation with a separate tree. As we did in derivations 13 and 15, draw the complete tree for the underlying structure (without triangles). For subsequent trees, you can use triangles for phrases that did not change from the previous tree.

1. Over the field they doggedly pursued their quarry.
      [Underlying structure: *They pursued their quarry over the field doggedly.* Apply T-AdvP twice.]
2. Foolishly Brenda passed every opportunity up.
3. The speaker finally got the message across to the audience.
4. During spring break, their uncle generously put the students up in his beach house.

Imperative Sentences

Traditional grammar classifies verbs as having different *moods*. All the sentences we have examined so far have been in the *declarative mood*, which means they make statements: e.g., *He is a boy scout.* Questions are in the *interrogative mood: Is she a girl scout?* (Some grammarians prefer to classify declarative and interrogative sentences as being two varieties of the same mood, which they call the *indicative mood*.) The *subjunctive mood* concerns hypothetical, not actual, situations: *If I were a cub scout. . . .* The final mood, and the one we will now consider, is the *imperative mood*. Imperative sentences are commands: *Be a good scout!*

In commands like *Be a good scout!* or *Open the door!* no subject noun phrase is stated, but it is understood to be the hearer (*you*) who is being directed to do something. In traditional grammar, it is said that the subject of an imperative sentence is "*you* understood." In other words, a sentence like *Be a good scout* has a subject (*you*) that is recognized but not spoken. In transformational terms, this is simply a way of saying that the subject is present in the underlying structure but deleted from the spoken structure.

It is important to realize that we are not claiming that our brains first generate the actual word "you" and then delete it. What we are saying is that the concept of the hearer is present as the underlying subject but does not become a spoken word. We will arbitrarily represent this concept as *HEARER*, written in upper-case letters, but we could as easily use *YOU* or *READER* or ☺ or any other symbol. Henceforth we will use uppercase letters to represent underlying concepts that may or may not get realized as spoken words.

16 **Imperative Transformation (T-Imp):** Delete the subject *HEARER* from an imperative sentence.

Here is the derivation of the command *Open the door!*

17

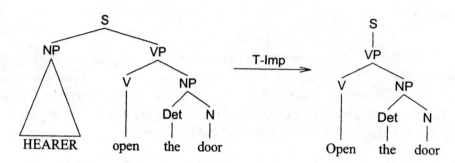

The subject noun phrase is simply deleted to form the spoken sentence. Alternatively, we can save some time and paper by using a "broken-line" diagram to show this transformation:

18

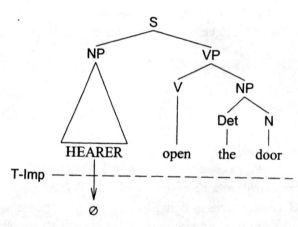

This diagram shows the operation of the transformation below the broken line. Here, T-Imp removes the subject, *HEARER*, so that it is absent from the spoken structure.

Exercises 8.3

Draw trees to show the derivations of these sentences:

1. Eat your oatmeal.
2. Stop!
3. Take the garbage out.   [More than one T-rule is needed to derive this sentence.]
4. Never raise your voice.   [Adv: *never*]

Indirect Objects

A noun phrase that follows a transitive verb is called a direct object. In addition to a direct object, a second noun phrase sometimes follows a verb, as in the sentences of 19. The italicized noun phrases that occur between the verbs and the direct objects in these sentences are called *indirect objects*.

19 a. Carmen gave *Jose* a lecture.
   b. George did *his mother* a favor.
   c. We told *him* a secret.
   d. The experience taught *Mona* a valuable lesson.
   e. I asked *the wise swami* a question.

In 19a, *a lecture* is the direct object (it is the thing that Carmen gave), and *Jose* is the indirect object. An ***indirect object*** names the person or thing to whom or for whom the action is performed. Sentence 19a would seem to have the following spoken structure:

20

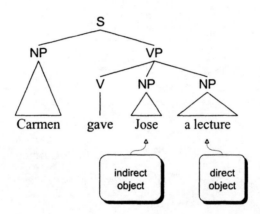

We can also observe that for each sentence with an indirect object, there corresponds an equivalent sentence with a prepositional phrase. These prepositional phrases generally begin with the prepositions *to, for,* or *of*:

21 a. Carmen gave a lecture *to Jose*.
   b. George did a favor *for his mother*.
   c. We told a secret *to him*.
   d. The experience taught a valuable lesson *to Mona*.
   e. I asked a question *of the wise swami*.

The question that faces us is how our grammar should account for indirect objects. We could decide to alter our VP rule to allow verbs to be followed by two noun phrases, but that would have two disadvantages. First, it would make the VP rule more complicated, and, second, it would not account for the similarity between the sentences of 19 and 21. Another solution—the one we will adopt—is to retain our current VP rule, which can generate the sentences of 21, and to claim that the sentences of 19 are derived from them by a transformational rule:

22   **Indirect-Object Transformation (T-IO)**: An indirect object can be created from a prepositional phrase that states to whom, for whom, or of whom an action is performed. The preposition *to*, *for*, or *of* is deleted, and the noun phrase that was the object of the preposition is moved forward to a position immediately following the verb.

Sentences 19a and 21a have identical underlying structures in this analysis; 19a is created by applying the transformational rule:

23   Carmen gave   a lecture to Jose

                                                            T-IO   ∅

Here is the complete derivation:

24

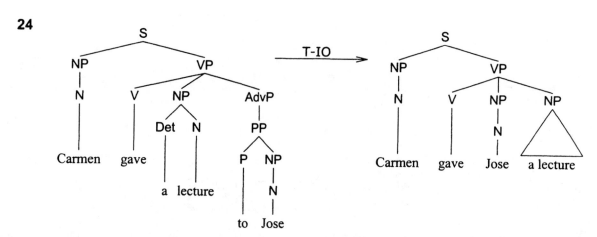

Exercises 8.4

1. Draw one line under each direct object and two lines under each indirect object (if there is one) in the following sentences. Draw trees to show their derivations. Draw a complete tree (with no triangles) for the underlying structure. You may use triangles in subsequent trees (if any) for a phrase whose structure has not changed from the previous tree.

    a. Earl gave <u>a firm handshake</u> to Isaac.   [No transformation is needed.]
    b. The team sent <u><u>the injured player</u></u> <u>a card</u>.   [Underlying: *The team sent a card to the injured player*]
    c. My brother-in-law got me a big discount.
    d. The sailor showed us his tattoos.
    e. Arlene rudely asked Lionel a question.   [More than one T-rule applies.]
    f. Heathcliff told Cathy a secret.

2. Redraw derivation 24, using the broken-line method.

(3.) Optional discovery exercise: Direct objects can be simple noun phrases, but they can also be complement clauses. Draw one line under the direct object in the following sentence and two lines under the indirect object. Then draw trees to show the derivation.

Heathcliff told Cathy that Hareton saw a ghost.

A transformational rule is obligatory when the underlying structure could not be a grammatical spoken sentence. Is T-IO optional or obligatory when the direct object of a sentence is a complement clause?

Must Transformations Apply in a Particular Order?

Some spoken sentences, we have seen, are derived through the operation of more than one T-rule. For example, consider the following sentence.

25   From the boat, the sailor threw us a lifeline.

To derive 25 from its underlying structure, T-AdvP moves the adverbial *from the boat*, and T-IO moves the indirect object *us*. Does one T-rule operate before the other? In this case, it does not seem to matter which order we choose. We could apply T-AdvP first:

26

The sailor threw a lifeline to us from the boat

↓ T-AdvP

From the boat the sailor threw a lifeline to us

↓ T-IO

From the boat the sailor threw us a lifeline

Or we could apply T-IO first:

27

The sailor threw a lifeline to us from the boat

↓ T-IO

The sailor threw us a lifeline from the boat

↓ T-AdvP

From the boat the sailor threw us a lifeline

The results are the same in either case, so it would appear that the order is irrelevant.
But now consider spoken sentence 28.

---

28   The chef whipped Melba up a fancy dessert.

Two transformations would seem to be required to derive this sentence: T-Prt to move *up* away from *whipped* and T-IO to make *Melba* the indirect object. What happens if we apply T-Prt first?

29

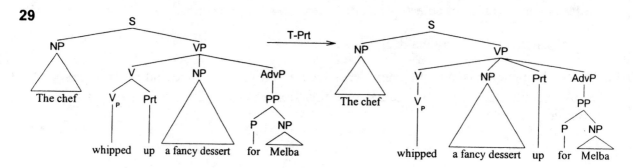

But if we now try to apply T-IO, which deletes *for* and moves *Melba* immediately after the verb, the result is an ungrammatical sentence:

30   * The chef whipped Melba a fancy dessert up.

We can conclude that applying T-rules in the order *first T-Prt, then T-IO* does not seem to work. What happens when we apply them in the reverse order? We start with T-IO:

31

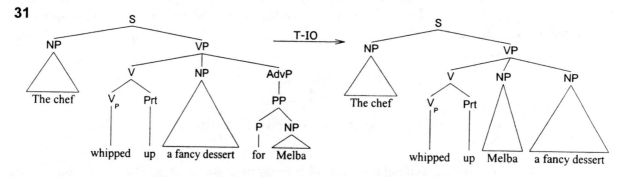

The result of the first transformation, *The chef whipped up Melba a fancy dessert*, is ungrammatical. But wait! What happens if we now apply T-Prt, which moves a particle to follow the first noun phrase in the verb phrase? It moves *up* so that it follows *Melba*:

32

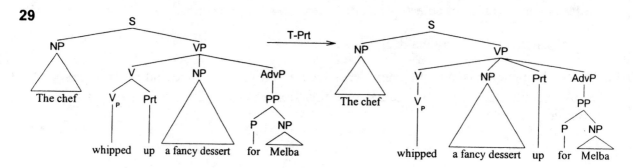

And voilà! The result is a grammatical spoken sentence. We can conclude that T-IO must apply before T-Prt. We can also conclude that when T-IO has applied to a structure with a phrasal verb, T-Prt then becomes an obligatory transformation.

Let us hypothesize that T-rules are ordered. That is, when more than one rule is applied in a derivation, one of those rules must be applied before the other. We will tentatively (and arbitrarily) select the following order, with the understanding that we are free to alter the order if we discover good reasons for doing so.

33   T-Rules (in relative order of application)

    1. T-AdvP

    2. T-IO

    3. T-Imp

    4. T-Prt

Exercises 8.5

Draw trees to show the derivation of each of the following spoken sentences. First decide what T-rules were used to produce this structure. Then draw the tree for the underlying structure, and show the application of the T-rules that result in the spoken structure. If more than one T-rule is needed, apply them in the relative order shown in list 33.

1. Take the garbage out.   [T-Imp (the third rule in the list) is applied before T-Prt (the fourth rule). Underlying: *HEARER take out the garbage*]
2. The candidate unintentionally did his opponent a favor.
3. At the signal, the proctor handed the exams out.
4. Tell the jury your whereabouts during the robbery.
5. Gently put the baby down on the bed.
6. During a storm, turn off the computer.
7. On your vacation, pick me up a souvenir.

       [All four T-rules are needed in this derivation. Remember it is not necessary that intermediate structures make acceptable spoken sentences.]

9

Pronouns:
Another Analysis

A Personal-Pronoun Transformation

In Chapter 4, a pronoun was defined as a word used in place of a noun phrase. We have used the second option in the following phrase-structure rule to generate personal pronouns such as *I*, *you*, and *they*:

1

$$NP \rightarrow \left\{ \begin{array}{l} (Det) \ (AdjP)^+ \ (Mod_{NP}) \ N \ (PP) \ (CompP) \\ Pro_P \end{array} \right\}$$

This rule allowed the grammar to produce sentences such as *She promoted him* and *They amazed us*.

   Another analysis of how pronouns are generated is also possible. Saying that pronouns "stand for" noun phrases is another way of saying that they are spoken representatives of those underlying noun phrases, derived from them by a transformation. The noun phrases (or, more accurately, the concepts that they represent) are present in the underlying structure, but they are replaced by pronouns in the spoken structure. Consider, for example, the following sentence:

2   Elizabeth praised the clerk, and he thanked her.

In this sentence, we understand the second clause to mean that the clerk thanked Elizabeth. What we understand is in fact the underlying structure, from which the sentence that is actually spoken is derived by this transformation:

3   **Personal-Pronoun Transformation (T-Pro$_P$):** A noun phrase may be replaced by the appropriate personal pronoun.

Under this analysis, here is the derivation of sentence 2:

4

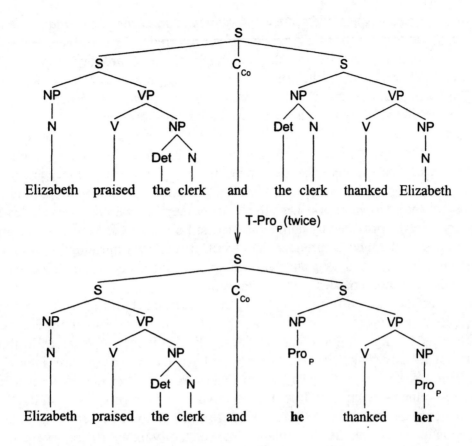

Alternatively, we could use the more economical broken-line diagraming method to show this same transformation:

5

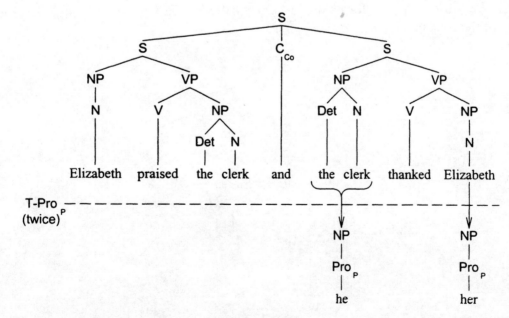

When using a broken-line diagram to show one constituent replacing another, repeat the lowermost label that does not change (in this case, NP) immediately below the broken line.

If we heard someone speak the sentence *Elizabeth praised the clerk, and he thanked her*, we would know which persons the pronouns *he* and *her* referred to (that is, we could reconstruct the sentence's underlying structure) because the noun phrases that the pronouns replace, *Elizabeth* and *the clerk*, are stated previously in the sentence. Such noun phrases that serve as guideposts to the underlying forms of pronouns are called ***antecedents*** of those pronouns. A personal pronoun is only useful and meaningful to hearers if it is accompanied by an antecedent. For example, if, out of the blue, someone blurted out, "He thanked her," we would be mystified, because we would lack antecedents for those two pronouns. Often, as in sentence 2, antecedents and pronouns appear within the same sentence. But speakers also have other means of providing antecedents. Antecedents might be spoken in an earlier sentence, either by the same speaker or by another party to the conversation ("What did Mom and Dad think of the surprise party?" "They loved it."). An antecedent can even be provided by nonverbal means: Pointing to an actor on TV, one could say, "He has the oddest smile," and the pronoun "he" would be perfectly meaningful. And with first- and second-person pronouns such as *I* and *you*, no spoken antecedents are necessary because the "antecedents" are the actual parties to the conversation.

A very important concept to understand—one that bears repeating—is that the underlying structure represents the sentence's idea or meaning. The words we write in our diagram across the bottom of the underlying tree represent that idea. But the words themselves in the underlying structure are not actually spoken or even necessarily formed as words in our minds. For example, if you say *I* in a sentence, that doesn't mean that your mind first thinks your name and then transforms it into the pronoun *I*. It does mean that you have the concept of yourself in mind and transform that concept into the word *I*. If you were to diagram such a sentence, however, in the underlying structure you might use your name or a sketch of yourself or some symbol to represent you. In this book, let us arbitrarily agree to use the term ***SPEAKER***, written in uppercase letters, as the underlying concept of oneself that is replaced in the spoken structure by the pronouns *I* or *me*. Likewise, we will use ***HEARER*** to represent the underlying concept for the pronoun *you*. We will use ***SPEAKERS*** for the plural forms *we* and *us*, and ***HEARERS*** for the plural *you*. Here is the derivation of the sentence *We trusted you*:

6

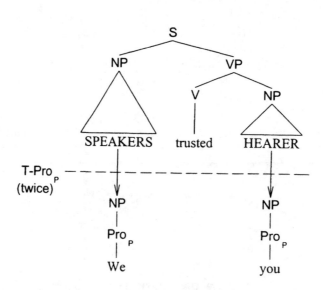

In this derivation the personal-pronoun transformation operates twice, once to change *SPEAKERS* to *we* and again to change *HEARER* to *you*. Because we are regarding *SPEAKERS* and *HEARER* as concepts rather than as actual words, we will not classify them as nouns or any other part of speech. Instead we will use triangles in underlying trees to signify that they are concepts, not words.

Exercises 9.1

1. Use T-Pro_P to derive the pronouns in the following sentences. Show the transformation either by drawing two trees or by using a broken-line diagram.

   a. Clementine brags that she speaks Hungarian.
   b. Dorothy dated Carl and Sean, but she disliked them.
   c. Linda and I petted the cat, but it scratched us.

2. For the following sentences, supply your own meaning for the pronouns; that is, invent appropriate underlying structures. Draw the derivations.

   a. It followed her to school.
   b. They fascinate him.

Deriving Possessive Pronouns

In Chapter 6, we observed that a possessive pronoun (Pro$_{P-S}$) was a variety of personal pronoun that functioned as a determiner, as in the following sentence:

7   Andre spent *his* allowance.

Because it was Andre's allowance that he spent, we can now assume that the pronoun *his* in 7 is derived (by the personal-pronoun transformation) from the underlying possessive noun phrase *Andre's*. We can show the derivation either by using two trees, as in 8, or by using a broken-line diagram, as in 9.

8

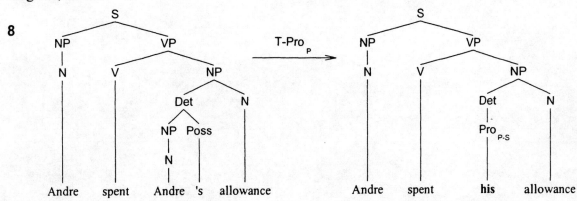

Notice that both *Andre's* and the possessive pronoun *its* that replaces it are determiners, not noun phrases.

A broken-line diagram is an equivalent way of showing this transformation:

9

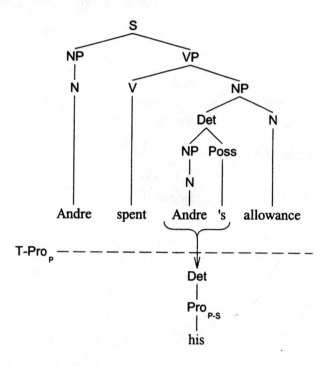

We can now update the personal-pronoun transformational rule (stated in 3) to include possessive pronouns:

10 **Personal-Pronoun Transformation (T-Pro$_P$):** A noun phrase may be replaced by the appropriate personal pronoun. A determiner that consists of a possessive noun phrase may be replaced by the appropriate possessive pronoun.

The same rule is used to derive both personal and possessive pronouns. The derivation of *I found my keys* is shown in 11.

11

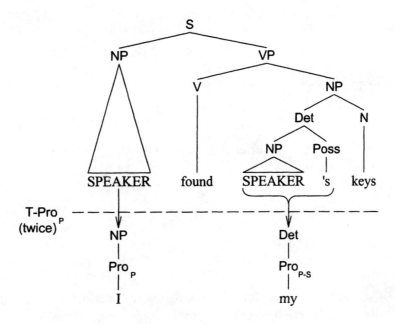

Here T-Pro$_P$ changes the noun phrase *SPEAKER* to the personal pronoun *I*, and it changes the possessive noun phrase *SPEAKER's* to the possessive pronoun *my*.

Exercises 9.2

Show the derivations of the following sentences with possessive and personal pronouns:

1. Lindy scraped her finger on the sharp rocks.
2. The lost child cried for its parents.
3. Jay dreamed that he dyed his hair.
4. You never forget my passion for chocolate.   HEARER never forget Speaker's passion for chocolate

T-Pro$_p$ —

you

my

Reflexive Pronouns

In addition to personal pronouns such as *him* or *them* and possessive pronouns such as *his* or *their*, we sometimes encounter still other pronouns:

12 a. Peter congratulated *himself*.
   b. The O'Hoolihan twins invited *themselves* to our party.

Like personal pronouns, these pronouns seem to stand for noun phrases, but they end in the suffixes *-self* or *-selves*. We will call them **reflexive pronouns** (abbreviated as **Pro$_{Rx}$**). It is clear in 12a that the person whom Peter congratulated was Peter. We can show the derivation of 12a as follows:

13

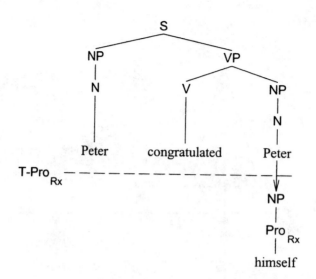

It is clear that reflexive pronouns are derived by a different transformational rule from that used to derive personal pronouns. If we applied T-Pro$_P$ to the underlying structure of 13 instead of T-Pro$_{Rx}$, we would have produced *Peter congratulated him*, which would be ungrammatical if *him* is intended to refer to Peter. Under what circumstances, then, do we apply T-Pro$_{Rx}$ rather than T-Pro$_P$? Let us examine some additional data before we decide.

Exercises 9.3

1. Which of the following sentences are grammatical? The pronoun *himself* is intended to refer to Peter in each sentence.

    a. Peter congratulated himself.
    b. Himself congratulated Peter.— don't name antecedent yet
    c. Jane said that (Peter) congratulated himself. part of same little clause
    d. Peter said that Jane congratulated himself.
    e. Peter said that himself congratulated Jane.

    antecedent has to be clearly → need pronoun

    Can you draw any conclusions from this data about when an underlying noun phrase can become a reflexive pronoun? If not, the additional data in exercise 2 may be of help.

2. The following are all underlying structures. For each, decide what would be the appropriate spoken structure that would be derived from it. That is, for each of the italicized noun phrases, substitute either a personal or a reflexive pronoun. You can assume that when a name such as *Mary* appears more than once in a sentence, it refers to the same person in each instance.

    a. Mary claimed that *Mary* understood trigonometry
    b. Maxwell looked at *Maxwell* in the mirror
    c. Clint tried hard, but *Clint* lost the race

d. Hugh and Maggie hosted a party in honor of *Hugh and Maggie*

e. Maria said that *Maria* injured *Maria*

In the following intermediate structure, T-IO has already applied to make the second *Fran* the indirect object. What pronoun transformations would now apply?

f. Fran promised *Fran* that *Fran* would study harder

3. Can you now state a rule for when a noun phrase can become a personal pronoun and when it can become a reflexive pronoun?

The answer to the last question is that a reflexive pronoun is used only when two identical noun phrases occur within the same clause:

14

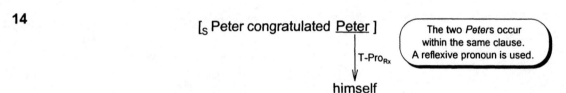

But a personal pronoun must be used when two identical noun phrases occur in different clauses:

15

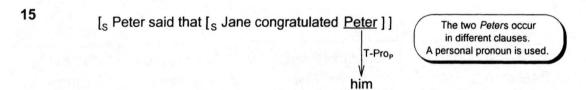

The second *Peter* in 15 cannot be pronominalized as *himself* ("pronominalize" means "made into a pronoun") because it is not in the same clause as the first *Peter*.

We can now state the reflexive-pronoun transformational rule:

16 **Reflexive-Pronoun Transformation (T-Pro$_{Rx}$):** When the same noun phrase occurs twice within the same clause, the second is changed to the appropriate reflexive pronoun.

Exercises 9.4

1. Show the derivations of these spoken sentences:

a. The astronaut blamed herself for the mishap.

b. Katrinka and Scott vindicated themselves.

Compare the following two sentences with personal and reflexive pronouns. To derive sentence *d*, first apply T-Pro$_{Rx}$ and then apply T-Pro$_P$:

c. Sandra regretted that Melvin embarrassed her.
d. Sandra regretted that she embarrassed herself.

The reflexive-pronoun transformation applies even when the antecedent occurs in a possessive noun phrase:

e. Stanley's description of himself was highly flattering.

For the following sentences, use *SPEAKER* to represent a noun phrase that underlies the pronoun *I*. First show the application of T-Pro$_{Rx}$ and then of T-Pro$_P$.

f. Carla and I treated ourselves to a fancy Chinese dinner.

2. Draw trees to show how spoken sentences would derive from exercise sentences 2a, 2b, and 2c on page 128.

English Pronouns—An Inventory

The personal, possessive, and reflexive pronouns of English are listed in table 17:

17	ENGLISH PRONOUNS	Personal Pronouns (T-Pro$_P$) Subject / Object		Possessive Pronouns (T-Pro$_{P-S}$)	Reflexive Pronouns (T-Pro$_{Rx}$)
Singular	1st Person (*SPEAKER*)	I	me	my	myself
	2nd Person (*HEARER*)	you	you	your	yourself
	3rd Person—Feminine	she	her	her	herself
	3rd Person—Masculine	he	him	his	himself
	3rd Person—Neuter	it	it	its	itself
Plural	1st Person (*SPEAKERS*)	we	us	our	ourselves
	2nd Person (*HEARERS*)	you	you	your	yourselves
	3rd Person—F, M, N	they	them	their	themselves

Conditions for Applying the Personal-Pronoun Transformation

We have seen that a noun phrase can become a reflexive pronoun only under certain specific conditions. That is, two identical noun phrases must occur within the same clause for one of them to become a reflexive pronoun. Furthermore, only the second of the two can be pronominalized. For example, T-Pro$_{Rx}$ can apply to the underlying structure in 14 to derive the spoken sentence *Peter congratulated himself* but not to derive **Himself congratulated Peter*.

Are there similar restrictions on when a personal pronoun can be derived? We have already seen that two identical noun phrases must occur in different clauses. Is it also true that only the second of these can be pronominalized? Let's look at some data before we decide. Consider the following underlying sentence, which contains a complement clause:

18   [$_S$ *Jen* announced [$_S$ that *Jen* won an award]]

In this instance, only the second occurrence of *Jen* can become a personal pronoun:

19 a.   Jen announced that **she** won an award.

   b.   **She* announced that Jen won an award.

Spoken sentence 19b is ungrammatical in this case because we would not understand *she* to refer to Jen. That is, we would not interpret it as deriving from underlying structure 18. Consequently, only the first of the following two derivations is allowed:

20 a.

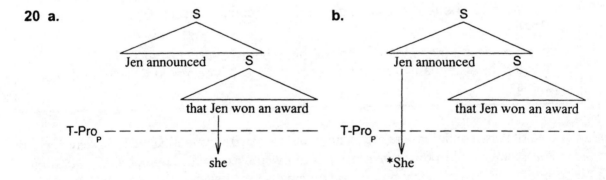

We have some evidence, then, for forming the hypothesis that only the second of two identical noun phrases can become a personal pronoun.

But now consider the following puzzling data. Here is another underlying sentence with a complement clause:

21   [$_S$ [$_S$ The fact that *Jen* won an award] surprised *Jen*]

In this instance it appears that *either* instance of the noun phrase *Jen* can become a personal pronoun:

22 a.   The fact that Jen won an award surprised **her**.

   b.   The fact that **she** won an award surprised Jen.

Pronouns: Another Analysis

That is, both of the following derivations appear to be allowed:

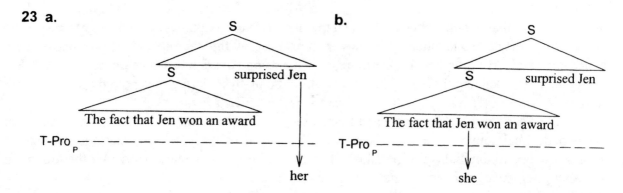

23 a.

b.

Surprisingly, sentence 22b (derived in 23b) is perfectly grammatical, even though the pronoun, *she*, is spoken before its antecedent, *Jen*. This contradicts and invalidates our hypothesis that only the second of two noun phrases can become a personal pronoun.

What new hypothesis, if any, can we devise in the face of these seemingly inconsistent data? How are we to know when a noun phrase can be pronominalized and when it cannot? From the data we have just examined, we are in a position to formulate a revised hypothesis:

24

> **Conditions for Applying T-Pro$_P$**
>
> When two identical noun phrases occur in different clauses of an underlying sentence, one of them can be replaced by a personal pronoun if it meets *either* of the following conditions:
>
> a. it is the second (rightmost) of the two noun phrases; or
> b. it is the lower of the two noun phrases—that is, if it occurs in a lower (embedded) clause.

If either or both of these conditions are met, a noun phrase can be pronominalized. In sentence 19a (derived in 20a), for example, pronominalization is allowed because the noun phrase in question is both the second of the two identical noun phrases and also the lower of the two. In 19b (derived in 20b), however, neither condition is met; pronominalization is not allowed because the noun phrase in question is both the first and the upper of the two. Only one of the two conditions needs to be met for the transformation to be allowed, as 23a and 23b demonstrate. In 23a the noun phrase is the second of the two, and in 23b it is the lower of the two.

These provisions may seem complicated at first, but if you test them you will discover that they perfectly describe the conditions under which a noun phrase can become a personal pronoun. Just remember the formula: "Second okay. Lower okay. But both first and upper, not okay."

Exercises 9.5

1. Let us test further to see if the conditions stated in 24 are accurate. The following underlying structure contains a complement clause. Assume that *Missy* refers to the same person in both instances.

she ————————→

The rumor that Missy watches cartoons embarrassed Missy

nominal-embedded clause — *her*

First draw the complete tree for the underlying structure, without using triangles. (If necessary, review nominal-complement clauses in Chapter 5.) Of the two identical noun phrases, which does hypothesis 24 predict can be pronominalized? Is the prediction accurate? Show the derivations for any acceptable spoken sentences. Then do the same steps for the following underlying structure:

he

The sergeant swore that the sergeant followed orders exactly *no guarantee it's same person, need antecedent first*

Do these sentences provide further support for hypothesis 24?

(2.) Optional discovery exercise: What happens when two identical noun phrases are embedded in different clauses at the *same* level (that is, if *neither* is the lower clause)? Consider the following underlying structure:

The fact that Moko barks at strangers shows that Moko is a good watchdog

Which of the two instances of *Moko* can be pronominalized? Show the derivation of each acceptable spoken sentence. Do we now need to revise the conditions in 24?

(3.) Optional discovery exercise: We have established conditions under which personal and reflexive pronouns can be used. But what about possessive pronouns? See if the following data can reveal the conditions under which a possessive noun phrase can be replaced by a possessive pronoun. First decide if each of the following can ever be a grammatical spoken sentence. The pronouns *he*, *his*, and *him* are intended to refer to Todd in each instance.

a. Todd said that his big mouth got him in trouble.
b. He said that Todd's big mouth got him in trouble.
c. Todd's big mouth got him in trouble.
d. His big mouth got Todd in trouble.

Now try to formulate a statement of the conditions for applying T-Pro$_P$ to derive possessive pronouns. Here are some additional sentences involving possessive and reflexive pronouns, all intended to refer to the same person, Todd. Determine which sentences are grammatical and whether your discoveries confirm or cause you to alter the conditions for applying T-Pro$_{Rx}$ or T-Pro$_P$.

e. Todd's description of himself is accurate.

---

f. His description of Todd is accurate.
g. Todd's description of himself pleased him.
h. Todd's description of himself pleased himself.
i. His description of himself pleased Todd.

An Order for Applying Transformations—An Update

Our grammar has now been expanded to include six transformational rules:

25   **T-Rules**

1. T-Pro$_{Rx}$ 4. T-Imp
2. T-AdvP   5. T-Pro$_P$
3. T-IO   6. T-Prt

   In the previous chapter, we speculated that when more than one transformational rule is applied in a given sentence, those rules should be applied consecutively and in a particular order. Now that we have expanded the list, let us claim, at least tentatively, that T-rules should apply in the relative order given in 25. What arguments can we discover to support (or to refute) this claim?

   Consider the derivation of the command *Excuse yourself*. Both the reflexive and imperative transformations need to apply to the underlying form to create that spoken sentence:

26

When applied in this order, the rules produce the desired spoken structure. What would happen if we tried to apply T-Imp before T-Pro$_{Rx}$?

27

The effect of the imperative transformation is to delete one instance of the noun phrase *HEARER*. But a requirement for the reflexive transformation is that two identical noun phrases must be present in the same clause. It could be argued that if T-Imp were applied first, the sentence would no longer have two identical noun phrases and so T-Pro$_{Rx}$ would be blocked. Consequently, we will order T-Pro$_{Rx}$ before T-Imp.

Now let us consider an argument for ordering T-Pro$_{Rx}$ before T-Pro$_P$. Let us examine the derivation of the following sentence with both a personal and a reflexive pronoun:

28   I astonished myself.

The derivation works nicely if we apply the rules in this order:

29

SPEAKER astonished <u>SPEAKER</u>

↓ T-Pro$_{Rx}$

<u>SPEAKER</u> astonished myself

↓ T-Pro$_P$

I astonished myself

What would happen if instead we applied T-Pro$_P$ first?

30
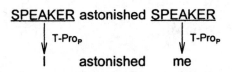

<u>SPEAKER</u> astonished <u>SPEAKER</u>

↓ T-Pro$_P$ ↓ T-Pro$_P$

I   astonished   me

It could be argued that, at this point, *I* and *me* are no longer identical noun phrases and that T-Pro$_{Rx}$ is prevented from applying. Consequently, we will order T-Pro$_{Rx}$ before T-Pro$_P$.

Let us tentatively accept the ordering of T-rules as in 25, with the understanding that we will revise the list if we discover reasons for altering the order of rules.

Exercises 9.6

1. In previous exercises when you have been asked to draw trees, you were given a spoken sentence and asked to show its derivations. In this exercise you will start out with a given underlying structure instead. Draw the tree for each of the following *underlying* structures, and then show the application of the specified T-rules to arrive at a *spoken* sentence.

   a. Phyllis cheered up Phyllis   [First apply T-Pro$_{Rx}$ and then T-Prt.]
   b. HEARERS give a reward to HEARERS   [First apply T-Pro$_{Rx}$, then T-IO, then T-Imp.]
   c. Martin told [that Martin played   [First apply T-AdvP (to move *often* in front of *played*), handball often] to SPEAKER   then T-IO, and finally T-Pro$_P$ twice.]

d. SPEAKER told [that Wesley played badly] to Wesley   [First apply T-IO, then T-Pro$_P$ twice. Is the reverse order also possible?]

2. For each of the following spoken sentences, decide what its underlying structure is and what T-rules must apply in order to derive it. Draw trees to show the complete derivation. If the derivation involves more than one T-rule, apply them in the relative order shown in 25.

   a. Rob rarely exerted himself.

   How might you determine the underlying structure of this sentence? The best method is to examine the sentence to see what T-rules were needed to produce this spoken structure. We know that adverbials such as "rarely" always start out in underlying structure at the end of the verb phrase. To come before the verb, as "rarely" does here, the T-AdvP rule had to apply. So we can decide that rarely will be the last word in the underlying form of this sentence. We also see the word "himself." We know that reflexive pronouns do not occur in underlying structure but are created by the T-Pro$_{Rx}$ rule. Consequently, we can decide that the underlying form of this sentence is "Rob exerted Rob rarely," and that two transformations, T-Pro$_{Rx}$ and T-AdvP, are applied to produce the spoken sentence, "Rob rarely exerted himself." Use a similar procedure to determine the underlying structures of the following sentences, and diagram the derivations.

   b. Brace yourself for a shock.
   c. Quickly shut the machine down.
   d. Give Hillary a catalogue.
   e. Take off your necktie.

10 More Embedded Sentences: Adverbial Clauses and Relative Clauses

Adverbial Clauses

Previously we have seen that an adverbial phrase can be either an adverb, as in 1a, or a prepositional phrase, as in 1b:

1

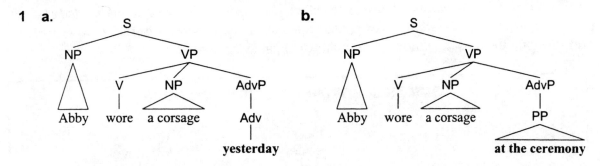

a. [tree diagram: S → NP (Abby), VP → V (wore), NP (a corsage), AdvP → Adv (yesterday)]

b. [tree diagram: S → NP (Abby), VP → V (wore), NP (a corsage), AdvP → PP (at the ceremony)]

Now let us consider a third option. An adverbial phrase can also be an entire clause:

2   Abby wore a corsage *when the class graduated*.

The embedded clause, *the class graduated*, is called an ***adverbial clause***. It is preceded by *when*, which is a ***subordinating conjunction*** (abbreviated **C_s**). Here are some other sentences with subordinating conjunctions and adverbial clauses:

3

   a. We bought a new car *because the old Camaro finally broke down.*

   b. They will arrive on time *unless their plane is delayed*.

   c. Jake dozed during class *although he had a good night's sleep*.

   d. Bob worried *almost until the plane taxied to the terminal*.

Our phrase-structure rule for adverbial phrases needs to be expanded to include adverbial clauses as an option:

4

$$\text{AdvP} \rightarrow (\text{Deg}) \left\{ \begin{array}{c} \text{Adv} \\ \text{PP} \\ \text{C}_\text{s} \ \text{S} \end{array} \right\}$$

If the last of these options is chosen, the grammar can generate sentences such as in 5:

5

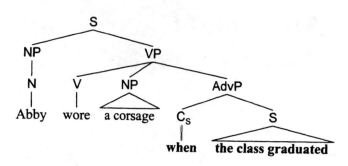

Unlike coordinating conjunctions such as *and* and *or* that connect two equal or *coordinate* clauses, subordinating conjunctions such as *when* connect unequal clauses. A subordinating conjunction introduces a clause that is embedded in—or subordinate to—the upper clause. The lower clause in 5 is a **subordinate clause** (also called a **dependent clause** or an **embedded clause**), while the upper clause is a **main clause** (also called an **independent clause** or a **superordinate clause**). Among the most common subordinating conjunctions are these:

6

COMMON SUBORDINATING CONJUNCTIONS		
after	if	until
although	lest	when
as	since	whenever
because	though	where
before	till	whereas
for	unless	while

Some other subordinating conjunctions, called **phrasal conjunctions**, consist of more than one word. Although the words that form them originally functioned as independent words, these phrasal conjunctions have come to act as if they were single words and can be treated as single words in the grammar. In some cases, such as *inasmuch* and *insofar*, the parts have even come to be joined together in spelling. Here are the most common phrasal subordinating conjunctions:

7

COMMON PHRASAL SUBORDINATING CONJUNCTIONS		
as if	even if	in order that
as soon as	even though	insofar as
as though	inasmuch as	so that

Rule 4 makes the claim that any adverbial can be preceded by a degree modifier. Does that apply to adverbial clauses as well? The following sentence shows that this claim is correct:

8

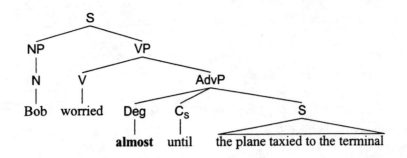

In 8 the degree modifier *almost* modifies the adverbial clause *until the plane taxied to the terminal*.

Exercises 10.1

Double underline each subordinating conjunction and underline each adverbial clause in the following sentences. Then draw trees to show the derivations of the sentences.

1. The coach has a tantrum <u>if</u> <u>a player commits a foolish foul</u>.
2. Jess hid <u>while</u> Marla searched for him.
3. Milton bought CDs <u>as if</u> money grew on trees. [Treat *as if* as if it were a single word.]
4. The gardener sees clearly <u>simply because</u> he got new glasses. [Adv: *clearly*; Deg: *simply*]
5. The pipes froze completely in January <u>although</u> Ray insulated the house.

Like other adverbials, adverbial clauses can be moved to other positions in a sentence. In the following sentence T-AdvP has applied twice to move two adverbials:

9   *While the family slept*, the burglar *deftly* entered the house.

Here is the derivation of 9:

10

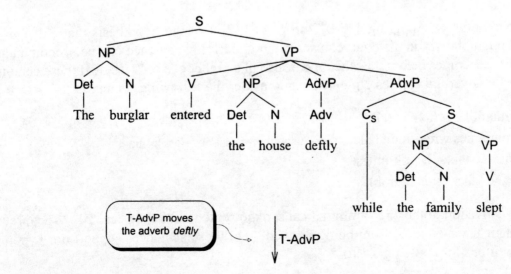

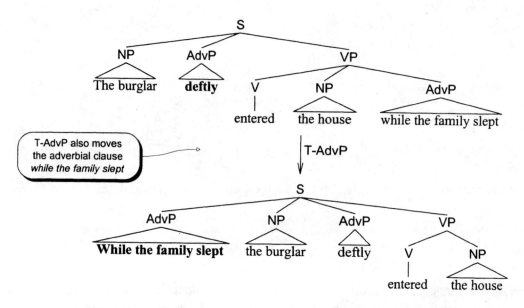

The first application of the adverbial-movement transformation moves the adverb *deftly* to a new position between the subject and the verb, and the second moves the adverbial clause to the front of the sentence. These two transformations could be shown in either order or, if we preferred, both at once.

Exercises 10.2

1. Show the derivations of the following spoken sentences:

   a. Lest the voters forget, the legislator reprinted the entire speech in his newsletter.
   b. The soprano, because the audience cheered lustily, sang an encore.
   c. Just before the rain came, Emily put away the lawnmower.   [Deg: *just*]
   d. Lately, whenever George snores, Martha pokes him.

2. The "Conditions for Applying T-Pro$_P$" on page 132 state the hypothesis that either of two identical noun phrases in different clauses of an underlying sentence can be pronominalized, except one that comes before the other and is also in a higher clause. Decide if these conditions hold true for adverbial clauses. In particular consider the following sentences:

   a. Jude mumbles when he talks.
   b. *He mumbles when Jude talks.   [ungrammatical if *he* refers to Jude]
   c. When Jude talks, he mumbles.
   d. When he talks, Jude mumbles.

   Show the derivation of the three grammatical spoken sentences, 2a, 2c, and 2d. What prevents ungrammatical sentence 2b from being derived? Do these sentences support our hypothesis about conditions for applying T-Pro$_P$?

(3.) Optional discovery exercise: In our ordered list of T-rules on page 134 we claimed that when a derivation requires both T-AdvP and T-Pro$_P$, T-AdvP must be applied first. Do exercises 1 and 2 support this hypothesis? In particular, attempt to derive exercise sentences 1d and 2c applying the T-rules in the reverse order. Be sure to keep in mind the conditions necessary for applying T-Pro$_P$ on page 132. Do your findings support or contradict the order specified on page 134?

Relative Clauses

We have encountered several kinds of sentences with multiple clauses. Coordinate sentences have two or more main clauses joined by a coordinating conjunction (for example: *He hates music, but she joined a band*). Other sentences have main and subordinate clauses. Subordinate clauses (also called "embedded" clauses) include complement clauses (*He claims that she joined a band*) and adverbial clauses (*He laughed when she joined the band*). Still other embedded clauses are *relative clauses*, whose purpose is to modify nouns. Relative clauses are printed in italics in the following sentences:

11 a. The woman *who joined the band* sings the blues. [handwritten: relative clause; use who because it is subject]
   b. The woman *whom the band hired* sings the blues. [handwritten: use whom because woman is direct object]
   c. Germaine devised the plan *that baffled her opponents*.
   d. Dixie admires the new shoes *that Amy wears*.
   e. Marvin reached a decision *which Jo Ann agreed with*.
   f. Marvin reached a decision *with which Jo Ann agreed*.
   g. Dawn helped the lady *whose car stalled on the bridge*.

Each of these relative clauses modifies—that is, provides some additional information about—the noun that it follows. More specifically, the clause identifies that noun. In 11a, for example, *who joined the band* identifies which particular woman is meant, and in 11c, *which baffled her opponents* identifies which plan is being discussed.

The Relative Pronoun as Subject

The relative clauses in 11a–11g begin with the words *who, whom, that, which,* and *whose*, which are called *relative pronouns* (abbreviated **Pro$_R$**). To call a word a pronoun is to say that the word "stands for" a noun phrase and, consequently, is derived from that underlying noun phrase by a transformation. If that is the case, we can ask what the relative pronoun *who* stands for in 11a. If we ask, "Who joined the band?," our answer is "The woman." Let us claim, then, that *the woman* is the underlying subject of the relative clause in 11a. If so, that sentence has the following derivation:

12

The woman [<u>the woman</u> joined the band] sings the blues

↓

The woman [who joined the band] sings the blues

Although it may seem odd at first, the underlying structure in 12 makes sense, because it captures the meaning of spoken sentence 11a. That is, if we were asked to paraphrase 11a, we might say, "The woman sings the blues—and because you don't know which woman I am talking about, let me identify her by telling you that *this woman joined the band*—that's the woman I mean!"

We can show the derivation of 11a in a tree diagram:

13

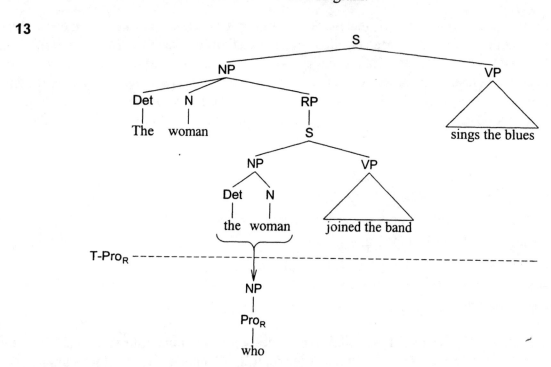

This derivation introduces a new label, RP, to refer to a relative clause. The "P" stands for "phrase," just as it does in the label "CompP," which we used to represent a complement clause. Clauses are a type of phrase, and our practice has been to label all groupings, including clauses, as phrases. In the next chapter we will also encounter instances where an RP can be a simple phrase rather than a complete clause.

Derivation 13 makes a number of interesting claims—claims that bear careful examination. Notice that our derivation assumes that the underlying form of the relative clause is a complete sentence (*the woman joined the band*), whose subject (*the woman*) is transformed into a relative pronoun (*who*). The relative clause is embedded in the main clause (*the woman . . . sings the blues*), where it follows and modifies the subject of the main clause (*the woman*), providing information about her—in this case, identifying which particular woman is meant. Notice that the phrase *the woman* appears in both the main clause and in the relative clause. In its underlying structure, a relative clause always contains a noun phrase identical to the noun phrase being modified.

The idea that a relative pronoun stands for (and replaces) a noun phrase in a sentence like 11a can be a difficult concept to see at first. The underlying structure in 13 may seem puzzling, but it does exactly what an underlying structure should do: It captures the essential meaning of the sentence. You may find it takes some more experience with relative clauses for that concept to become clear. If you are still confused or skeptical, bear with our discussion a while longer.

To account for our analysis, we must include in our grammar revised phrase-structure rules (14) and a new transformational rule (15):

14   NP → (Det) (AdjP)⁺ N (PP) **(RP)** (CompP)
       RP → S

15   **Relative-Pronoun Transformation (T-Pro$_R$):** A noun phrase is replaced by a relative pronoun if it occurs in a relative clause that follows and modifies an identical noun phrase.

Notice how this rule is applied in derivation 13, where the noun phrase *the woman* is replaced by the relative pronoun *who* because it is located in a relative clause that modifies that same noun phrase (*the woman*) in the main clause.

Any noun phrase in a sentence can be modified by a relative clause. In sentence 11c, diagrammed below, the direct object of the main clause (*the plan*) is modified by a relative clause:

16

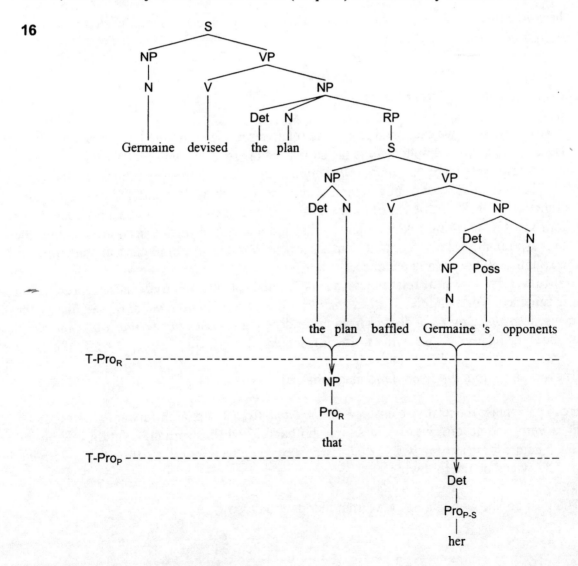

Exercises 10.3

1. Underline relative clauses in each of the following spoken sentences. Then write the underlying structure below it, with relative clauses in brackets. Finally, draw trees to show the sentence's derivation. T-Pro$_R$ is performed before T-Pro$_P$.

   a. The outfits <u>that fit Archie well</u> were too expensive.
      Underlying structure: *The outfits [the outfits fit Archie well] were too expensive*

   b. Clark knew the nun who visited Martin in jail.
      Underlying structure:

   c. A young woman who lives in my apartment plays golf professionally.
      Underlying structure:

   d. People who take foolish risks have an unpleasant fate which awaits them.
      Underlying structure:

2. One relative clause can be embedded in another. Show the derivation of the following sentence:

   The owner thanked the veterinarian who cured the racehorse that won the Derby.

The Relative Pronoun as Direct Object

In the relative clauses we have examined so far, the relative pronoun has acted as the *subject* of the relative clause. In 11a, for example, *who* is the subject of the relative clause *who joined the band*, and in 11c, *that* is the subject of *that baffled her opponents*. Can relative pronouns ever act in any other role? They can, and we will now examine sentences, such as 11b and 11d, where relative pronouns function as the *direct object* of their clauses. (Once again, let me issue a brief advisory: I know from years of teaching relative clauses that the discussion in this section is among the trickiest to grasp initially. I also know that in a short time it does become clear to students who follow the argument with care and patience.)

Central to our discussion of relative clauses is the claim that a relative clause represents an underlying sentence. For example, in 11a (*The woman who joined the band sings the blues*), the relative clause *who joined the band* derives from the underlying sentence *the woman joined the band*. But what about the relative clause in the following sentence?

17 The woman *whom the band hired* sings the blues.

If we were to paraphrase the relative clause *whom the band hired* as a straightforward sentence (with a subject, a verb, and so on), we would say, "The band hired the woman." Could this be the underlying structure for *whom the band hired*? Let us explore that possibility. If so, the underlying structure of 17 would be the following:

18 The woman [the band hired the woman] sings the blues

On the level of meaning, at least, this structure makes perfect sense. After all, we could paraphrase 17 just as we earlier paraphrased 11a: "The woman sings the blues—and because you don't know which woman I am talking about, let me identify her by saying that *the band hired this woman.*"

But how can we derive the spoken relative clause *whom the band hired* from the underlying clause in 18? Presumably T-Pro$_R$ would replace *the woman* in the relative clause with a relative pronoun:

19   The woman [the band hired <u>the woman</u>] sings the blues

                                                          ↓ T-Pro$_R$

                     The woman [the band hired whom] sings the blues

But the result (*The woman the band hired whom sings the blues*) is not 17; in fact, it is not even an acceptable spoken sentence. To resolve our dilemma, let us claim that another T-rule now comes into play:

20   **The *Wh*-Fronting Transformation (T-WH):** When a relative pronoun is not the first word in a relative clause, move it to the front of that clause.

We will call this rule the **wh-fronting rule**, because it moves relative pronouns (*who, whom, which, whose,* and *that*), all but one of which begin with the letters *wh*. Notice how it can be applied following T-Pro$_R$ to give us the derivation of sentence 17:

21   The woman [the band hired <u>the woman</u>] sings the blues

                                                      ↓ T-Pro$_R$

                     The woman [the band hired <u>whom</u>] sings the blues

                          ↑⎯⎯⎯ T-WH ⎯⎯⎯⎦

Moving *whom* to the front of the clause gives us sentence 17, *The woman whom the band hired sings the blues.* Consequently, we will claim that 21 represents the derivation of 17.

Several significant claims have been made about the derivation of relative clauses. Let us review what we have discovered:

1. Every relative clause derives from a straightforward underlying sentence. (In 11a, for example, *who joined the band* derives from the sentence *the woman joined the band.* In 17, *whom the band hired* derives from the sentence *the band hired the woman.*)
2. Every relative clause contains in its underlying structure a noun phrase identical to the noun phrase that the relative clause modifies. (The relative clauses in both 11a and 17 modify the noun phrase *the woman,* and *the woman* also appears in the underlying structure of both relative clauses.)
3. That noun phrase in the relative clause is transformed by T-Pro$_R$ into a relative pronoun. (In 11a, *the woman* is transformed into the relative pronoun *who.* In 17, *the woman* is transformed into *whom.*)

4. Every relative clause must begin with a relative pronoun. When a relative pronoun is in a different position, it must be moved by T-WH to the beginning of the clause. (In 11a, *who* is the subject of the relative clause and so begins the clause, so no movement is necessary. In 17, however, *whom* is the direct object of the clause, so T-WH must move it to the front of the clause.)

These principles all apply in the derivation of sentence 17, shown here in its entirety:

22

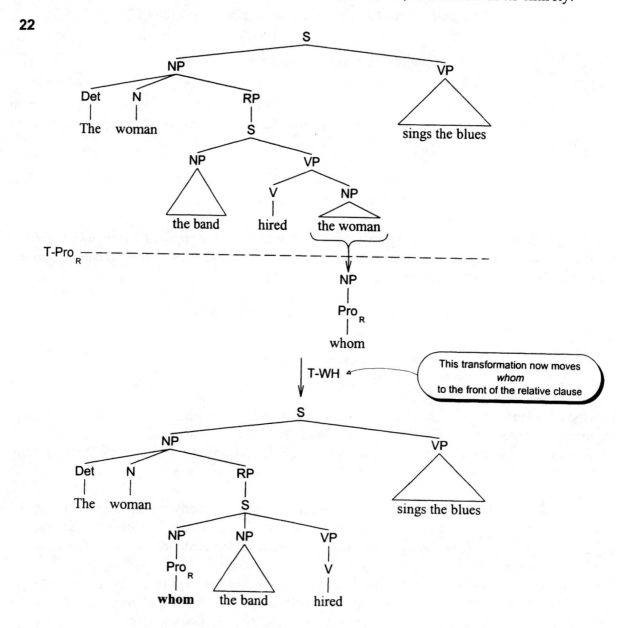

As another example, let us analyze sentence 11d, *Dixie admires the new shoes that Amy wears*. When analyzing a spoken relative clause to determine its underlying structure, it is useful to start with the verb. In the case of the clause *that Amy wears*, the verb is *wears*. To find the underlying subject of that clause, ask, "Who wears them?" The answer: "Amy does," so *Amy* is the underlying subject of the clause. To find the object, ask, "Wears what?" The answer: "the new shoes," which is the direct object. Consequently sentence 11d has this underlying structure:

23   Dixie admires the new shoes [Amy wears the new shoes]

The derivation of the spoken sentence requires two transformations:

24   Dixie admires the new shoes [Amy wears <u>the new shoes</u>]

$\downarrow$ T-Pro$_R$

Dixie admires the new shoes [Amy wears <u>that</u>]

T-WH

We can now draw trees to show that derivation. This time we'll use the broken-line method to show the T-WH transformation.

25

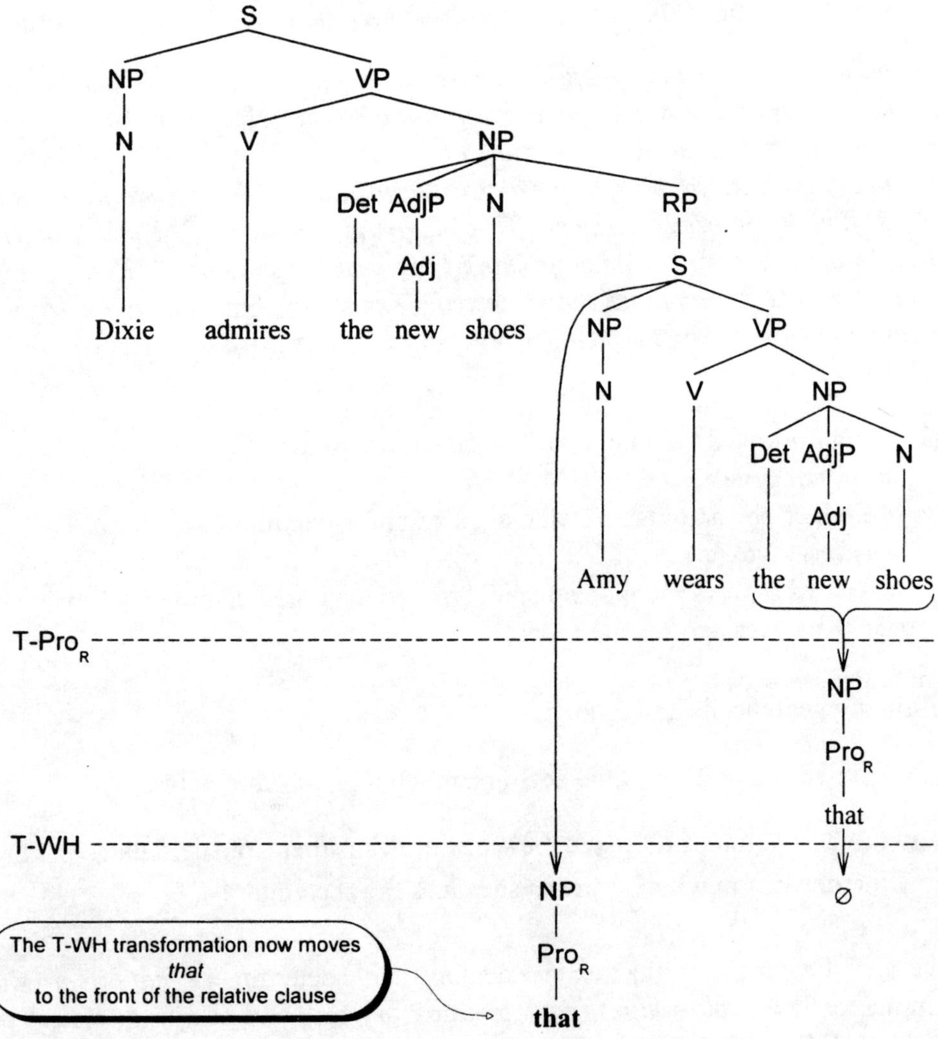

The T-WH transformation now moves *that* to the front of the relative clause

We can now update our list of T-rules:

26   **T-Rules**

    1. T-Pro$_{Rx}$ 5. T-IO
    2. T-Pro$_R$ 6. T-Imp
    3. T-WH   7. T-Pro$_P$
    4. T-AdvP   8. T-Prt

Exercises 10.4

1. For each of the following spoken sentences, underline any relative clauses. Then write the underlying structure below it, with relative clauses in brackets. Finally, draw trees to show the derivation of each sentence.

   a. The students <u>whom the magician hypnotized on stage</u> quacked like ducks.
      Underlying structure: *The students [the magician hypnotized the students on stage] quacked like ducks*

      Remember that the underlying structure of a relative clause is always a standard complete sentence with a subject, a verb, and so on. Here is a useful procedure for determining the underlying structure of a relative clause: First, find the verb. In sentence a the verb in the relative clause is "hypnotized." Second, find the subject by asking, Who hypnotized? Answer: "The magician hypnotized." Third, ask, Hypnotized whom/what? Answer: "The magician hypnotized the students." Finally, include any other elements to complete the underlying sentence: "The magician hypnotized the students on stage." Just remember that your analysis always starts with the first step: find the verb.

   b. The troops followed the plan that the general devised.
      Underlying structure:
   c. The fire which the arsonists set damaged a famous landmark.
      Underlying structure:
   d. The fellow who plays the glockenspiel ignored the notes that the composer wrote.
      Underlying structure:

2. The following sentence is ambiguous:

   Harry invited the brother of the accountant whom Consuelo dates.

   a. Show the derivation of the sentence when it means that Consuelo dates the brother.
   b. Show the derivation when it means she dates the accountant.

3. We have seen the word *that* function as a demonstrative determiner (*That tomato was delicious*), as a complementizer (*Nelly claims that a tomato is a fruit*), and now as a relative pronoun (*The tomato that Hal bought is rotten*). When a clause is introduced by *that*, you may sometimes find

it difficult to tell whether *that is* a complementizer or a relative pronoun. Remember that a relative pronoun stands for a noun phrase; in the sample sentence (*The tomato that Hal bought is rotten*), *that* is a relative pronoun because it stands for *the tomato* (underlying structure of the clause: *Hal bought the tomato*). In contrast, a complementizer stands for nothing and has no meaning; in the sentence *Nelly claims that a tomato is a fruit*, *that* is a complementizer because it does not replace any word in the clause, which is a complete sentence by itself (*a tomato is a fruit*). Another simple test is to see whether the word *that* can be replaced by another relative pronoun such as *which* or *who*. If it can (*The tomato which Hal bought is rotten*), it is a relative pronoun and the clause is a relative clause. If it cannot (**Nelly claims which a tomato is a fruit*), *that* is a complementizer and the clause is a complement clause. For the following sentences, underline each relative clause and double-underline each complement clause:

a. Peter bought the pastry <u>that Sadie liked</u>.   [test: Peter bought the pastry *which* Sadie liked.]
b. Peter knew <u>that the family liked pastry</u>.   [test: *Peter knew *which* the family liked pastry.]
c. The fact that you wore a funny hat at the party surprised us.
d. The hats that you wore amused the partygoers.
e. We understood the theory that Einstein developed.
f. We rejected the theory that flowers feel pain.
g. I bought the book that Judy said that she enjoyed.

Draw trees to show the derivations of exercise sentences 3e, 3f, and 3g. Remember that relative clauses require transformations for their derivations, but complement clauses do not. Apply T-rules in the relative order shown in 26.

4. Consider the following ambiguous sentence:

   We believed the theory that Mona proposed to Antoine.

   a. First draw the derivation when the sentence means that Mona proposed a theory to Antoine and we believed that theory.
   b. Then draw the derivation when it means that we believed someone's claim that Mona made a proposal of marriage to Antoine.

(5.) Optional discovery exercise: At times, we have the option of omitting a relative pronoun. Instead of 11b, for example, we could say *The woman the band hired sings the blues*. But we cannot omit *who* in 11a: **The woman joined the band sings the blues*. Examine the sentences of 11 and other sentences with relative clauses in this chapter, and note which of them have relative pronouns that can be omitted. What principle determines when a relative clause can be omitted? Is it similar to the principle of when a complementizer can be omitted in complement-clause sentences (see exercise 5 on page 63)? Why do you think the language has such restrictions? Do they help us avoid confusion?

The Relative Pronoun as the Object of a Preposition

Having seen that a relative pronoun can replace an underlying subject or an underlying direct object in a relative clause, we would probably feel confident in predicting that a relative pronoun can also replace an underlying object of a preposition. Consequently, let us predict that the following underlying structure can result in a grammatical spoken sentence:

27   Marvin reached a decision [Jo Ann agreed with the decision]

Let's see if we are right. If we apply T-Pro$_R$ and T-WH to this structure, the result is a grammatical sentence, as we predicted:

28   Marvin reached a decision [Jo Ann agreed with a decision]
$$\downarrow \text{T-Pro}_R$$
Marvin reached a decision [Jo Ann agreed with which]
$$\uparrow\text{———— T-WH ————}$$

That is, it results in the following spoken sentence:

29   Marvin reached a decision which Jo Ann agreed with.

The principles we have already described can account for 29. But how can we account for the following spoken sentence?

30   Marvin reached a decision with which Jo Ann agreed.

Sentences 29 and 30 are identical in meaning, so presumably they would have the same underlying structure. What differentiates 30 from the other spoken sentences in this chapter is that its relative clause, *with which Jo Ann agreed*, begins not with a relative pronoun but with a preposition. We can account for this sentence if we claim that T-WH allows us two options—namely, we can either move a relative pronoun that is the object of a preposition, as in 28, or else we can move the *entire prepositional phrase*, as in 31:

31

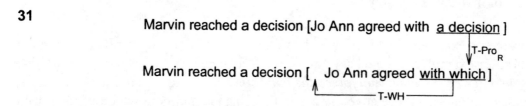

To account for 31, we need to revise 21, our statement of the *wh*-fronting transformation:

32   **T-WH (revised):** When a relative pronoun is not the first word in a relative clause, move that relative pronoun, *or a phrase that contains it*, to the front of that clause.

Revised rule 32 allows us to move either the relative pronoun, as we did in 28, or the entire prepositional phrase, as we did in 31. If we use T-WH to move just the relative clause, we derive sentence 29:

33

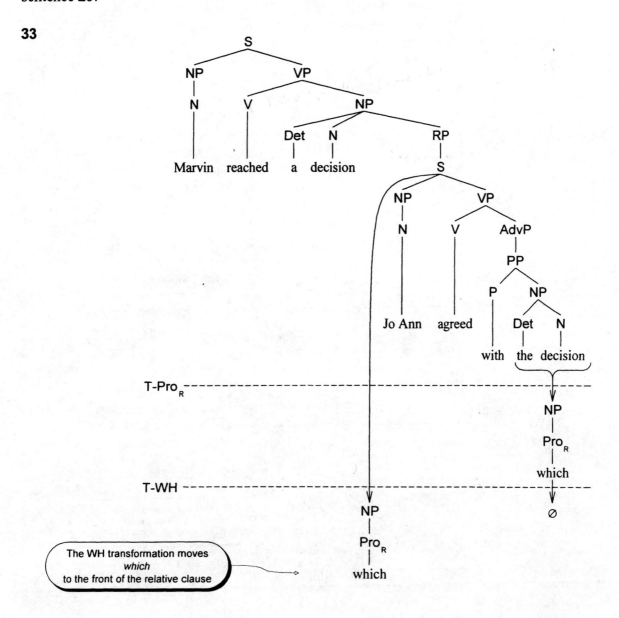

Alternatively, we could use T-WH to move the entire adverbial phrase and so derive sentence 30:

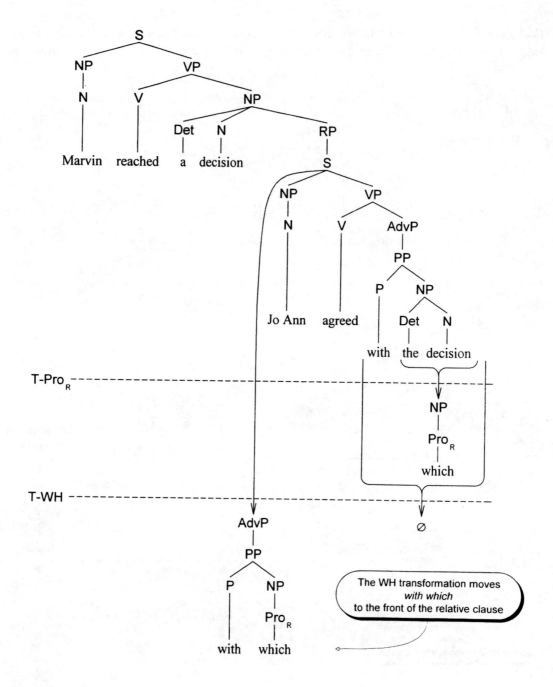

Exercises 10.5

1. Underline the relative clauses in each of the following spoken sentences. State the underlying structure, and draw trees to show the sentence's derivation.

   a. Ella envied the singer <u>to whom Stevie gave the award</u>.

      Underlying structure: *Ella envied the singer [Stevie gave the award to the singer]*

   b. The bench which the spectators sat upon collapsed.

      Underlying structure:

c. The obstacles that the scientists fought against never defeated them.
   Underlying structure:
d. Socrates posed no questions to which Alcibiades knew the answer.
   Underlying structure:
e. The crew built a grandstand from which the dignitaries viewed the parade.
   Underlying structure:
f. The lawyer with whom we talked made a statement that we had many objections to.
   Underlying structure:

2. The following sentences have relative clauses embedded within other relative clauses (represented in brackets). Draw trees to show the derivations of these sentences.

   a. The junior found the book [that the sophomore [who lived in the dorm] lost].
   b. Jan scolded the orator [who aroused the crowd [that began the riot [to which the police responded]]].

Possessive Relative Clauses

Now let us consider 11g, *Dawn helped the lady whose car stalled on the bridge*. At this point you may have already surmised the underlying form of the relative pronoun *whose* in this sentence — namely, *the lady's*. The underlying structure for sentence 11g is this:

35   Dawn helped the lady [the lady's car stalled on the bridge]

Here the noun phrase *the lady* is modified by a relative clause that contains that same phrase in a possessive form (*the lady's*). That possessive noun phrase is then replaced by a relative pronoun (*whose*) that is also possessive. The sentence has the following derivation:

36
           Dawn helped the lady [the lady's car stalled on the bridge]
                                      ↓ T-Pro$_R$
           Dawn helped the lady [whose car stalled on the bridge]

Because *whose* replaces a possessive noun phrase, it is called a ***possessive relative pronoun*** (abbreviated **Pro$_{R-S}$**). Our statement of T-Pro$_R$, the relative-pronoun transformation (15), needs to be revised to account for the derivation of a Pro$_{R-S}$ as well as a Pro$_R$.

37   **T-Pro$_R$ (revised)**: A noun phrase *or a phrase containing it* is replaced by a relative pronoun if it is located in a relative clause that follows and modifies an identical noun phrase.

The complete derivation of sentence 11g is shown in 38:

38

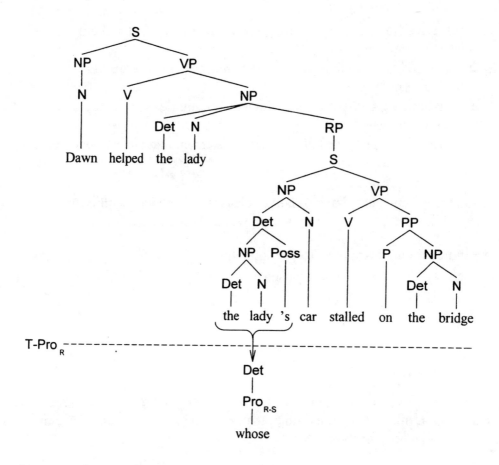

Notice that the possessive relative pronoun *whose*, like the phrase it replaces, is a determiner.

The fronting transformation, T-WH, is not needed in 38, but it can apply when *whose* is not the first word in the relative clause, as in the following derivation of *Anna thanked the man whose tools the workers used*:

39

Anna thanked the man [the workers used <u>the man's</u> tools]

           T-Pro_R

Anna thanked the man [the workers used <u>whose tools</u>]

           T-WH

In 39 T-WH moves not just the possessive relative pronoun (*whose*) but the entire noun phrase that contains it (*whose tools*). The complete derivation of that sentence is shown in 40.

40

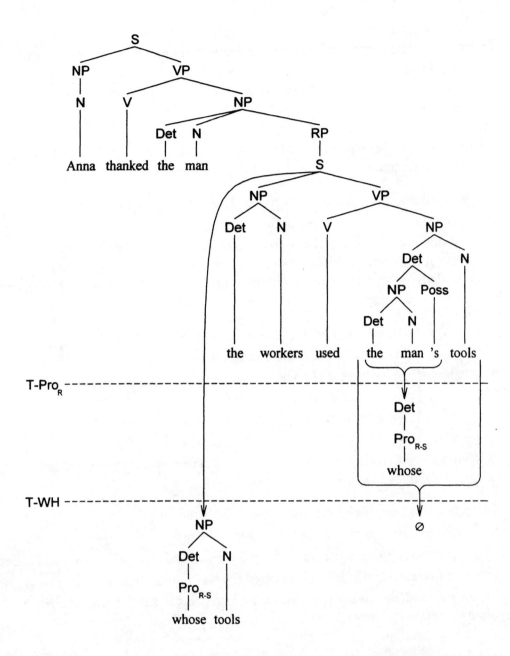

The T-WH transformation moves the entire noun phrase *whose tools* to the front of the clause.

Exercises 10.6

1. Underline the relative clauses, state their underlying structures, and draw trees to show the derivations:

   a. Hester had a daughter <u>whose name was Pearl</u>.

      Underlying structure: *Hester had a daughter [a daughter's name was Pearl]*

   b. Several artists whose etchings we saw in the Louvre lived during the Renaissance.

Underlying structure:
c. The intruder whose outburst interrupted the performance shocked the audience.
   Underlying structure:
d. The committee awarded the job to a man whose application they rejected previously.
   Underlying structure:

2. Reread statement 32, the explanation of the T-WH transformation, before drawing the derivation of the following sentence:

   The hikers thanked the family in whose house they took shelter.

3. A relative pronoun can take many different roles within a relative clause: It can be the subject of the clause, its direct object, the object of a preposition, or a possessive noun phrase. The following underlying structures represent these different roles. For each of the five sentences, state the corresponding spoken structure, and show the derivation.

   The student {
     the student lost the keys to the car *who*
     Heidi drove *the student* to school *whom* d.o.
     Corey expected a visit from *the student* *whom* was late — *object of preposition*
     the student's car had a flat tire *whose*
     Yolanda borrowed *the student's* notes *whose*
   }

4. The following are underlying structures. For each, state a spoken sentence that can be derived from it, and draw trees to show the derivation.

   a. The noise [Winthrop heard the noise] came from the attic
   b. Merlin owns an owl [the owl's screech shatters glass]
   c. The organization [Byington resigned from the organization] discriminates against oenophiles
   d. The color [the woman [HEARER married the woman] prefers the color] is hot pink
   e. The owner fired the cooks [the cooks' negligence caused the fire [the fire damaged the restaurant [the cooks worked in the restaurant]]]

(5.) Optional discovery exercise: Having seen that a relative pronoun can be an underlying subject, a direct object, an object of a preposition, or a possessive noun phrase within a relative clause, we might make the generalization that *all* noun phrases within a relative clause can become relative pronouns. You can test this hypothesis on one noun-phrase role that we did not examine: indirect object. Can the italicized indirect object in the following structure become a relative pronoun?

   Jamar pitied the people [the movie gave *the people* a headache]

If the result of applying T-Pro$_R$ and T-WH to this structure is not an acceptable spoken sentence in your dialect, does it mean that our hypothesis ("all noun phrases within a relative clause can become relative pronouns") is incorrect? Notice that the given structure is an intermediate, not an underlying, structure, because T-IO has already been applied. Does this have any implications for the relative order of applying the T-rules T-IO and T-Pro$_R$? What is the result if the T-rules are applied to the underlying structure in the order shown in 26?

Clauses with Relative Adverbs

Relative pronouns such as *who* and *which* are called "pro*nouns*" because they stand for nouns (to be more precise, for noun phrases). Adverbials in relative clauses can also be replaced by the pro-forms *where, when,* and *why*. Although "relative pro-adverbials" would be a more accurate term, we will use the traditional term ***relative adverbs***, which we will abbreviate **Pro$_{R\text{-}A}$**. Consider these sentences:

41 a. The tour visited the house <u>*where*</u> Mozart lived.

    b. The relatives recalled the day <u>*when*</u> Cliff rescued the puppy.

    c. Loretta explained the reason <u>*why*</u> the price of wheat futures rose.

who, where, why, when...
w/ noun in front
is relative adverb

Relative adverbs such as *when, where,* and *why* in 41 replace underlying adverbials. Here are the corresponding underlying structures:

42 a. The tour visited the house [Mozart lived *in the house*]

    b. The relatives recalled the day [Cliff rescued the puppy *on the day*]

    c. Loretta explained the reason [the price of wheat futures rose *for the reason*]

In 41a, the relative adverb *where* replaces the adverbial phrase *in the house*. In 41b, *when* replaces *on the day*. And in 41c, *why* replaces *for the reason*. In drawing trees, we can use triangles to represent underlying relative adverbials, as in the following derivation of 41a:

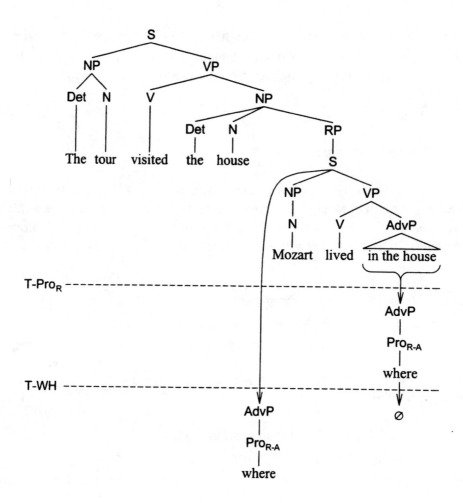

Our revised T-rules, T-Pro$_R$ (37) and T-WH (32), are sufficiently broad to accommodate sentences with relative adverbs.

Exercises 10.7

1. Draw trees for the derivations of sentences 41b and 41c.

2. In the following sentences, underline the relative clauses, state the underlying structures, and show the derivations.

   a. The map shows the cave <u>where the pirates hid the loot</u>.
      Underlying structure: *The map shows the cave [the pirates hid the loot in the cave]*

   b. The reason why Dick was late was a faulty alarm clock.
      Underlying structure:

   c. The gremlins await the hour when the goblins are asleep.
      Underlying structure:

d. The plaque marks the spot where Washington delivered the speech.

   Underlying structure:

3. The word *when* can be either a relative adverb or a subordinating conjunction (see page 138). Decide which role *when* plays in each of the following sentences, and draw the derivations:

   a. Doris memorized the dates when the kings of England reigned.
   b. Cosmo returned to school when the vacation ended.

4. Here is a sentence with both relative and complement clauses (you can consult page 59 to review complement clauses). See if you can show its derivation.

   Hilda remembers the exact moment when she learned that the tenor whose voice caused a sensation died.

Some Notes on Usage

Of the relative pronouns, *who* and *whom* are used for people, *which* is used for things, and *that* and *whose* are used for both people and things. At times you may hear it said that *that* should only be used for things, but this claim is not supported by actual usage: Phrases such as *the person that I most admire* are frequently used by literate speakers of English. Another persistent claim is that a sentence may not end with a preposition. However, not only is the sentence *Marvin reached a decision which Jo Ann agreed with* standard English, but it is derived using T-Pro$_P$ and T-WH in exactly the same way that all other sentences with relative clauses are derived. Contrary to the claim, a preposition is a part of speech that educated speakers and writers frequently end their sentences with.

Because the word *whom* seems to be disappearing from general use, an increasing number of people find the distinction between *who* and *whom* puzzling. The distinction is no longer part of the unconscious knowledge of most speakers of English; in order to know it, they must learn it consciously. Traditionally, *who* has been the nominative form, used to replace a subject noun phrase (*the child who helped me*), and *whom* has been the objective form, used to replace a direct object (*the child whom I helped*) or an object of a preposition (*the child whom I smiled at*). Increasingly, however—especially in speech—*who* is being used for objective as well as nominative forms, with *whom* appearing consistently only when it directly follows a preposition (*the child at whom I smiled*). This is consistent with the centuries-long trend of the English language to lose its inflected forms.

11 Restrictive and Nonrestrictive Clauses and Phrases

Restrictive and Nonrestrictive Relative Clauses

Although the italicized relative clauses in the following two sentences look similar, they function in very different ways:

1 **a.** Natalie dislikes all men *who dip snuff*, [restrictive has to be there]
   b. Dana dislikes Kenny, *who is my best friend*, [nonrestrictive doesn't have to be there]

Sentence 1a tells us which men Natalie dislikes. The relative clause *who dip snuff* is an essential part of the sentence. If it were omitted, not only would we not know which men were being talked about but the meaning of the main clause (*Natalie dislikes all men*) would be drastically changed.

In sentence 1b, on the other hand, the relative clause is not essential to the main idea. It only provides supplemental information about Kenny; if it were omitted from the sentence (*Dana dislikes Kenny*), the idea of the main clause would be left intact.

As another demonstration of the different functions of the two relative clauses, we could appropriately insert a phrase such as *by the way* or *incidentally* after the relative pronoun in 1b, but we could not do so in 1a; there is nothing incidental about the relative clause in that sentence:

2 **a.** Natalie dislikes all men who (*by the way*) dip snuff.
   b. Dana dislikes Kenny, who (*by the way*) is my best friend.

A relative clause such as *who dip snuff* in 1a is called a ***restrictive relative clause***, because it *restricts* the scope of the noun phrase it modifies. In 1a the group of men that Natalie dislikes is restricted to just those men who dip snuff. Presumably there are many non-snuff-dipping men whom Natalie does not dislike at all. A restrictive clause can also be said to *identify* the noun phrase it modifies; in 1a, the question "Which men does she dislike?" is answered by the clause: men *who dip snuff*. All the relative clauses we encountered in Chapter 10 were restrictive.

In contrast, sentence 1b introduces another kind of relative clause called a ***nonrestrictive relative clause***, so called because the clause does not restrict the noun it modifies. The nonrestrictive clause in 1b (*who is my best friend*) is not used to limit the "Kenny" category in the way that the restrictive clause in 1a limits the "men" category to certain particular men. If sentence 1b were spoken in a conversation, the listener would already know who Kenny is. The relative clause does not tell the listener "which Kenny" Dana dislikes but provides additional information about him.

To make the distinction between restrictive and nonrestrictive clauses clearer, let's look at a few more sample sentences. See if you can identify which of the following italicized clauses is restrictive and which is nonrestrictive:

3 **a.** Zebras, *which are horselike mammals*, feed mostly on grasses.

  b. Zebras *which have orange and green stripes* exist only in the world of imagination.

A restrictive clause occurs only in 3b. The purpose of the relative clause in 3b (*which have orange and green stripes*) is to restrict the class of zebras being discussed to just ones with those strange colors. The statement being made ("exist only in the world of imagination") applies only to those zebra, not to other zebras.

Sentence 3a, on the other hand, contains a nonrestrictive relative clause (*which are horselike mammals*). The clause does not restrict the class of zebras to just certain ones. Instead, it provides supplemental information about zebras in general.

Can you now identify which of the following relative clauses are restrictive and which nonrestrictive?

4 **a.** Barry recognized the street *on which they filmed the movie.*

  b. Patti borrowed Moe's blanket, *which we sat on during the concert.*

  c. The Andersons, *whose dog bit three children*, are unpopular with the neighbors.

  d. The woman *whose dog you petted* is a famous artist.

The clauses in sentences 4a and 4d are restrictive; without them the listener wouldn't know which street (4a) or which woman (4d) the speaker was discussing. In contrast, the clauses in 4b and 4c are nonrestrictive. Moe's blanket (4b) and the Andersons (4c) do not require further identification; the relative clauses merely provide supplemental information about them.

Several tests can be used to determine whether a relative clause is restrictive or nonrestrictive:

5

Tests for Restrictive and Nonrestrictive Relative Clauses

  a. **The "which" test**: Is the purpose of the clause to tell us *which* members of the modified noun phrase are being discussed? If so, the clause is restrictive.

  b. **The "that" test**: The relative pronoun *that* can occur only in restrictive clauses. Does *that* appear in the clause, or can *that* be substituted for *who, whom,* or *which* in the clause without changing meaning? If so (as in 1a and 3b), the clause is restrictive. (This test does not apply if the relative pronoun is *whose*, as in 4d, or if *which* immediately follows a preposition, as in 4a.)

  c. **The "by the way" test**: Can the phrase *by the way* appropriately be inserted after the relative pronoun? If so (as in 1b, 3a, 4b, and 4c), the clause is nonrestrictive.

  d. **The pause test**: When you read the sentence aloud, do you pause briefly before and after the relative clause? If so (as in 1b, 3a, 4b, and 4c), the clause is nonrestrictive.

Let us see how these tests can be applied to the following sentences:

6   **a.**   Jason's boat, which is an old trawler, sleeps six comfortably.

      b.   The boat which Helen bought from Hector is a catamaran.

The relative clause in 6a is *which is an old trawler*. (1) We can apply the "which" test and ask if the purpose of the clause is to identify *which boat* we mean. The answer is no—we already know we are talking about Jason's boat—so the clause is nonrestrictive. (2) If we try substituting *that* for *which*, the result is unsatisfactory: *Jason's boat, *that is an old trawler, sleeps six comfortably.* This test also shows that the clause is nonrestrictive. (3) As we would expect for a nonrestrictive, the clause passes the "by the way" test: *Jason's boat, which (by the way) is an old trawler, sleeps six comfortably.* (4) When a nonrestrictive is spoken aloud, the speaker is likely to pause briefly before and after the relative clause: *Jason's boat, [pause] which is an old trawler, [pause] sleeps six comfortably.* In our writing system, we usually place a comma before and after a nonrestrictive clause to represent these pauses.

In 6b, the relative clause is *which Helen bought from Hector.* (1) The purpose of the clause is to tell us *which boat* is being discussed, so it is restrictive. (2) Likewise, we can substitute *that* for *which*: *The boat that Helen bought from Hector is a catamaran.* (3) As expected, the clause fails the "by the way" test: *The boat which (*by the way) Helen bought from Hector is a catamaran*—the clause is no afterthought but a crucial component of the noun phrase. Finally, (4) we do not pause in speech after *boat* and *Hector.* For this reason, commas are not placed before and after a restrictive clause.

Exercises 11.1

1. Underline each relative clause in the following sentences, and identify it as either restrictive or nonrestrictive. The commas that would normally appear before and after nonrestrictive clauses have been omitted in these exercises.

    a. Dad, <u>who is a baseball fan</u>, roots for Toronto.   [nonrestrictive]

    b. I prefer the lasagna which Gino bakes. restrictive

    c. Genevieve took a course in history, which is my favorite subject. nonrestrictive

    d. Irwin visited the cottage in which Wordsworth lived. restrictive

    e. Stories which people tell about fishing bore me. restrictive

    f. Our horse, which we treat like a member of the family, never won a race. non

    g. Stevie never drinks beer, which is an alcoholic beverage. nonres

    h. Steve never eats food <u>that</u> is green and fuzzy. res

[handwritten margin note: that is always restrictive]

2. The following sentences are ambiguous in that they can be read in either a restrictive or a nonrestrictive sense. What would the sentence mean if the clause is restrictive? What would it mean if the clause is nonrestrictive?

a. The world owes a debt to the ancient Egyptians who invented hieroglyphics.

b. The students in this class who are brilliant linguists deserve high grades.

Accounting for Nonrestrictive Clauses

It has been our assumption that a structurally ambiguous sentence (more accurately, two identically worded sentences with different meanings) must have two different tree structures. So it must be for a sentence with a relative clause that can have either a restrictive interpretation (as in 7a) or a nonrestrictive interpretation (as in 7b):

7 **a.** The world owes a debt to the ancient Egyptians *who invented hieroglyphics*.

—a restrictive relative clause

   b. The world owes a debt to the ancient Egyptians, *who invented hieroglyphics*.

—a nonrestrictive relative clause

Interpreted in the restrictive sense of 7a (with a debt owed just to those particular ancient Egyptians who did the inventing), the sentence would have one tree structure. Interpreted in the nonrestrictive sense of 7b (with a debt owed to ancient Egyptians as a whole), it would presumably have a different tree structure.

What might those two different structures look like? By now, it should be evident that syntax is not a subject where the student has little to do but accept and memorize a body of unquestioned truths. It is, in fact, more like a puzzle that all of us—teachers and students alike—have a hand in trying to solve. As here, we are often presented with specific problems to which we must bring insight and ingenuity. Just how, we must now ask, can we account for the differences between restrictive and nonrestrictive clauses so as to reflect their different functions and to capture our intuitions about their structures? We could easily propose several different hypotheses. The following represents one of these.

First, let us review the structure we proposed last chapter for a restrictive clause. Here is the structure of the restrictive clause in 7a:

8

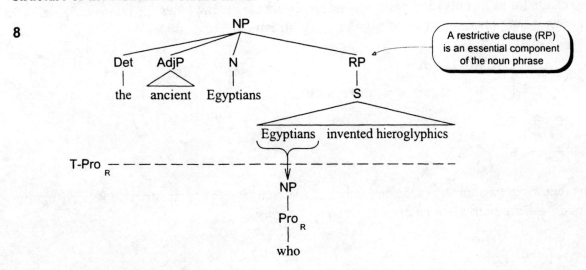

A restrictive clause (RP) is an essential component of the noun phrase

This structure makes sense for restrictive clauses, which are essential components of the noun phrases they modify. Note that the noun *Egyptians* in the main clause has three modifiers, all essential for telling us which Egyptians we mean: *the* Egyptians, *ancient* Egyptians, and Egyptians *who invented hieroglyphics*. Like the determiner and the adjective, the restrictive relative clause is essential to identify the noun. Consequently, we will continue to diagram a restrictive clause as a direct constituent of the NP label.

On the other hand, a nonrestrictive clause (a "by the way" clause) doesn't *identify* the noun but merely provides supplemental information. Consequently, it has a kind of independence from the rest of noun phrase. We need to devise a way to show that both the nonrestrictive clause and the noun phrase it modifies are separate, independent entities. Consequently, let us hypothesize that the phrase in 7b has this structure:

9

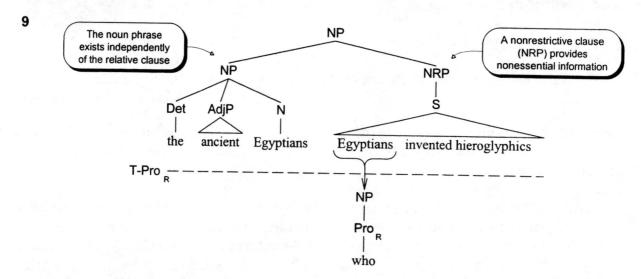

In the last chapter, we said that RP stood for "relative phrase/clause." Let us change that, so that **RP** stands for "restrictive phrase/clause." We can then introduce a new category, **NRP**, which stands for "nonrestrictive phrase/clause."

Examine the underlying structure of 9 carefully. Notice that the NP label occurs twice: once for the phrase *the ancient Egyptians* (to show that it can stand on its own and does not depend on the relative clause for its identity) and again for the larger phrase that includes the relative clause. We have to revise our phrase-structure rules to generate structures like 8 and 9:

10

$$NP \rightarrow \left\{ \begin{array}{c} \text{(Det)} \ \text{(AdjP)}^+ \ \text{(Mod}_{NP}) \ \text{N} \ \text{(PP)} \ \text{(CompP)} \ \textbf{(RP)} \\ \textbf{NP} \ \ \textbf{NRP} \end{array} \right\}$$

$$RP \rightarrow S$$

$$NRP \rightarrow S$$

The following diagram shows the derivation of a sentence with a nonrestrictive relative clause: *Cara studied white sharks, which are dangerous predators.*

11

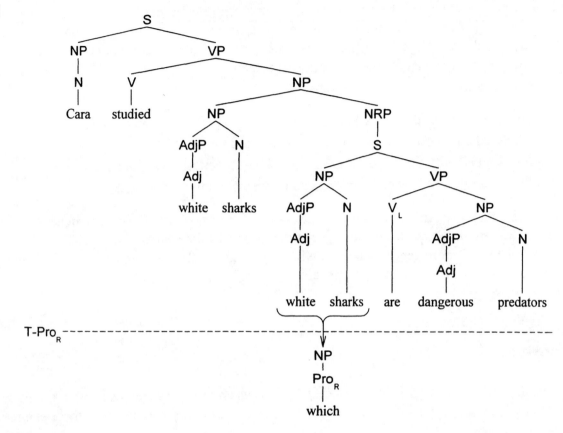

Exercises 11.2

1. Show the derivations of these sentences with nonrestrictive clauses:

    a. The astronomer admired the new moon, which appeared on Friday.
    b. Toby, whom Wanda supported, won the nomination.
    c. Olivia served fresh prawns, which tickle Hiram's fancy.
    d. The boss fired his son-in-law, whose surliness alienated the entire staff.
    e. The pet that Sheila kept in the dorm was a tarantula, which terrified her roommate.

2. The following sentence is ambiguous. Explain what it means when the relative clause has a restrictive interpretation, and draw a tree to show its derivation. Then explain what it means when the relative clause has a nonrestrictive interpretation, and show that derivation as well.

    Dancing(,) which incites lust(,) is sinful.

(3.) Optional discovery exercise: Nonrestrictive relative clauses generally modify noun phrases, but consider the following sentence:

    a. The chimps mimicked the trainer, which amused the onlookers.

If we asked what amused the onlookers, the answer isn't *the trainer* but the fact that *the chimps mimicked the trainer*. It appears that the relative clause doesn't modify a noun phrase but the entire main clause. The relative pronoun *which* apparently stands for that entire clause as well. How might you account for the derivation of sentence *a*?

Now consider the following sentences:

b. The man without shoes—which is an odd way to dress—attracted stares.
c. Kit dived under the bed, which is an obvious hiding place.
d. Julie argued with the customers, which is a bad practice for cashiers.
e. The children were curious, which is an important quality in students.

It appears that nonrestrictive clauses can modify not just noun phrases and sentences but many other kinds of phrases as well. How might the rule in 10 for nonrestrictives (NP → NP NRP) be replaced by a more general rule that would account for all these sentences? Remember that we have used XP to stand for "any phrase."

Apposition

An *appositive* is a noun phrase that immediately follows and further explains another noun phrase. Like relative clauses, appositives can be either restrictive or nonrestrictive, as in these examples:

12 a. My brother *Claude* lives in Idaho.   —a restrictive appositive
   b. My mother, *a chinchilla rancher*, lives in Montana.   —a nonrestrictive appositive

The subjects of these two sentences are the noun phrases *my brother* and *my mother*, respectively, and each is followed by an appositive. In 12a, *Claude* is a noun phrase "in apposition with" the noun phrase *my brother*. It is restrictive because it identifies which particular brother the speaker means. In 12b, however, *a chinchilla rancher* is a nonrestrictive appositive, because its purpose is not to identify which mother is meant but to provide supplementary information about the speaker's mother. Just as with nonrestrictive relative clauses, speakers pause briefly before and following a nonrestrictive appositive; in writing, these pauses are represented by commas. On the other hand, speakers do *not* pause before and following restrictive appositives, nor are commas usually used when restrictive appositives are written.

Appositives act just like relative clauses: They modify noun phrases, and they can be either restrictive or nonrestrictive. Let us broaden our RP and NRP rules to include them:

13
$$ RP \rightarrow \left\{ \begin{array}{c} S \\ NP \end{array} \right\} \qquad NRP \rightarrow \left\{ \begin{array}{c} S \\ NP \end{array} \right\} $$

The two appositives in 12 can be diagramed as in 14.

14   **a.**

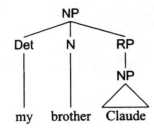

my   brother   Claude

b.

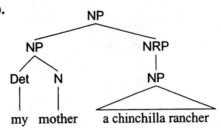

my   mother   a chinchilla rancher

Exercises 11.3

Underline the appositives in the following sentences and label them as restrictive or nonrestrictive. For nonrestrictive appositives, supply the commas that have been omitted. Then draw trees to show the derivation of each sentence.

1. The tourists visited Oslo <u>the capital of Norway</u>.   [nonrestrictive; a comma should follow *Oslo*]
2. Nigel mispronounced the word "ptisan."
3. Nelson an avid reader admires the poet Keats.
4. The expression "a pound of flesh" comes from Shakespeare's play *The Merchant of Venice*.
5. The youngest person in the room Anna loves bebop a style of jazz.

Restrictive and Nonrestrictive Adjectival Phrases

Adjectival phrases can also follow noun phrases, either restrictively or nonrestrictively, as in these examples:

15 a. A person *angry with the world* makes a poor neighbor.
— a restrictive adjectival phrase

b. The governess, *weary from her long journey*, went to bed early.
— a nonrestrictive adjectival phrase

The noun phrases in 15 can be diagramed as follows:

16 a.

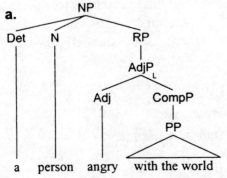

a   person   angry   with the world

b.

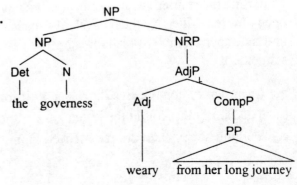

the   governess   weary   from her long journey

The NP label occurs twice in the nonrestrictive example, to signify that *the governess* is independent of the nonrestrictive phrase, which provides supplemental information only. An adjectival phrase that follows a noun phrase can take a complement, just like an adjectival phrase that follows a linking verb (an AdjP$_L$). The complement can be either a prepositional phrase, as in the examples of 16, or a complete clause, as in 17:

17 a. A person *certain that the whole world is against him* never listens to reason.

— a restrictive adjectival phrase

    b. Lavonne, *irate that her neighbor played music at a deafening volume*, complained to the landlord.

— a nonrestrictive adjectival phrase

We have seen that restrictive and nonrestrictive modifiers can be not only relative clauses but also appositive noun phrases and adjectival phrases. We can revise our rules to account for these options:

18 a.

$$\text{RP} \rightarrow \left\{ \begin{array}{c} \text{S} \\ \text{NP} \\ \text{AdjP}_L \end{array} \right\}$$

b.

$$\text{NRP} \rightarrow \left\{ \begin{array}{c} \text{S} \\ \text{NP} \\ \text{AdjP}_L \end{array} \right\}$$

Exercises 11.4

1. Underline the restrictive and nonrestrictive adjectival phrases in the following sentences (commas have been omitted), and identify them as either restrictive or nonrestrictive. Then draw trees to show the derivation of each sentence.

    a. Trees <u>heavy with fruit</u> await the harvest.   [restrictive; no commas are needed]

    b. The vanguard of the army unsure of its footing paused at the edge of the swamp.

    c. The patriarch wise and benevolent greeted the prodigal's return with eyes wet with tears.

    d. Allyson fearful that punishment awaited her surrendered to the authorities.

         [You may wish to review adjectival-complement clauses beginning on page 67.]

    e. People aware that lightning endangers computers unplug them during electrical storms.

2. Underline the restrictive and nonrestrictive modifiers in the following sentences (commas have been omitted). Identify them as relative clauses, appositive noun phrase, or adjectival phrases— and as either restrictive or nonrestrictive. Finally, draw trees to show the derivations of the sentences.

    a. Milton a millionaire lived in a shack fit for a pauper.

    b. The family that found the kitten gave it the name "Growltiger."

    c. Daphne happy and carefree married Dominic a misanthropic hermit.

     d. Guinevere who worries about her appearance frequently wears the color orange which flatters her.

3. Nonrestrictives can be set off in writing by commas, dashes, or parentheses. What effect does each of these forms of punctuation have in the following sentences? Are these punctuation marks interchangeable, or would it make a difference if one were substituted for another in these sentences?

     a. His all-time favorite ballplayer was the Sultan of Swat (Babe Ruth).

     b. Hunger and malnutrition—which afflict over a third of the world's inhabitants—are found even in wealthy industrialized nations.

     c. Ivy, content with her job, never sought a promotion.

(4.) Optional discovery exercise: The rules of 18 show that at least three different kinds of phrases can be restrictive or nonrestrictive modifiers. Can we add adverbial phrases to the list of options as well? Consider the following sentences:

     a. The train, usually on time, arrived late on Thursday.

     b. The guests, here at last, apologized for the delay.

If so, is our list of restrictive and nonrestrictive modifiers now complete, or can we generalize further and replace those rules with the following?

$$RP \rightarrow XP \qquad\qquad NRP \rightarrow XP$$

(5.) Optional discovery exercise: In addition to following the phrases they modify, nonrestrictive modifiers can also precede them:

     a. Curious but rude, the intruder barged through the door.

     b. A man totally without tact, Wesley insulted LaShanda.

Assume that the modifiers in the two sentences are moved by a transformation. Formulate that rule (you can call it "nonrestrictive movement" or "T-NRP"), and use it to draw the derivations of sentences *a* and *b*. (You should also check to see if restrictive modifiers can also be moved in such a way.)

(6.) Optional discovery exercise: In Chapter 9, we examined reflexive pronouns such as *myself* and *themselves*. The same words that act as reflexive pronouns can also act in a different function— as **intensive pronouns**. Intensive pronouns are appositives whose function is to reinforce (or "intensify") the noun phrases that they follow, as in these examples:

     a. I *myself* have no fear of goblins.

     b. Blanche's best friend is Blanche *herself*.

Are intensive pronouns restrictive or nonrestrictive? Is a new transformational rule needed to derive intensive pronouns? Show how we might derive sentences *a* and *b*.

(7.) Optional discovery exercise: In exercise 3 on page 165, we saw that relative clauses can modify phrases other than noun phrases. Can appositives also modify phrases other than noun phrases? Consider the following sentences:

    a. Doc put the key under the doormat—an unfortunate location.
    b. Doc put the key under the doormat—an unfortunate action.

Show the derivations of these sentences. Do any rules need to be modified to accommodate them?

(8.) Optional discovery exercise: For every appositive or adjectival phrase that follows and modifies a noun phrase, there exists a corresponding relative clause beginning with a relative pronoun and a linking verb:

    a. Jorge, *the leader of the uprising*, . . .
    b. Jorge, *who was the leader of the uprising*, . . .

    c. My friend *the insurance adjustor* . . .
    d. My friend *who is the insurance adjustor* . . .

    e. Noreen, *happy with the arrangements*, . . .
    f. Noreen, *who was happy with the arrangements*, . . .

This similarity has led some linguists to speculate that both members of each pair are derived from the same underlying form. For example, under this hypothesis both *a* and *b* would be derived from the following:

    Jorge [Jorge was the leader of the uprising] . . .

If so, formulate the rule that would be needed to derive phrases *a*, *c*, and *e* in this exercise, and then show the derivations. Does the hypothesis seem a reasonable one?

Summary and Review: Chapters 7–11

We have reached a convenient point to sum up and review what we have so far discovered about the structure of the English language. Our grammatical model now has the following phrase-structure and transformational rules. The T-rules are listed in their relative order of application.

PS RULES

$$S \rightarrow NP \quad VP$$

$$NP \rightarrow \begin{Bmatrix} (Det) \quad (AdjP)^+ \quad (Mod_{NP}) \quad N \quad (PP) \quad (CompP) \quad (RP) \\ CompP \\ NP \quad NRP \end{Bmatrix}$$

$$VP \rightarrow \begin{Bmatrix} V \quad (NP) \\ V_L \begin{Bmatrix} NP \\ AdjP_L \\ AdvP_L \end{Bmatrix} \end{Bmatrix} (AdvP)^+$$

$$(V \rightarrow V_P \quad Prt)$$

$$Det \rightarrow \begin{Bmatrix} Art \\ Dem \\ Quant \\ NP \quad Poss \end{Bmatrix}$$

$$Mod_{NP} \rightarrow (AdjP)^+ \quad (Mod_{NP}) \quad N \quad (PP)$$

$$AdjP \rightarrow (Deg) \quad Adj$$

$$AdjP_L \rightarrow (Deg) \quad Adj \quad (CompP)$$

$$AdvP \rightarrow (Deg) \begin{Bmatrix} Adv \\ PP \\ C_s \quad S \end{Bmatrix}$$ ← *complementizer*

$$AdvP_L \rightarrow (Deg) \begin{Bmatrix} Adv_{(Time/Place)} \\ PP_{(Time/Place)} \end{Bmatrix}$$

$$CompP \rightarrow \begin{Bmatrix} C_{Cl} \quad S \\ PP \end{Bmatrix}$$

$$PP \rightarrow P \quad NP$$

$$XP \rightarrow XP \quad C_{Co} \quad XP$$

$$RP \rightarrow \begin{Bmatrix} S \\ NP \\ AdjP_L \\ AdvP_L \end{Bmatrix}$$

$$NRP \rightarrow \begin{Bmatrix} S \\ NP \\ AdjP_L \\ AdvP_L \end{Bmatrix}$$

T-RULES

1. $T\text{-}Pro_{Rx}$ — *reflexive*
2. $T\text{-}Pro_R$ — *± relative — frontingrule*
3. T-WH
4. T-AdvP
5. T-IO
6. T-Imp
7. $T\text{-}Pro_P$ — *personal pronouns*
8. T-Prt

Exercises 11.5

1. Use grammar 19 to show the derivations of the following sentences. Commas that would normally appear with nonrestrictive modifiers have been omitted. Review previous sections and chapters as needed to draw the trees.

   a. Benjy insulted Kitty because she offended him.
   b. The extremely expensive curtains that Carla bought hang in the den.
   c. Give Tommy the money.
   d. Fred claimed that the treasurer improperly spent the club's funds.
   e. Frank who forgets things threw the bills out.
   f. Mom diapered the baby, while Jimmy dressed himself.
   g. The boy whose mother rode that motorcycle drives a respectable Buick with four doors.
   h. Never put yourself down.
   i. Bo made a pilgrimage to Graceland the house where Elvis lived.
   j. When they arrived, the twins received a warm welcome.
   k. A snowstorm rarely occurs in April which is a very mild month.
   l. Fido whose fleas tormented him scratched himself constantly.
   m. The cop knows that the man that he arrested has a long record.
   n. Show Vince the parchment on which the pirate drew the treasure map.
   o. Bart the son in the cartoon gave his sister Lisa a kiss.
   p. Willie and Libby unaware of the time almost missed the bus.
   q. Stop the behavior that annoys Deborah.
   r. After the attorney explained the agreement, she drew the contract up.
   s. The children know that Ken wanted the candy that Barbie hid in the dresser.
   t. The circus fired the clown whose antics caused the riot.
   u. While Maxwell sunned himself, Bertha very contentedly read a book.
   v. If you see the papers, throw them out.
   w. The doctor who examined Edna wrote the prescription that Dad took to the drugstore.
   x. Even when he works quickly, Van seldom makes a mistake.

2. Supply the commas that were omitted before and after nonrestrictive modifiers in exercise 1. If any modifier is ambiguous—that is, if it could have either a restrictive or a nonrestrictive interpretation—explain the different meanings the sentence would have under each interpretation.

3. Assume that in exercise sentence 1j *they* refers to the twins. Could *they* also refer to the twins in the following sentence: *They received a warm welcome when the twins arrived*? Use both sentences as examples to explain the conditions under which T-Pro$_P$ can apply (see page 132). Also use them to discuss the order in which T-AdvP and T-Pro$_P$ are performed.

12 Verb Inflections

Present and Past Tenses

Until now, we have ignored the different verb tenses and other verb inflections. For example, we have treated *I go* and *I went* exactly the same in our grammar. In this chapter, we will examine the way such verbs are formed.

Tense is frequently described as the property that relates a verb's action to the time when it is performed. In traditional grammar study, verbs in English are said to take twelve tenses. Here, for example, are the traditional tense forms of the verb *go*:

1

TRADITIONAL ANALYSIS OF ENGLISH VERB TENSES

Common Forms

Present Tense:	I go, you go, she goes, we go, they go
Past Tense:	I went, you went, she went, . . .
Future Tense:	I will go, you will go, . . .
Present Perfect Tense:	I have gone, you have gone, . . .
Past Perfect Tense:	I had gone, you had gone, . . .
Future Perfect Tense:	I will have gone, you will have gone, . . .

Progressive Forms

Present Progressive Tense:	I am going, you are going, she is going, . . .
Past Progressive Tense:	I was going, you were going, . . .
Future Progressive Tense:	I will be going, you will be going, . . .
Present Perfect Progressive Tense:	I have been going, you have been going, . . .
Past Perfect Progressive Tense:	I had been going, you had been going, . . .
Future Perfect Progressive Tense:	I will have been going, you will have been going, . . .

This traditional analysis can be misleading, however, because it does not reflect the way in which English verb ***inflectional endings*** (such as *-s* and *-ed*) are actually supplied. In English, unlike many other languages, verbs by themselves have only two distinct tense forms, present and past.

All the other "tenses" in list 1 are formed by using **auxiliary** (or "helping") **verbs** such as *will* or *have*. In this chapter, we will examine how the grammar produces these verb forms.

Every English verb has a present and a past form. For the majority of verbs, known as **regular** (or **weak**) **verbs**, the past tense is formed by adding *-ed* or *-d* to the present-tense form. Examples of the two tenses for regular verbs are *talk/talked, bake/baked,* and *need/needed.* In contrast, **irregular** (or **strong**) **verbs** form the past tense in irregular ways: *do/did, have/had, take/took,* and *go/went.* Linking verbs are even less regular, with multiple forms in both present tense (*am, are, is*) and past tense (*was, were*).

Let us hypothesize that the grammar has some way of marking verb tense in the underlying structure and then assigning the proper spoken form to the verb. We can represent this in our model of the grammar by incorporating into the verb phrase a new element to hold tense information. We can call this element an **auxiliary marker** (abbreviated **Aux**). According to this hypothesis, the following represents the underlying structure of the sentence *Pete went to Chicago:*

2

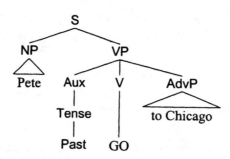

This tree shows that the spoken verb will be the past tense of the verb *GO.* You will remember that in earlier chapters we wrote certain underlying elements in capital letters (*HEARER, SPEAKER*) to indicate that they represent concepts rather than words that are actually spoken. Let us continue to use that convention. In underlying structure 2, the spoken form of the verb has not yet been assigned, and so, to show that, we will represent the verb by giving its basic, uninflected form (also called its **infinitive form**), written in capital letters. From the infinitive form *GO,* all the inflected forms of that verb are derived: *go, goes, went, going,* and *gone.*

Our revised grammar will need to include these phrase-structure rules:

3
$$VP \rightarrow \textbf{Aux } \textbf{V } \textbf{NP } \textbf{(AdvP)}^+$$

$$Aux \rightarrow \textbf{Tense}$$

$$Tense \rightarrow \left\{ \begin{matrix} \textbf{Pres} \\ \textbf{Past} \end{matrix} \right\}$$

These rules will produce the underlying structure in 2. A transformational rule will then be needed to assign the proper spoken form to the verb. The various forms a word takes are called its **inflections**, so we will call this rule the **inflection-assigning transformation** (abbreviated **T-Infl**).

In showing the derivation of verb inflections, we will use a broken-line diagram together with a new convention, shown in diagram 4, which represents the derivation of *Pete went to Chicago:*

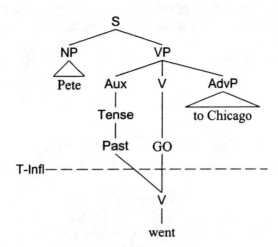

4

In showing the operation of the T-Infl rule, we will draw lines down from both the Tense and V categories to represent that these two elements act together to derive the inflected form of the verb. Speakers of English know the past tense form of *GO* because we store information about the various forms of verbs in our memories—which is another way of saying in our mental lexicons. Derivation 4 does nothing more complicated than demonstrate that the grammar assigns the proper spoken form to the verb. We could describe what happens here by saying that T-Infl sees that the past tense of the verb *GO* is called for, and it supplies the proper form to the spoken structure—namely, *went*.

For an example of a sentence with a verb in the present tense, consider the derivation of *Ingrid loves anchovies*:

5

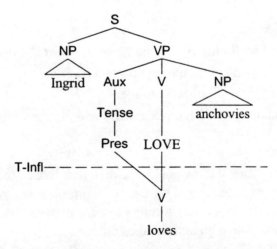

Diagram 5 shows that the inflection-assigning transformation (T-Infl) consults both the verb (*LOVE*) and the tense marker (*Pres*) in assigning the inflected verb form (*loves*) to the sentence. What the diagram does not show, however, is that T-Infl also must consult the subject (*Ingrid*), because the subject determines which of two possible present-tense forms (*love* or *loves*) is selected. For third-person-singular nouns such as *Ingrid*, the form *loves* is assigned (see page 46 for a discussion of person and number), whereas *love* is assigned for other present-tense forms (*I love, you love, they love,* . . .). To account for the role of the subject in the assignment of verb forms, we could draw a third line in 5 from the noun phrase *Ingrid* to the inflected verb *loves*. However, for the sake of simplicity in our tree-drawing, let us agree not to do so, provided that we keep in mind that the transformation consults the subject as well as the tense marker when it assigns tense inflection to the verb.

Exercises 12.1

1. Underline the verb in each of the following sentences, and indicate whether its tense is present or past. Using derivations 4 and 5 as your models, show how the sentences are derived:

    a. Arthur <u>hates</u> okra.   —present tense

    The infinitive form of "hates" is "HATE." To determine the infinitive form of any verb, find the form that would complete a sentence such as "I used to _____" or "I like to ____."

    b. Bethany captured a lemming.
    c. The anthropologists puzzled the chimpanzees.
    d. I sleep soundly.

2. We usually think of the present tense as describing actions taking place at the present time and of the past tense as describing past actions. This is sometimes, but by no means always, the case. For the following sentences, identify the tense of each italicized verb, and note whether the time it describes is the present, the past, the future, or an ongoing time.

    a. Tomorrow I *drive* to Cincinnati.
    b. Your disguise *fooled* me.
    c. "So then this big oaf *walks* up to me, and he *says*, '*Beat* it, buster!'"
    d. A gentleman never *wipes* his mouth on his sleeve.
    e. I *wonder* what I would do if he *spoke* to me.
    f. Lefty *winds* up. He *delivers*. McGraw *swings* and *misses*. The game *is* over.

As the last exercise makes clear, we routinely use different tenses in complex and sophisticated ways. The relationship between tense and time is not a simple one. As we continue our study of verb forms, be prepared for instances where a verb's tense is used to serve grammatical purposes that have little to do with the time when an action takes place.

Modal Auxiliaries

Although we sometimes use the present tense to describe future actions (see the preceding exercise sentence 2a), usually we indicate the future by using the words *will* or *shall*, as in *They will go* and *I shall return*. Words like *will* and *shall* are sometimes called "helping verbs." They are better described as ***modal auxiliaries*** (abbreviated **M**). In addition to *will* and *shall*, a number of other English helping verbs are classified as modal auxiliaries. Here are modals in the present- and past-tense forms:

6

MODAL AUXILIARIES	
Present	**Past**
will – *made up mind*	would
shall – *have intent*	should
can – *physically able*	could
may – *person*	might
must – *obligation*	(no past-tense form)

Your first reaction to chart 6 is likely to be that you do not usually think of *will* as being in the present tense nor of *might* as being the past form of *may*. Nevertheless, those tense labels provide the best classification of these forms. The present-tense forms in 6 function in our grammar much like other present-tense verbs, and the past forms *would, should, could,* and *might* developed historically as the past-tense forms of *will, shall, can,* and *may*. As we have seen, tense is best described as a category that determines which form of a verb will be spoken; it only loosely indicates the time at which the action of the sentence is performed. As is often the case in grammar, the concept of tense can be described more accurately in terms of structure than in terms of meaning.

Let us add the modal auxiliary as an optional constituent of the auxiliary category. The Aux rule in 3 will then need to be revised to include it:

7   Aux → Tense **(M)**

$$M \rightarrow \left\{ \begin{array}{c} WILL \\ SHALL \\ CAN \\ MAY \\ MUST \end{array} \right\} \varnothing$$

These rules state that the auxiliary category always has a tense marker but that a modal is optional. A modal will consist of one of the five listed verbs, plus the ***null symbol*** ($\varnothing$). The purpose of the null symbol is simply to indicate that the verb that follows a modal will not take an inflectional ending in the spoken structure—that is, it will remain in its uninflected form. You will see how this will work in the following derivation.

With these rules, we can now derive sentences with modal auxiliaries, such as 8a, *Myra will retire,* and 8b, *Gordon might need a bandage.*

8 a.

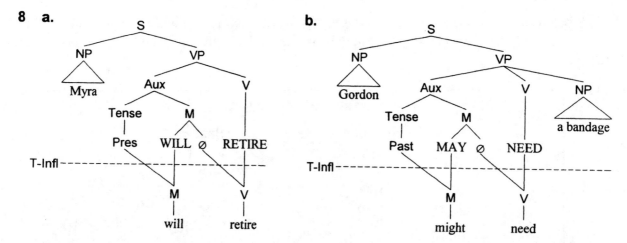

There are many important observations to be made about these derivations. Notice first that in the underlying form of sentences, verbs are always shown in their uninflected forms. This is true of auxiliary verbs such as modals (*WILL, MAY*) as well as main verbs (*RETIRE, NEED*). The T-Infl rule assigns the appropriate form of both main and auxiliary verbs in the spoken structure. Notice too that modals have uninflected forms (the five forms listed in the modal rule in 7) and that the tense stated in the Aux category determines whether modals like *MAY* or *WILL* are assigned the present-tense form (*may, will*) or the past-tense form (*might, would*). In 8a, the tense-marker *Pres* and the modal *WILL* are paired to produce the spoken form *will*. Similarly in 8b, the tense-marker *Past* and the modal *MAY* are paired to produced *might*.

Finally, notice in 8a and 8b that the tense-marker affects *only* the modal, not the main verb. The form of the main verb is determined by the item immediately to its left, the null symbol ∅. The null symbol indicates that no inflection is added to the verb that follows it. Consequently in 8a, ∅ and *RETIRE* are paired to produce the uninflected form *retire*—in other words, no change is made to the form of that verb.

We can now describe the inflection-assigning transformation more fully:

9   **Inflection-Assigning Transformation (T-Infl):** Starting with the tense marker and moving to the right, pair off all the constituents of the *Aux* and *V* categories, and assign to each pair the appropriate spoken verb form.

Notice how 9 describes the operation of T-Infl in the derivations of 8.

Exercises 12.2

1. In each of the following sentences, draw two lines under the main verb and one line under each modal auxiliary. Identify the tense of the sentence, and show the sentence's derivation.

    a. Audrey <u>can</u> <u>ski</u> expertly.   [*Can* is the present tense of *CAN*]
    b. Jeremy <u>could</u> <u>be</u> the boss.   [*Could* is the past tense of *CAN*]
    c. The children must take baths.
    d. The restaurant may hire Candace as a cook.

e. The medics should assist the surgeons in an emergency.

(2.) Optional discovery exercise: In addition to the modals in chart 6, certain two-word combinations also perform a modal-like function. These **quasi-modals** include *have to, had to, used to,* and *ought to.* Although written as two words, they act as single words in modern English and are even pronounced like single words in normal, rapid speech (*hafta, hadda, useta, oughta*). Show the derivations of the following sentences; treat the quasi-modals like single words in your diagrams.

a. Quasimodo had to ring the bell.
b. Trains used to be a popular form of transportation.
c. Young Clampett ought to learn proper manners.

Notice that *had to* in 2a fills the void left by the absence of a past form of *must.*

(3.) Optional discovery exercise: In the regional dialect spoken where I live (eastern North Carolina), it is possible in informal speech to have more than one modal auxiliary in a verb phrase (*I might can go, We used to could sleep late*). Are such forms possible in your dialect? If not, how would you express the ideas stated in those two sentences? How may the rules of 7 be different for dialects that allow these expressions?

Perfect and Progressive Auxiliaries

In addition to the modal auxiliaries, two other auxiliaries that can precede verbs are forms of *HAVE* and *BE.* For example, we have verb phrases such as *have taken* and *is taking,* not to mention phrases with multiple auxiliaries such as *could have been taking.*

To understand how the system of verbs works in our language, we need to discover when and how these various auxiliaries occur. To do so, we will find it useful to have a body of data to examine. The following exercise can help us discover more about how English verbs are used.

Exercises 12.3

Elements from the three columns below can be combined to produce sentences:

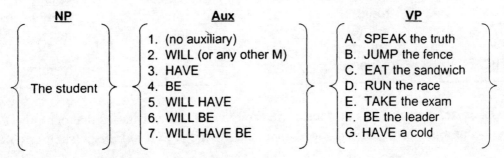

NP	Aux	VP
The student	1. (no auxiliary) 2. WILL (or any other M) 3. HAVE 4. BE 5. WILL HAVE 6. WILL BE 7. WILL HAVE BE	A. SPEAK the truth B. JUMP the fence C. EAT the sandwich D. RUN the race E. TAKE the exam F. BE the leader G. HAVE a cold

In most cases, the selection of one item from each column will result in a grammatical spoken sentence after inflections are assigned to the verbs. For example, if we start a sentence with *The student* and then add choices 5 (the auxiliary *WILL HAVE*) and C (the verb phrase *EAT the sandwich*), the result is *The student will have eaten the sandwich*. The resulting spoken sentence for 4A is *The student is speaking the truth*, and the sentence for 1B (with no auxiliary) is *The student jumps the fence*.

1. Try all possible combinations—there are too many to write down, so just say them aloud—and see if your unconscious knowledge allows you to assign the correct inflections in each case. A few of the combinations will be odd (such as 4G), and a few will be downright awkward (such as 6F), but most should result in perfectly acceptable sentences.

2. From the preceding, can you gain any conscious insight into what your brain knows unconsciously about verb inflections? That is, can you discover how you knew which inflections to assign in exercise 1?

3. The chart lists eight possible combinations of auxiliaries. Are any other combinations possible (such as *BE WILL* or *BE HAVE WILL*)?

The data from this exercise may seem hopelessly confusing, a jumble beyond our capacity for comprehending. Clearly, however, some principle must be at work here because our brains know unconsciously which inflections to apply. If we analyze our data carefully and systematically, we should begin to find order where at first seemed only chaos.

We have already noted the two forms that verbs can take when they occur without any preceding auxiliaries: the present-tense forms (such as *speak/speaks*) and the past-tense form (*spoke*). We have also seen that verbs that follow modals take no inflection (*can speak*). In addition, we now see that verbs that are preceded by other auxiliaries can have different inflected forms (such as *spoken* and *speaking*). These are called the **perfect** and **progressive** forms respectively. From the sample sentences in the exercise, we can now list the various forms that each verb can take:

10

VERB INFLECTIONS				
Uninflected (ø-ending)	Present	Past	Perfect (-en/-ed ending)	Progressive (-ing ending)
SPEAK	speak(s)	spoke	spoken	speaking
JUMP	jump(s)	jumped	jumped	jumping
EAT	eat(s)	ate	eaten	eating
RUN	run(s)	ran	run	running
TAKE	take(s)	took	taken	taking
BE	am/is/are	was/were	been	being
HAVE	have/has	had	had	having

From the exercise, it also seems that there are three classes of auxiliaries that can precede a verb. These can occur alone or in combination. One class is the **modal auxiliary** (such as *CAN, WILL,*

MAY, and so on). Another consists of forms of the verb *HAVE*—known as the **perfect auxiliary**. The perfect auxiliary is always followed by the perfect form of the verb (*have spoken*). The third consists of forms of the verb *BE*—known as the **progressive auxiliary**. The progressive auxiliary is always followed by the progressive form of the verb (*is speaking*).

How does the grammar know which verb forms to use with each auxiliary? We have already devised a way in rule 7 to show that modals are always followed by verbs that take a "null" ending (that is, they remain in their uninflected form). In our diagrams we have represented this "ending" by the null symbol ∅. Let us do something similar to show that the perfect auxiliary *HAVE* is always followed by a perfect verb form, as in *have spoken* or *has jumped*. We will represent the perfect ending by the symbol *-en/-ed*, because most perfect verbs end in those letters. Finally, because the progressive auxiliary *BE* is always followed by a progressive verb form, as in *is speaking* or *am jumping*, let us represent the progressive ending by the symbol *-ing*.

One further discovery from the data in our exercise is that any or all of the three types of auxiliary verbs can occur together in a verb phrase, but when they do so, they must occur in a certain order. When they occur together, modals always come before perfect and progressive auxiliaries, and perfects always come before progressives. This knowledge now allows us to write phrase-structure rules that we hope will produce grammatical combinations of auxiliaries and verb endings. If so, we can conclude that they model the rules your brain uses as you produce these grammatical forms.

11   VP → Aux V (NP) (AdvP)$^{+}$

Aux → Tense (M) (Perf) (Prog)

$$M \rightarrow \left\{ \begin{array}{c} \text{WILL} \\ \text{SHALL} \\ \text{CAN} \\ \text{MAY} \\ \text{MUST} \end{array} \right\} \varnothing$$

Perf → HAVE -en/-ed

Prog → BE -ing

Although these rules may seem quite complex, you will soon see (with a little practice) that they operate with an elegant simplicity. Observe in 12 how we can use these rules, plus the T-Infl transformation, to generate a sentence with multiple auxiliary verbs, such as *The gamblers had been cheating Sam*.

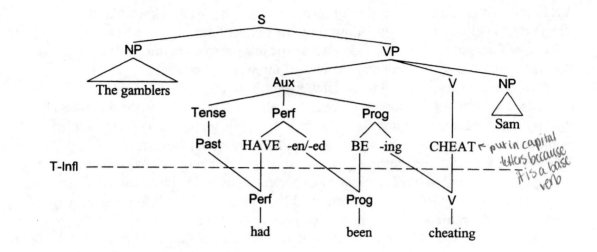

Notice in 12 how T-Infl pairs the elements of the Aux and V categories: *Had* is the past tense of *HAVE*; *been* is the *-en/-ed* form of *BE*; and *cheating* is the *-ing* form of *CHEAT*.

Let us look at one more example, the derivation of *Joel must have finished the job*:

13

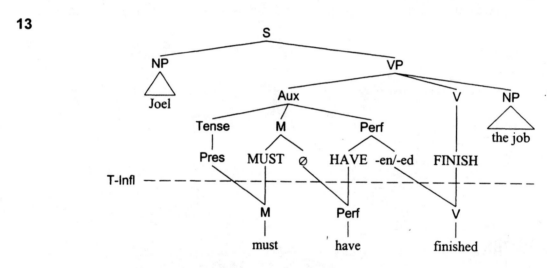

Here too, as you can observe, the rules we have devised have resulted in exactly the spoken form produced by our mental grammar. The solution we have devised is elegant, and, as you will see in the following exercise, it works every time. Our analysis of auxiliaries is an impressive demonstration of the effectiveness of transformational grammar in describing the unconscious rules we observe as we use our language.

Exercises 12.4

For each of the following sentences, first draw two lines under the main verb, and then draw one line under each auxiliary verb. Identify each auxiliary as a modal auxiliary, a perfect auxiliary (a form of *HAVE*), or a progressive auxiliary (a form of *BE*). Examine the first auxiliary, and determine if it is in the present or the past tense. Finally, follow the rules of 11 to show the derivation of each sentence. Your trees will resemble those of 12 and 13.

1. The river <u>has</u> <u>been</u> <u>rising</u> quickly.   Tense: present [The first auxiliary, *has,* is the present-tense form of
            Perf Prog   V   *HAVE.*]

2. The show should have ended.

3. Pamela is trying eagerly.

4. Gophers could have been causing the problem.

5. Daisy might have left already.   [For some verbs, the *-en/-ed* form does not always end in those
                                      letters. Adv: *already*]

6. The cooks will have been working for an hour.

7. I must have a car.   [Here *HAVE* is the main verb, not an auxiliary.]

8. Colin had been a spy.   [Here the main verb is the linking verb *BE*.]

9. The hyenas may be laughing at the jackals.

10. The waiter has apologized for the mixup.

13 Negatives and Questions

Negative Sentences

For each sentence that makes a positive statement, there can also be a corresponding negative sentence containing the word *not*. For example, corresponding with the positive sentence *Howard will pump iron* is the negative sentence *Howard will not pump iron*. The word *not* is added to form such sentences, but how? To answer this question, we need more data to examine.

Negative Sentences with Auxiliary Verbs

Let us see what various sentences with negatives look like. The following tree shows the underlying structure for sentences with different combinations of auxiliary verbs. We would like to identify the negative version of each of these seven combinations:

1

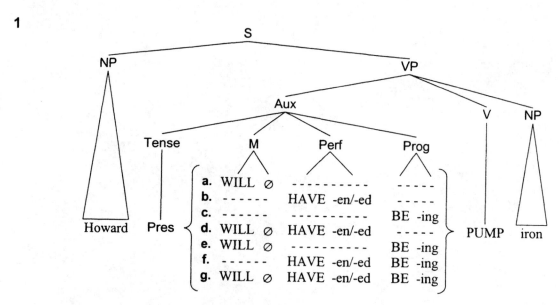

In this chart, **1a** represents the underlying structure of *Howard will pump iron*; **1d** of *Howard will have pumped iron*; and **1g** of *Howard will have been pumping iron*.

Exercises 13.1

1. For each of the seven positive sentences in 1, supply the corresponding negative sentence. For example, the negative of **1a** is *Howard will not pump iron.*

2. Can you state a generalization about how we form the negative for a sentence with one or more auxiliary verbs? Does your generalization also apply to the past-tense versions of the sentences in 1?

You undoubtedly noticed that the negative is formed by placing *not* immediately after the first auxiliary, as in *Howard has not been pumping iron,* where *not* comes immediately after *has.* No matter how many auxiliary verbs precede the main verb, *not* always follows the first one. How can we revise our grammar to incorporate this observation?

If we continue to assume that the underlying structure of a sentence captures its meaning, then we would expect the negative element *not* to be present in the underlying structure of a negative sentence. One solution would be to say that the auxiliary marker includes an optional negative element, which we can represent as **Neg.** But how do we insert it into our auxiliary rule 2 so that *not* always follows the first auxiliary?

2   Aux → Tense (M) (Perf) (Prog)

It appears that we cannot. Rule 2 can generate any combination of the three auxiliaries, so no matter where we insert Neg into this rule, there is no way to assure that it will follow the first auxiliary.

We have faced dilemmas like this before, and, fortunately, transformational rules have provided us with a handy solution to the problem. So too here. We can generate the Neg element in a fixed position somewhere in the Aux and then have a T-rule move one or more elements so that *not* follows the first auxiliary. First, let us revise rule 2 so that it includes the negative element:

3   Aux → (**Neg**) Tense (M) (Perf) (Prog)
    Neg → *not*

In 3, the negative element *not* comes before the tense marker, where it will not be in the way when T-Infl pairs up the other constituents of Aux. Let's see how our revised grammar generates the sentence *Howard has not been pumping iron.* After T-Infl is applied to the underlying structure generated by 3 we would have:

4   Howard not has been pumping iron

Let us assume that a T-rule then reverses the positions of *not* and *has.* The effect is the same whether we move *has* forward or *not* backward. Let us arbitrarily pick the former:

5   Howard   not <u>has</u> been pumping iron

We can call this operation the negative transformation, which we can state as follows:

6   **Negative Transformation (T-Neg):** Following the operation of T-Infl, the first auxiliary verb is moved so that it precedes *not*.

With rules 3 and 6, we can now show the complete derivation of *Howard has not been pumping iron*:

7

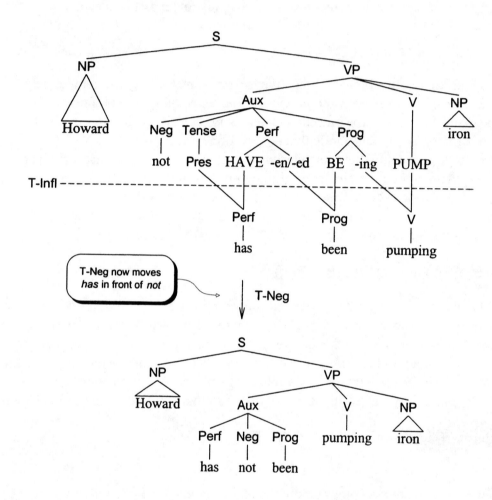

Alternatively, we could use a broken-line diagram to show the entire derivation, as in 8. Use whichever method you find clearer when you draw derivations of negative sentences.

8

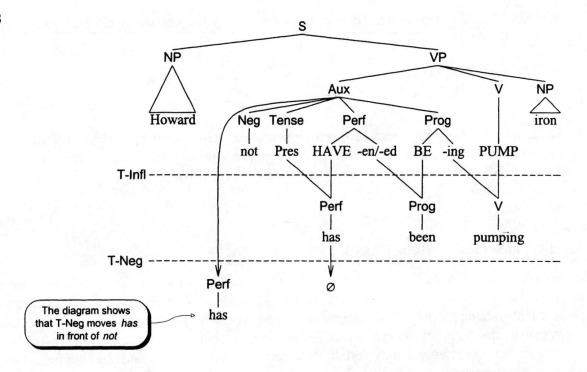

The diagram shows that T-Neg moves *has* in front of *not*

Exercises 13.2

1. Underline each auxiliary and main verb in the following sentences. Then use rules 3 and 6 to show the derivations of the sentences. You may use either a separate tree, as in 7, or a broken-line diagram, as in 8, to show the operation of T-Neg.

   a. The officials <u>have</u> not <u>been</u> <u>losing</u> sleep over the decision.

   b. Tyrone cannot speak Hungarian.   [The fact that *cannot* is written as a single word is a typographical convention. Treat *can* and *not* as separate words in your derivation.]

   c. Seth would not have remembered my birthday.

   d. The workers are not taking a break.

   e. Ginny has not forgotten her promises.

   f. The driver is not leaving without the passengers.

   g. The assassins could not have been posing as guards.

   h. Melanie and Frederick had not been wasting any time.

2. When an auxiliary such as *has* is followed by *not*, the two words are frequently combined, especially in speech, to form a ***contraction***, such as *hasn't*. We could say that an optional transformational rule, which we may call **T-Cont**, can apply following T-Neg to produce the contracted forms, as diagramed on the right. State the contracted versions of the auxiliary verbs in

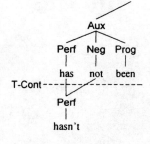

sentences 1a–1h. Then draw the derivations of the following sentences, showing the operation of the T-Cont rule.

   a. The plane hasn't landed yet.

   b. Lance won't be attending the meeting.

3. Rules 3 and 6 correctly produce negative sentences with auxiliary verbs. But what about sentences with no auxiliaries? What is the negative sentence that corresponds with *Howard pumps iron*? What did you have to do to produce the negative sentence?

Negatives of Sentences without Auxiliary Verbs

Several centuries ago, it was possible for speakers of English to form the negative of a sentence with no auxiliaries by moving the main verb to precede *not*, as in *Howard pumps not iron* (although it is unlikely that "pumping iron" was an expression known to the Elizabethans). The English language is constantly changing, and in our century such constructions are no longer grammatical. If a negative sentence lacks an auxiliary verb in its underlying structure, one must be supplied. For this purpose, the ***supporting auxiliary DO*** is used in such sentences, so that in our era the negative version of *Howard pumps iron* is *Howard does not pump iron*.

Notice that the *DO* auxiliary is quite different from the modals and other auxiliaries that we have encountered. Each of those auxiliaries has some effect on the meaning of the sentence. In contrast, the supporting auxiliary has no effect on meaning whatever. It is merely a dummy word, whose only purpose is a structural one: to provide the required auxiliary that is necessary in a negative sentence.

We can state this observation in the form of a transformational rule:

9   **Supporting-Auxiliary Insertion (T-Supp)**: If a negative sentence lacks an auxiliary verb in its underlying structure, the supporting auxiliary (DO + ∅) is inserted following the tense marker.

The derivation of *Howard does not pump iron* is shown in 10.

10

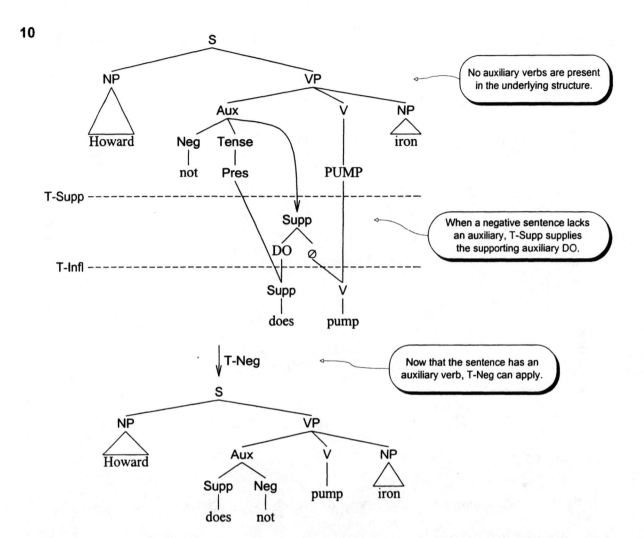

No auxiliary verbs are present in the underlying structure.

When a negative sentence lacks an auxiliary, T-Supp supplies the supporting auxiliary DO.

Now that the sentence has an auxiliary verb, T-Neg can apply.

Notice how T-Supp adds *DO* to the Aux marker and how T-Infl then combines the Aux and V elements to provide inflections.

In a multi-step derivation such as 10, with its three different transformations, the grammar can appear complex—as it most certainly is! The very least you will gain from this course is an appreciation of the remarkably sophisticated tasks our minds constantly (and effortlessly) perform as we use language. On the other hand, we should not allow these derivations to seem any more complicated than they are. For example, writing a transformational rule like T-Neg is simply another way of showing that we put the first auxiliary before *not* when we speak. Drawing a separate tree in our diagram to show this simple step makes it look deceptively complicated. When we understand what these derivations are actually showing, however, they will seem both reasonable and straightforward.

Derivation 10 shows the operation of T-Neg by drawing a separate tree. As an alternative, we could have used the broken-line method to show the entire derivation, as in 11:

11

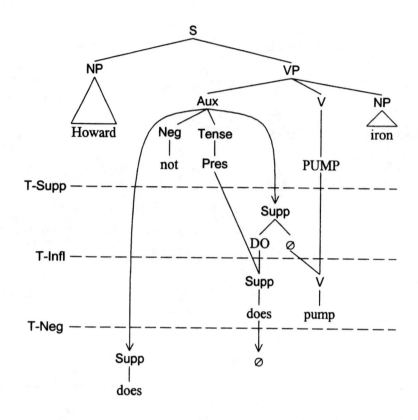

Exercises 13.3

1. State the negative sentence that corresponds to each of the following positive sentences:

   a. Meg likes spicy foods.
   b. The bright lights dazzled Stella.

2. Draw trees to show the derivations of the following sentences. Use either a separate tree or the broken-line method to show the operation of T-Neg.

   a. Old stories did not bore Alphonse.
   b. The mountaineers do not use ropes.
   c. This telephone does not have a cord.
   d. The mistakes didn't matter in the long run.

3. In the preceding sentences, the supporting auxiliary *DO* was inserted for purely structural reasons: simply to supply a meaningless auxiliary so that T-Neg could be performed. In addition to this purpose, the supporting auxiliary can sometimes be used to influence meaning: to make an assertion emphatic (for example, in this exchange: "You've never respected me." "But I *do* respect you.") In each of the following sentences, assume that the underlying structure lacks an auxiliary and that *DO* is inserted by T-Supp. Draw the derivations of these emphatic sentences.

a. Ethnic stereotypes do annoy Maurice ["Maurice is insensitive when it comes to ethnicity." "You're wrong; ethnic stereotypes *do* annoy Maurice."]

b. The outfit did cause a sensation.

c. Brigid does do her homework faithfully.

(4.) Optional discovery exercise: We made the claim that all sentences with *not* require an auxiliary verb. Consider, however, the following sentences:

a. A spider is not an insect.

b. She hasn't a care in the world.

How must we modify that claim? That is, are certain verbs able to form negatives without auxiliaries? Is the supporting auxiliary an optional alternative with any of these verbs?

Questions

All of the sentences we have considered so far in this book have been either statements—otherwise known as sentences in the declarative mood—or commands—sentences in the imperative mood. (See page 115 to review the concept of grammatical mood.) Now let us consider questions, which are sentences in the ***interrogative mood***. Questions are of two kinds: ***yes/no questions*** that call for a yes or no answer (for example, *Did you enjoy the movie?*) and ***"wh"-questions*** that begin with words such as *who* or *what* and that call for more substantive answers (*Who directed the movie?*).

Yes/No Questions

For each declarative sentence, there is a corresponding yes/no question. For example, the yes/no question form of *Howard will pump iron* is *Will Howard pump iron?* To discover how these questions are formed, we need once again to assemble a body of data to examine.

Exercises 13.4

For each of the following declarative sentences, state the corresponding yes/no question:

1. The officials have been losing sleep over the decision.
2. Tyrone can speak Hungarian.
3. Seth would have remembered my birthday.
4. The workers are taking a break.

From the data you have produced, can you describe how you formed such yes/no questions?

Similar to negative sentences, where the first auxiliary verb is moved to the front of the Aux marker, yes/no questions are formed by moving the first auxiliary to the front of the sentence, as follows:

12   Howard <u>has</u> been pumping iron

Notice that this analysis makes the claim that interrogative sentences have the same underlying form as declarative sentences—that is, it assumes that the structure of declarative sentences is somehow basic and that questions constitute a variation on the basic pattern rather than an entirely different, unrelated pattern. Notice that in earlier chapters we made the same assumption about imperative sentences and relative clauses, where in each case we assumed a declarative pattern as the underlying structure. We cannot "prove" that these assumptions are correct, but we have support for them both in our intuitions and, more substantially, in the fact that our grammar model, which is based on these assumptions, "works," because it consistently produces grammatical sentences. Unless we find evidence to the contrary, let us continue to act on these assumptions.

Another assumption we have made is that different sentences must have different underlying structures. Consequently, the grammar must have some means of denoting the underlying difference between a declarative sentence (*Howard has been pumping iron*) and an interrogative sentence (*Has Howard been pumping iron?*). In other words, the mood of the sentence needs to be indicated in the underlying structure. Let us add the element of mood to our rule for the auxiliary marker:

13   Aux → **Mood** (Neg) Tense (M) (Perf) (Prog)

$$\text{Mood} \rightarrow \left\{ \begin{array}{l} \text{Dec} \\ \text{Q} \\ \text{Imp} \\ \text{Sbj} \end{array} \right\}$$

These rules add a **_mood marker_** to the auxiliary category to designate each sentence as **_declarative_** (abbreviated **Dec**), **_interrogative_** (**Q**), **_imperative_** (**Imp**), or **_subjunctive_** (**Sbj**).

In addition, the grammar must have a transformational rule to move the auxiliary in forming a yes/no question, which we can tentatively state as follows:

14   **Auxiliary Fronting (T-AuxFront)**: In an interrogative sentence, the first auxiliary verb is moved to the front of the sentence.

With rules 13 and 14, we can now show the derivation of *Has Howard been pumping iron?*

15

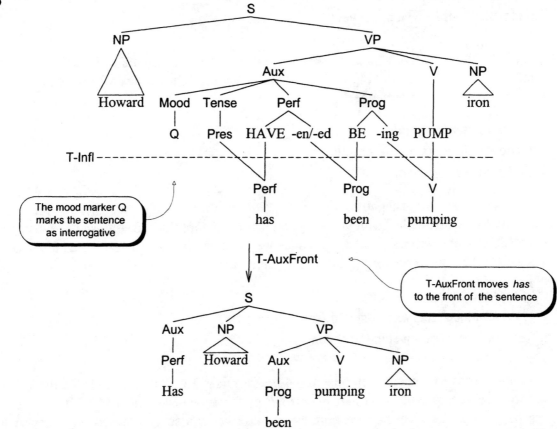

The mood marker Q triggers the T-AuxFront transformation. If the mood marker in the underlying structure had been Dec instead of Q, the fronting transformation would not have been invoked, and the declarative sentence *Howard has been pumping iron* would then have been produced as the spoken form. Once the mood and tense markers have served their purpose, they are deleted and do not appear in the spoken form of the sentence.

Notice that T-AuxFront splits the auxiliary marker in two, detaching the first part (the perfect auxiliary *has*) and moving it to the front of the sentence. The other auxiliary verb, *been*, remains in its original position.

The broken-line method could also have been used to show the operation of T-AuxFront in 15.

Exercises 13.5

1. Underline the auxiliary verbs and the main verb in each of the following yes/no questions. Then show the derivation of each sentence. You may use either a separate tree or the broken-line method to show the operation of T-AuxFront.

   a. <u>Should</u> Noah <u>have built</u> a bigger boat?
   b. Have you been nibbling at the fruitcake?
   c. Is the semester coming to an end?

---

d. Could the soprano have been singing for three hours?

e. Has Jamie ordered a pizza yet?

2. All of the interrogative sentences that we have seen so far contain at least one underlying auxiliary verb. The following three sentences have no auxiliaries. What yes/no questions correspond with these sentences?

a. Meg likes spicy foods.

add DO

b. The bright lights dazzled Stella.

c. Old stories bore Alphonse.

Yes/no questions, like negative sentences, require an auxiliary verb. When an underlying interrogative sentence lacks an auxiliary, one must be supplied. Rephrase the T-Supp rule on page 188 so that it applies to interrogative as well as negative sentences. Then use T-Supp and T-AuxFront to draw trees for the following three questions:

d. Does the bookstore sell toiletries?

e. Did Grandpa receive a postcard from Zimbabwe?

f. Do many students watch the soaps?

(3.) Optional discovery exercise: In question 4 of Exercises 13.3 on page 191, we discovered that negative sentences with the linking verb *BE* or the transitive verb *HAVE* do not require an auxiliary verb. Can yes/no questions with these verbs also be formed without auxiliaries? Consider the following:

a. Are you the black sheep of the family?

b. Have you any wool?

Are *BE* and *HAVE* the only main verbs that can be fronted to form yes/no questions? Can the supporting auxiliary *DO* be used with either of these verbs? Revise T-Supp on page 188 to allow for these exceptions.

Negative Yes/No Questions

We have formed negative sentences and yes/no questions. What happens when we combine them, as in 16?

16   Won't Gertrude be coming to dinner?

Both the first auxiliary (*will*) and the negative (*not*) are fronted in this case. Here is the derivation of 16:

17

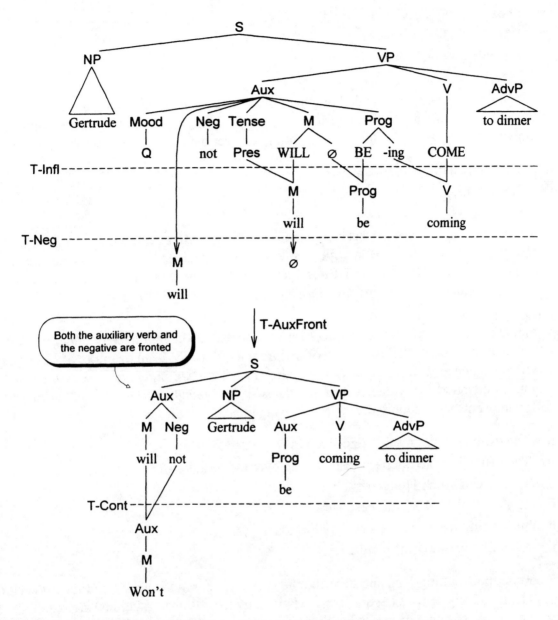

T-AuxFront can be revised as follows:

18   **Auxiliary Fronting (T-AuxFront):** In an interrogative sentence, the first auxiliary verb and Neg (if present) are moved to the front of the sentence.

The T-AuxFront transformation could also be shown using a broken-line diagram.

Exercises 13.6

1. Show the derivations of the following sentences:

---

a. Shouldn't the party have started?

b. Doesn't Andy work here?

c. Haven't we met before?

2. The rules of 13 assume that underlying trees must have a way of specifying the sentence's mood. Why is or isn't this a worthwhile assumption? Using these rules, draw the derivations of the following two sentences. Do they help you to answer the previous question?

a. You study hard.   —statement

b. Study hard!   —command

3. State the imperative sentence that corresponds to the declarative sentence *You sing in the shower*. Then state the negative declarative version of that sentence. Finally, state the negative imperative version. Revise the T-Supp transformation one more time to account for negative imperative sentences, and show the derivation of *Do not sing in the shower*.

(4.) Optional discovery exercise: Every declarative sentence can be followed by a *tag question*, can't it? The phrase "can't it?" at the end of the previous sentence is an example of a tag question. Another sentence with a tag question is *Howard has been pumping iron, hasn't he?* The negative version of that sentence is *Howard hasn't been pumping iron, has he?* For each of the following sentences, supply the appropriate tag question at the end:

a. The officials have been losing sleep over the decision.

b. The officials have not been losing sleep over the decision.

c. Tyrone can speak Hungarian.

d. Lily cannot speak Portuguese.

e. Seth would have remembered my birthday.

f. A small boy drew this picture.

Examine the resulting data and describe the series of operations your mind had to perform in producing the appropriate tag questions. How many steps (transformations) are required? Your answers to these questions must surely impress you. A very great many steps are required for us to produce tag questions, and yet you can state the correct tag question for any given sentence almost instantaneously, can't you? The operation of the grammar in your mind is indeed a wondrous thing. You can also understand, from the complexity of forming tag questions, why most three-year-olds have not yet learned how to produce them. Tags are, in fact, among the last grammatical skills that children master as they learn English.

Wh-Questions

The questions we have so far examined are requests for yes or no answers. Other types of questions call for more substantial replies. These questions are called *"wh"-questions*, because those two letters are found in the words that begin these questions: *who, whom, what, when, where, why, which, whose,* and *how.* The following are all *wh*-questions:

19 a. Who bought a computer?

   b. What has Eloise bought?

   c. To whom can she send e-mail?

   d. When will Eloise be using the computer?

   e. Where did she get such a bargain?

   f. Why didn't she buy a printer too?

   g. How could she afford it?

   h. Which model did Eloise get?

   i. Whose software is she borrowing?

   j. How big is the computer's hard drive?

   k. How quickly did she learn the program?

Interrogative Pronouns

Of the *wh*-words, *who, whom,* and *what* are **interrogative pronouns** (abbreviated **Pro$_Q$**). Interrogative pronouns take the place of underlying noun phrases, just as these same words do when they act as relative pronouns. An interrogative pronoun replaces an **indefinite noun phrase**, an unidentified someone or something whose identity is being sought. We can use the abbreviation *SME* to represent an indefinite someone or something in the underlying structure. Here, for example, is the derivation of *Who bought a computer?*

20

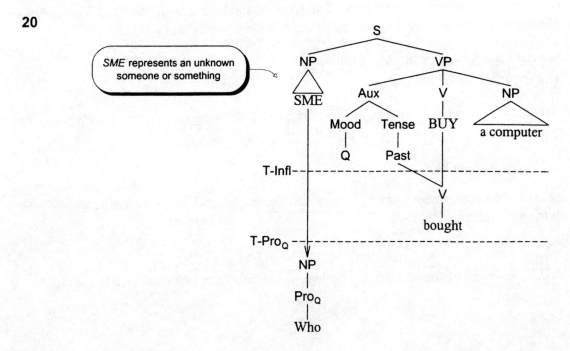

In 20, the underlying indefinite element *SME* represents the unknown quantity, the someone whose identity is being asked for by the question. In the spoken sentence, it is replaced by the interrogative pronoun *who*.

Exercises 13.7

1. Show the derivations of the following *wh*-questions:

   a. Who should have washed these dishes?
   b. What fell from the sky?
   c. What has been happening since I left?
   d. Who was that woman in the red beret?

2. When *SME* occurs in a *wh*-interrogative sentence, as in 20, it is replaced by an interrogative pronoun (Pro_Q) such as *who*. However, when *SME* occurs in a declarative sentence, it is replaced by an **indefinite pronoun (Pro_I)**, such as *someone, something,* or *somebody*. If, for example, the mood marker in 20 were Dec instead of Q, the spoken structure would have become *Someone bought a computer*. Write the rules for the T-Pro_Q and the T-Pro_I transformations. Use the latter to show the derivations of these sentences:

   a. Someone stole the last piece of pie.
   b. The investigators suspect somebody of the crime.
   c. Something is causing interference on my TV.

(3.) Optional discovery exercise: In addition to declarative sentences, indefinite pronouns can also be used in yes/no interrogative sentences. The words *anyone, anything,* and *anybody* are other indefinite pronouns. Show the derivations of the following sentences:

   a. Shouldn't someone pick up the telephone?
   b. Does anyone want lemonade?

   Does the underlying tree for sentence *b* differ from the underlying tree for the following spoken sentence?

   c. Who wants lemonade?

   If it does not, what adjustments might you make to the grammar to differentiate between the two underlying structures?

In 20, *SME* represented the underlying subject of the sentence. Consider now the following sentence:

21   What has Eloise bought?

The person doing the buying is Eloise, so she is the underlying subject of sentence 21. The underlying structure of 20, then, corresponds to the following:

22   Eloise has bought SME

To derive spoken sentence 21, not only is the indefinite element *SME* transformed into the interrogative pronoun *what*, but it is also moved to the beginning of the sentence. *Wh*-questions, as you may have noticed, are very similar to relative clauses. As with relative clauses, when a *wh*-word is not the first word in the clause, it must be moved to become the first word. The T-WH transformation that we used for relative clauses (see page 150) also applies to *wh*-questions. In *wh*-questions, T-AuxFront also applies, so that the following steps are involved in the derivation of 21 (ignoring T-Infl for the moment):

23

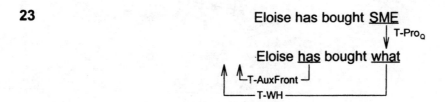

The four T-rules involved in the derivation of 23 are T-Infl, T-Pro$_Q$, T-AuxFront, and T-WH. Here is the complete derivation of *What has Eloise bought?*

24

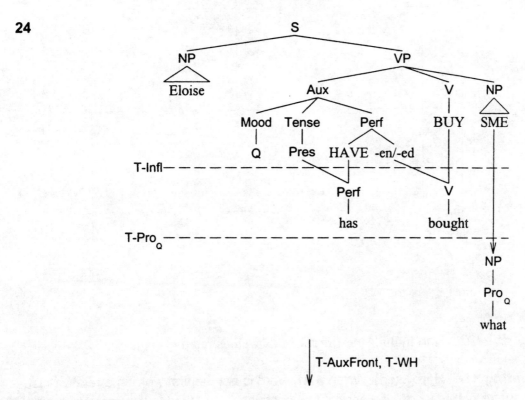

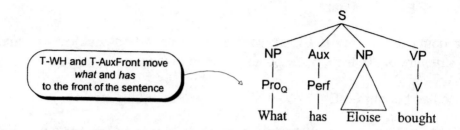

T-WH and T-AuxFront move
what and *has*
to the front of the sentence

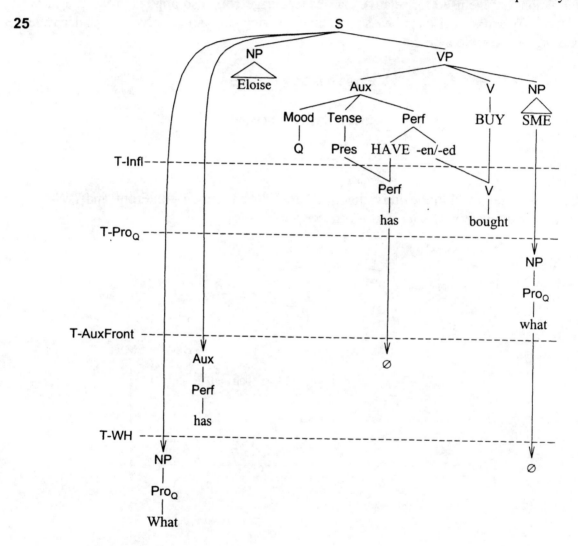

When using a new tree to show the final transformations in a derivation, as in 24, we can save some time by showing the operations of both T-AuxFront and T-WH in the same tree. If we use the broken-line method, however, it is best to show each of these transformations separately:

25

We can now revise T-WH to include *wh*-questions as well as relative clauses:

26   ***Wh*-Fronting (T-WH**, revised): When a *wh*-word is not the first word in a relative clause or a *wh*-question, that word, or a phrase that contains it, is moved to the front of the clause.

Exercises 13.8

1. Show the derivations of the following questions:

   a. What might Stella have been plotting?
   b. Whom has Chloris been dating lately?
   c. What was I thinking?
   d. Whom should the tourists ask for directions?
   e. Who has been complaining about the food?

2. A *wh*-word in a prepositional phrase acts the same in a *wh*-question as in a relative clause. Show the derivations of these questions. You may want to review how *wh*-words in prepositional phrases were moved within relative clauses (starting on page 150).

   a. What has Morey sat on?
   b. With whom will Tammy elope?
   c. Whom can we turn to in an emergency?

3. When an underlying question lacks an auxiliary verb, one is supplied by T-Supp. Show these three derivations:

   a. Whom did Marguerite admire?
   b. What does Charles expect?
   c. On what do you base your assumptions?

   But note that T-Supp is not needed when *SME* is the underlying subject of the sentence:

   d. Who admired Marguerite?

Interrogative Adverbs

The question words *when, where, why,* and *how* are ***interrogative adverbs***. Each replaces an adverbial phrase that contains the indefinite element *SME*. For example, the interrogative adverb *when* replaces an underlying phrase whose approximate meaning is "at some time." Underlying structures, of course, represent concepts rather than spoken words, and we will represent the underlying adverbials in capital letters. Because interrogative adverbs replace adverbials, they might also be called "interrogative pro-adverbials" (compare relative adverbs on page 157). We will abbreviate them as **Pro**$_{Q-A}$. Here is the derivation of *When will Eloise be using the computer?*

27

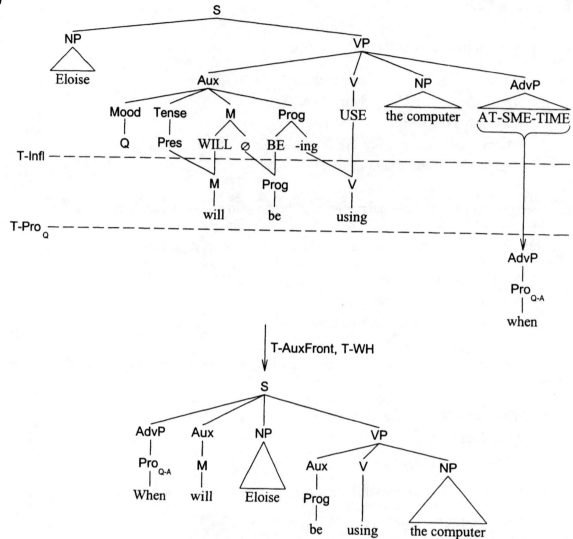

In a similar manner, the adverbial concept *AT-SME-PLACE* becomes the interrogative adverb *where*, *IN-SME-MANNER* becomes *how*, and *FOR-SME-REASON* becomes *why*.

Exercises 13.9

1. Derivation 27 shows the T-Pro$_Q$ transformation creating the interrogative adverb *when*. Is this rule adequate as written, or does it need to be revised in order to do this? Does the T-WH rule need to be revised to accommodate interrogative adverbs?

2. Show the derivations of these questions with interrogative adverbs:

   a. Where has Mitch been storing the supplies?
   b. How can we repay you for your kindness?

c. When will the boat be sailing?

d. Why did Josh insult those thugs?

(3.) Optional discovery exercise: Consider the following sentences:

a. Where is the party?

b. When was the deadline?

Presumably the underlying structure of sentence *a* is *The party is AT-SME-PLACE*. Are our rules adequate to account for the derivations of sentences like *a* and *b*? Take into account your answers to the optional discovery exercises in Exercises 13.3 on page 191 and Exercises 13.5 on page 194. Show the derivations of these two questions.

Interrogative Determiners

Which, what, and *whose* act as **interrogative determiners** (abbreviated **Pro$_{Q-D}$**) when they modify nouns, as in these three questions:

28 a. Which ⎫
   b.   What ⎬ car should Bernie wash?
   c.   Whose ⎭

Each of these *wh*-words replaces an indefinite determiner in the underlying structure. For example, the underlying form of 28a (after T-Infl) corresponds roughly to the declarative sentence *Bernie should wash some car*. Here is the derivation:

29

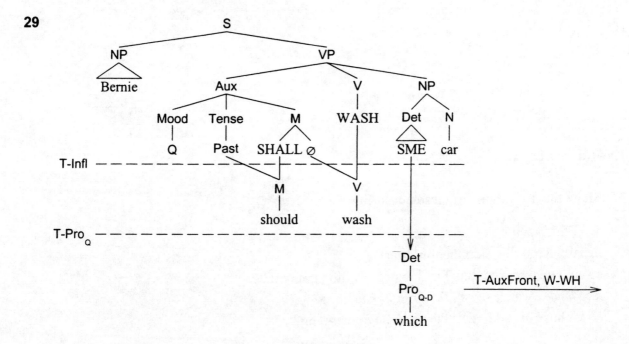

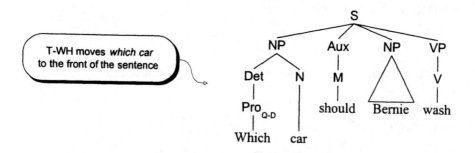

In this derivation, T-Pro$_Q$ replaces *SME* with the interrogative determiner *which*. T-WH then moves not just the *wh*-word but the entire noun phrase, *which car*, to the front of the sentence. *SME* is the underlying form for both *which* and *what*.

Whose is a **possessive interrogative determiner** (abbreviated **Pro$_{Q-D-S}$**). Following is the derivation of *Whose glass is empty?*

30

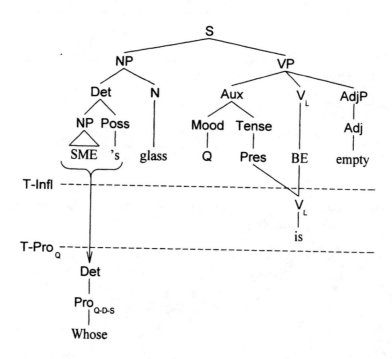

Exercises 13.10

1. Show the derivations of these questions:

    a. Which actor won an Oscar?
    b. What movies did Quentin direct?
    c. In which theater has Frankie been selling popcorn?
    d. Whose watch shows the time in Australia?
    e. Whose birthday will the party be celebrating?

2. The declarative equivalent of the interrogative determiners *what* and *whose* is the **indefinite determiner** *some*, which we can abbreviate as Pro_{I-D}. Show the derivations of the following sentences with indefinite determiners:

    a. Some actor won an Oscar.
    b. Phil ate lunch in some strange truckstop in Nebraska.

   See if you can also determine the derivations of the following sentences with indefinite pro-forms:

    c. Wilma found somebody's wallet.
    d. Cliff put the message somewhere.

3. Each of the sentences below is derived using one or more of the following transformational rules, applied in this relative order:

1. T-Supp	5. $T\text{-}Pro_I$
2. T-Infl	6. T-AuxFront
3. T-Neg	7. T-WH
4. $T\text{-}Pro_Q$	8. T-Cont

   For each sentence, double underline the main verb, and underline each auxiliary verb. State the mood and tense of the sentence. Finally, show the sentence's derivation.

    a. Adam <u>has</u> not <u>been</u> <u>facing</u> reality.   [Mood: Dec   Tense: Pres]
    b. Might Beatrice have misunderstood the question?
    c. Does Chuck need a haircut?
    d. What causes sunspots?
    e. What will the farmer be planting in the field?
    f. Won't Felicity need scissors?
    g. From whom has Greg inherited his money?
    h. What didn't Hilda want in the contract?
    i. What will Isaiah write with?
    j. Don't laugh at Jacqueline.
    k. When is Ken leaving?
    l. Whose cat dug the hole?
    m. Minerva wanted some respect.
    n. What news did the emissary report?

(4.) Optional discovery exercise: Consider the following questions:

    a. *How smoothly* did the meeting go?
    b. *How fresh* is the milk?

The word *how* in both of these sentences is an *interrogative degree modifier* (**Pro$_{Q-Deg}$**). Determine how the italicized phrases are derived, and show the derivations of these sentences.

(5.) Questions that ask for information are called *direct questions*. All the questions we have examined so far have been direct questions. When a sentential-complement clause is introduced by a *wh*-word, it is called an *indirect question*, as in these examples:

a. I wonder *who is kissing her now.*
b. We know *what we like.*
c. Jerry asked *when the show will start.*
d. The women guessed *which box held the treasure.*
e. *What damages the jury would award* remained a mystery.

Unlike direct questions, indirect questions are not requests for information. What differences do you notice between the ways direct and indirect questions are formed? In particular, how are auxiliaries affected in the two kinds of questions? From your experience with sentential-complement clauses in Chapter 5, with relative clauses in Chapter 10, and with *wh*-questions in this chapter, see if you can determine how these indirect questions are formed. Draw the derivations of the five sample sentences.

(6.) The sample sentences in exercise 5 can all be called *"wh"-indirect questions*, because the clauses are introduced by *wh*-words that replace the underlying *SME* marker. Can *yes/no indirect questions* also be formed? Consider the following data: We have seen that for every declarative sentence, there is a corresponding yes/no direct question. For example, the yes/no question corresponding to *The rain will end* is *Will the rain end?* Can a yes/no indirect question be formed from the following underlying structures?

a. I wonder [the rain will end]
b. The children asked [the museum charges admission]

In Chapter 5, we assumed that the words *whether* and *if* were complementizers, generated by phrase-structure rules. Might they instead be added by a transformation? Draw the derivations of sentences *a* and *b*. Are any new T-rules needed to account for them?

14 The Passive Voice

Active and Passive Voice

Verbs can occur in either the active or the passive voice. The difference between the two voices is best described in terms of meaning. When a verb is in the *active voice*, the subject of the sentence performs the action, and the direct object receives the action. When the verb is in the *passive voice*, the subject receives the action, and the performer of the action is stated in a prepositional phrase beginning with the word *by*. Here are examples:

1 a. Olga *ate* the apple.   —*Ate* is in the active voice.

   b. The apple *was eaten* by Olga.   —*Was eaten* is in the passive voice.

As we examine these two sentences, we can make several observations about them. Both sentences describe the same event and communicate the same information. In 1a, however, greater attention seems to be paid to Olga, whereas in 1b, focus is placed on the apple. In the active sentence, 1a, the subject noun phrase *Olga* performed the action—that is, she was the one who did the eating. In the passive sentence, 1b, the subject noun phrase *the apple* received the action—it didn't eat but got eaten. To put it in another way, *the apple*, which is the receiver of the action in both sentences, is the direct object in 1a but the subject in 1b. The doer of the action, *Olga*, is the subject of the active sentence but the object of the preposition *by* in the passive sentence. Finally, we can observe that although the action occurred in the past in both sentences, the past form of the verb *EAT* is used in the active sentence but not in the passive, where the past form of *BE* is used, followed by the *-en/-ed* form of the verb *EAT*.

Verbs in both tenses, with or without auxiliaries, can have active and passive versions. Here are some further examples:

2 a. Veronica *prefers* soft drinks.   —Active, no auxiliary verbs

   b. Soft drinks *are preferred* by Veronica.   —Passive, no auxiliary verbs

3 a. Marlene *can ride* bucking broncos.   —Active, with modal auxiliary

   b. Bucking broncos *can be ridden* by Marlene.   —Passive, with modal auxiliary

4 a. The workers *are repairing* the potholes. —Active, with progressive auxiliary

b. The potholes *are being repaired* by the workers. —Passive, with progressive auxiliary

5 a. The pirates *might have hidden* the treasure. —Active, with modal and perfect auxiliaries

b. The treasure *might have been hidden* by the pirates. —Passive, with modal and perfect auxiliaries

Note carefully the differences between the sentences in each pair. Notice that the same auxiliaries occur in both the active and passive versions, although the passive sentences have an additional auxiliary, a form of *BE*. Be certain that you understand why the *a* sentences are active and the *b* sentences are passive.

Exercises 14.1

Draw two lines under the main verb in each of the following sentences, and draw one line under any auxiliary verbs. Identify each sentence as active or passive. If it is active, state also the corresponding passive version. If it is passive, state its active counterpart. Make certain that the two versions have the same tense and the same auxiliaries. But note: A form of the auxiliary *BE* must be added as you transform an active into a passive sentence and removed as you do the reverse.

1. The tomato <u>was</u> <u>sliced</u> by Willie.   [Passive. Active: *Willie sliced the tomato.*]
2. Jill could have fired Greg.
3. The committee was debating the merits of the new constitution.
4. Common courtesy is observed by all members of this crew.
5. The actors had performed a play by Shakespeare.
6. The decorations will astound you.
7. The joke might have been appreciated by a more sophisticated audience.
8. The boys were being punished by the principal.
9. Evelyn was told a lie by Barney.
10. Tallulah looks up to Marjean.

Deriving Passive Sentences

In each pair of active and passive sentences that you have examined, the two sentences have different word orders and different focuses, but they consist of the same words and communicate the same essential meaning. Linguists do not agree about whether active and passive sentences derive from the same underlying structure, but, for the sake of argument, let us hypothesize that they do, because that is consistent with our assumption that sentences with the same meaning have essentially the same underlying forms. We are always free to consider alternative hypotheses in the future if we discover reasons to do so.

As we have throughout this book, let us assume that an active declarative pattern is the basic form of every underlying sentence. Consequently, we will assume that a passive sentence is a variation on the basic active pattern, rather than the reverse. We can find support for this assumption in our intuition that a *performer-verb-receiver* order (active order) is more "natural" and "basic" in our language than a *receiver-verb-performer* order (passive order). More substantially, we can observe that active sentences occur far more frequently than passive sentences and that children learn to speak active sentences before they learn to speak passive sentences.

Let us hypothesize, then, that active and passive sentences are derived from the same underlying structure, with only a voice marker in the auxiliary to denote the sentence as active or passive. Let us revise our auxiliary rule one more (and final) time:

6   Aux → **Voice Mood (Neg) Tense (M) (Perf) (Prog)**

$$\text{Voice} \rightarrow \left\{ \begin{array}{c} \text{Act} \\ \text{Pass} \end{array} \right\}$$

According to our hypothesis, sentences like 1a and 1b have identical underlying structures, except that 1a has Act (that is, "active") as its voice marker, while 1b has Pass ("passive") as its voice marker. We can also observe that four different steps are required to transform an underlying active structure into a spoken passive sentence. Let us incorporate these steps into a passive transformational rule:

7 **Passive Transformation (T-Pass):** When a sentence is marked as passive, the following four operations are performed:
   a. The underlying subject noun phrase is replaced by the noun phrase that follows the verb.
   b. The passive auxiliary (*BE + -en/-ed*) is added as the final constituent of the auxiliary marker.
   c. The position vacated by the noun phrase that followed the verb is left empty (⌀).
   d. A prepositional phrase, consisting of the preposition *by* and the underlying subject noun phrase, is added to the end of the verb phrase.

This rule seems complex, but the operations it describes will become clear as you experience some examples.

The underlying structure for sentences 1a and 1b is the same, except for the voice marker. The following shows how T-Pass operates on this underlying structure in the derivation of passive sentence 1b, *The apple was eaten by Olga*.

8

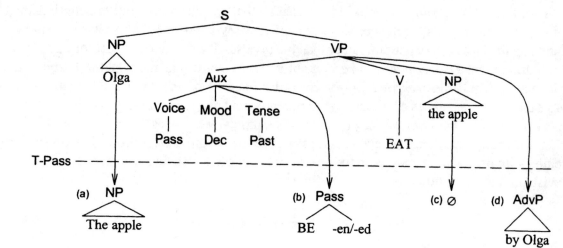

The four steps of **T-Pass** are shown below the broken line. In step *a*, the underlying subject *Olga* is replaced by the underlying direct object *the apple*. In step *b*, the passive auxiliary is added. In *c*, the place formerly occupied by the direct object is left vacant (symbolized by ⊘). Finally, in *d*, the underlying subject *Olga* is added to the verb phrase as the object of the preposition *by*.

    T-Infl can now supply the appropriate verb inflections. Here is the complete derivation of *The apple was eaten by Olga:*

9

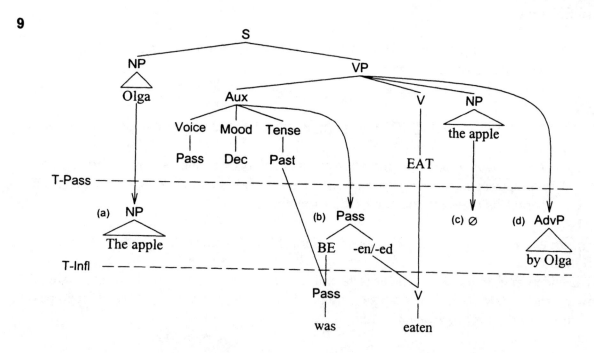

The passive voice marker in the underlying structure triggers the **T-Pass** transformation. Had the voice marker been active instead of passive, T-Pass would not have been performed and the active sentence *Olga ate the apple* would have been produced.

    The passive transformation also works with sentences that have other auxiliary verbs. The derivation of passive sentence 5b, *The treasure might have been hidden by the pirates*, is shown in 10.

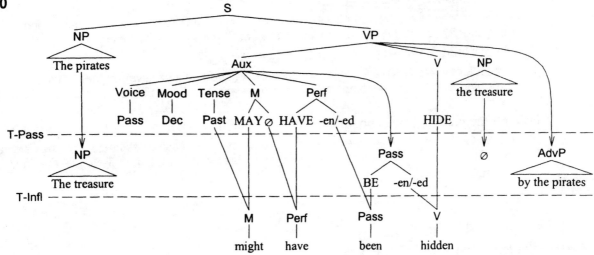

Exercises 14.2

1. For each of the following passive sentences, do the following: (a) Draw two lines under the main verb; (b) Then draw one line under each auxiliary verb; (c) Label each auxiliary verb as to type: M, Perf, Prog, or Pass; (d) State the corresponding active sentence; (e) Finally, show the derivation of each sentence. Remember: Elements will be in active order in the underlying structure, and the passive auxiliary *BE* will not appear in the underlying tree. In determining the underlying subject of a sentence, it is often useful to ask yourself, "Who did it?"

   a. The fortress <u>should</u> <u>have</u> <u>been</u> <u>stormed</u> by the barbarians.
      M   Perf Pass
      [Active: *The barbarians should have stormed the fortress.*]

   b. The mice are being exterminated by the piper.

   c. Lancelot was banished by the king.

   d. The roses could have been sent by a secret admirer.

   e. The elections have been postponed again by the tribunal.

   f. Accidents are caused by carelessness.

   g. The house may be saved by the firefighters.

   h. Gamblers had waged large bets on the game.   [Don't be tricked by this one.]

2. Passive sentences can also be negative or interrogative. Show the derivations of the following sentences:

   a. The fortress should not have been stormed by the barbarians.

      [Except for the Neg element (*not*), this negative passive sentence has the same underlying structure as sentence 1a. In drawing the derivation, perform T-Pass and T-Infl before T-Neg.]

   b. Are the mice being exterminated by the piper?

      [Except for the Mood (Q), this passive yes/no question has the same underlying structure as sentence 1b. Perform T-Pass and T-Infl before T-AuxFront.]

c. Who was banished by the king?

> [Except for the Mood (Q) and the indefinite direct object (*SME*), this passive *wh*-question has the same underlying structure as sentence 1c. Perform T-Pass and T-Infl before T-Pro_Q.]

d. By whom could the roses have been sent?

> [Except for the Mood (Q) and the indefinite subject (*SME*), this passive *wh*-question has the same underlying structure as sentence 1d. Perform T-Pass and T-Infl before T-Pro_Q, T-AuxFront, and T-WH.]

e. Haven't the elections been postponed again by the tribunal?

> [Except for the Mood (Q) and the negative element (*not*), this passive yes/no question has the same underlying structure as sentence 1e. Perform T-Pass and T-Infl before T-Neg, T-AuxFront, and T-Cont.]

Passive Sentences with Indefinite Agents

Not every passive sentence names the agent or performer of the action in a *by*-phrase. Step *d* of T-Pass rule 7 is omitted if the underlying subject is *SME*—that is, if the subject is an indefinite someone or something. Here, for example, is the derivation of the passive sentence *Horseplay is forbidden*:

11

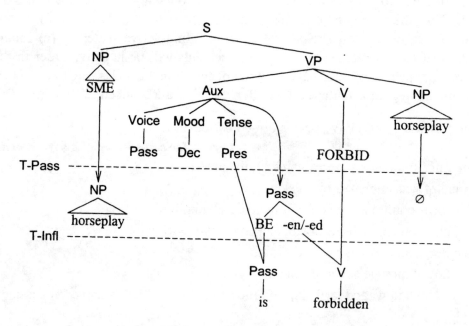

The person or persons doing the forbidding are not specified. Because the underlying subject is an unidentified someone (*SME*), no *by*-phrase is needed in the spoken structure.

Exercises 14.3

1. Revise the passive transformational rule, 7, to account for sentences with indefinite agents.

Chapter 14

2. Underline and label all main and auxiliary verbs in the following sentences. For each, state the equivalent active declarative sentence. Finally, show the derivation of each sentence. Remember: Passive sentences with indefinite agents have *SME* as their underlying subjects.

   a. Soup <u>is</u> <u>served</u> in bowls.   [Active declarative: *Someone (SME) serves soup in bowls*]
           Pass   V

   b. That insult should have been avenged.

   c. The children may be excused.

   d. One step of the passive transformation is omitted with indefinite subjects.

   e. Will taxes be raised?

   f. Rudeness must not be tolerated.

   g. What had been decided?   [The underlying structure has both an indefinite subject (someone = *SME*) and an indefinite object (something = *SME*).]

Passive Sentences with Indirect Objects

Consider the derivation of the passive sentence *A secret was told to Gina by Arnold*. In general terms, its derivation is approximately the following:

12

According to rule 7, our statement of the passive transformational rule, "the noun phrase that follows the verb" in an active sentence is moved forward to become the subject of the passive sentence. Consequently, *a secret*, the noun phrase that follows the verb *told* in the active sentence of 12, is moved forward to become the subject of the passive sentence.

However, "the noun phrase that follows the verb" is not always a direct object. As you recall from Chapter 8, the transformational rule T-IO can move an indirect object forward so that it directly follows the verb. For example, if we apply T-IO to the underlying structure of 12 before we apply T-Pass, the following derivation results:

13

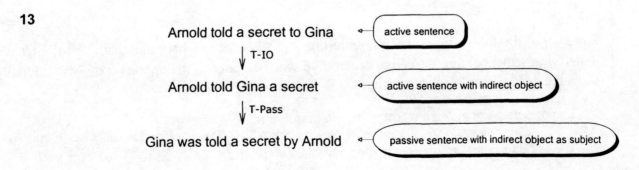

The Passive Voice

In 13 *Gina* is moved forward by T-IO, so that "the noun phrase that follows the verb" is now *Gina*, an indirect object. T-Pass then applies to make this noun phrase the subject of the passive sentence.

Here is the derivation of *Gina was told a secret by Arnold*:

14

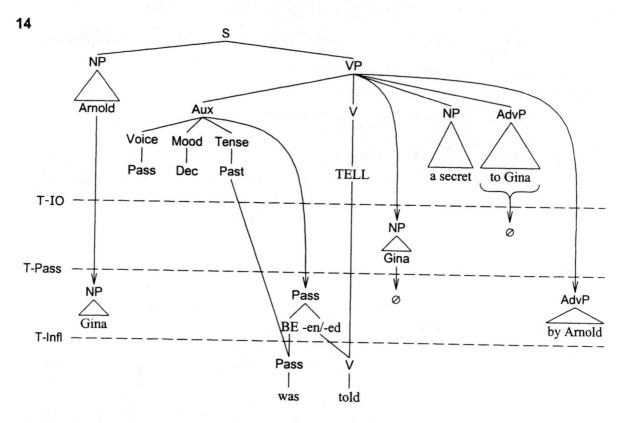

Carefully study derivation **14** to be certain that all the steps in the derivation are clear to you. Note especially the following: (1) The underlying structure, above the first broken line, corresponds with the active sentence *Arnold told a secret to Gina*. (2) Then the first of three transformations, T-IO, moves the indirect object *Gina* in front of the direct object, *a secret*. At this point of the derivation, the structure corresponds with the spoken sentence *Arnold told Gina a secret*. (3) T-Pass then moves the indirect object *Gina* to make it the subject of the passive sentence. (4) Finally, T-Infl assigns the appropriate verb forms to produce the spoken passive sentence *Gina was told a secret by Arnold*.

Exercises 14.4

For each of the following sentences, underline and label the auxiliary and main verbs. State the underlying sentence (i.e., the active declarative sentence prior to the operation of T-IO). Finally, show the derivation of each sentence.

1. The drivers <u>were</u> <u>given</u> a warning by the patrolman.
         Pass   V   [Active declarative before T-IO: *The patrolman gave a warning to the drivers*]
2. The voters will be promised the moon by the candidates.

3. Donnie has been taught a trick by the magician.
4. The future has been shown to Dionne by the psychic.   [Don't be tricked by this one.]
5. The finder of the jewels is being offered a reward.
3. Was the scandal given wide coverage by the press?
4. Who hasn't been told the good news?

Summary and Review: Chapters 12–14

Derivation 14 demonstrates the relative order in which three transformational rules (T-IO, T-Pass, and T-Infl) must be performed. This marks a good time to sum up the current state of our grammar. Here are the phrase-structure rules that we have revised or added since our last summary on page 171, as well as a list of T-rules in the relative order in which they are performed.

15

PS Rules

. . .

$$VP \rightarrow Aux \left\{ \begin{array}{l} V\ (NP) \\ V_L \left\{ \begin{array}{l} NP \\ AdjP_L \\ AdvP_L \end{array} \right\} \end{array} \right\} (AdvP)^+$$

Aux → Voice Mood (Neg) Tense (M) (Perf) (Prog)

$$Voice \rightarrow \left\{ \begin{array}{l} Act \\ Pass \end{array} \right\}$$

$$Mood \rightarrow \left\{ \begin{array}{l} Dec \\ Q \\ Imp \\ Sbj \end{array} \right\}$$

Neg → not

$$Tense \rightarrow \left\{ \begin{array}{l} Pres \\ Past \end{array} \right\}$$

$$M \rightarrow \left\{ \begin{array}{l} WILL \\ SHALL \\ CAN \\ MAY \\ MUST \end{array} \right\} \emptyset$$

Perf → HAVE -en/-ed

Prog → BE -ing

T-Rules

1. T-IO
2. T-Supp
3. T-Pass
4. T-Infl
5. T-Neg
6. T-Pro$_R$
7. T-Pro$_Q$
8. T-AuxFront
9. T-WH
10. T-Cont
11. T-Pro$_{Rx}$
12. T-AdvP
13. T-Imp
14. T-Pro$_P$
15. T-Prt

Exercises 14.5

1. So far we have considered passive sentences in the declarative and interrogative moods. Passive sentences can also be imperative. Show the derivations of these sentences:

   a. Be feared by potential enemies.
   b. Do not be fooled by trick questions.
   c. Be respected for your integrity.   [Underlying: *SME respect HEARER for HEARER's integrity*]
   d. Don't be annoyed.

2. Do we have to revise T-Supp (page 188) in order to derive exercise sentences 1b and 1d?

3. The verb *BE* has very different functions in the following three sentences. Show their derivations:

   a. The boys should have been studying.
   b. The boys should have been good athletes.
   c. The boys should have been punished.

4. The following sentences review the additions to our grammar in Chapters 12 through 14. For each sentence, underline and label all auxiliary and main verbs. State the equivalent active declarative sentence. Finally, draw the derivations.

   a. The lion <u>chased</u> the tiger.   [Active declarative: *The lion chased the tiger.* In your derivation,
           V   show the auxiliary category, including voice, mood, and tense.]
   b. <u>Had</u> the plumbers <u>fixed</u> the leak?
        Perf   V   [Active declarative: *The plumbers had fixed the leak.*]
   c. Maxine did not know about the party.
   d. What caused the earthquake?
   e. Whom did the students elect as secretary?
   f. A panic was caused by the appearance of ghosts.
   g. The pictures might be taken tomorrow.
   h. The poodle should have been given an award by the judges.
   i. Is the new guy liked by the staff?
   j. Who hasn't received a schedule?
   k. What was being demolished by the workers?
   l. Which person will be told the names of the winners?
   m. Where does Kareem shop for groceries?
   n. Whom was this poem written by?
   o. By whom was Astrid shown the secret passageway?
   p. Don't be intimidated by the new technology.

(5.) Optional discovery exercise: Sometimes "the noun phrase that follows the verb" in the underlying structure is an object of a preposition, as in these passive sentences:

a. The chair was sat upon by a giant.
b. The matter was looked into by the panel.
c. The children have been read to by their father.

But other objects of prepositions do not seem able to become the subjects of passive sentences:

d. * The table was rolled off by the pen.
e. * Norway is come from by Olaf.
f. * The bridge has been flowed under by this river for centuries.

Add to the above data by considering still other active sentences in which a verb is followed by a prepositional phrase, and see if the object of the preposition can become the subject of an equivalent passive sentence. Can you determine any principle for when such a transformation can and cannot take place?

(6.) In speaking imperative sentences, we normally delete the underlying subject (*HEARER*), as in *Open the door*. On occasion, to emphasize a command, the subject is sometimes spoken as the pronoun *you*, as in *You open the door right this minute!* Notice that when this is done with a negative imperative sentence (*Don't be late*), we don't say *You don't be late!* but *Don't you be late!* That is, the auxiliary is spoken before, not after, the subject *you*. Decide what transformations are needed in the derivation of *Don't you be late!* and draw the derivation. Does this cause you to reconsider the derivations of sentences 1b, 1d, and 4p on the previous page?

15 Infinitives

Infinitive Verb Forms

We have seen that every English verb can take many different forms. These include an underlying form, such as *BE*, *TALK*, or *SING*, and numerous inflected forms. Inflected forms of the linking verb *BE* are *am*, *is*, *are*, *was*, *were*, *been*, and *being*. Other verbs have fewer inflected forms; for example, inflected forms of *TALK* are *talk*, *talks*, *talked*, and *talking*; and inflected forms of *SING* are *sing*, *sings*, *sang*, *sung*, and *singing*.

The basic, underlying form of a verb is usually known as its ***nonfinite*** (or ***infinitive***) ***form***. In previous chapters, when we showed sentence derivations, we used nonfinite forms, written in uppercase letters, to represent verbs in the underlying structure. The inflection-assigning transformation (T-Infl) then assigned the appropriate ***finite*** (or ***inflected***) ***form*** of the verb to the spoken structure. The terms *finite* and *nonfinite* derive from how these verb forms represent time. Because inflected forms are often related to a particular tense (a limited time), they are called *finite*. In contrast, uninflected forms are not limited to a particular tense and are in that sense "infinite."

You can determine the nonfinite form of any verb by using it in a phrase beginning with the word *to*, as in "I like to *sing*" or "I try to *be* honest." A verb phrase with a nonfinite verb introduced by *to* is known as an ***infinitive phrase***. Infinitive phrases are italicized in the following sentences:

1. a. Hindus believe cows *to be sacred animals*.
    b. Any hopes for the strike *to end quickly* are fading fast.
    c. Stanley is happy *to have a job*.
    d. Mom's dream is for Ruth *to become an orthodontist*.
    e. Ruth intends *to become a philosopher*.
    f. *To err* is human.
    g. Dad requires the kids *to be working*.
    h. For Poirot *to be baffled by a case* was a rarity.
    i. The immigrants struggled *to achieve a better life*.
    j. The manager *to replace Filsner* is Drimble.
    k. It is easy for reporters *to find Rex*.
    l. Rex is easy for reporters *to find*.

The word *to* in infinitive phrases is a different word from the proposition *to* in a sentence like *Josie went to the movies*. In all the sentences of 1, *to* has no meaning of its own, serving only to alert us that an infinitive phrase is being introduced. For that reason, we will call this use of *to* an **infinitive marker**, or **IM**. The part of an infinitive phrase that consists of just the verb and the infinitive marker *to* is often called simply an **infinitive**. In 1a, *to be* is an infinitive.

The infinitive phrases in 1 may seem similar, but, as we shall see, they derive from a great many different underlying structures. This variety makes infinitive phrases among the most interesting and controversial constructions in the English language. We will spend this chapter examining them.

Complement Infinitives

Analyzing the meaning of sentences with infinitives can give us a clue to their underlying structures. First, let us consider three sentences of a type that we studied in a previous chapter. Each contains a complement clause. (Because there will be many references to complements in this chapter, you may wish to review our earlier discussion of complement clauses, which began on page 59.)

2 a. Hindus believe *that cows are sacred animals*.   —sentential-complement clause
   b. Any hopes *that the strike will end quickly* are fading fast.   —nominal-complement clause
   c. Stanley is happy *that he has a job*.   —adjectival-complement clause

We can note the striking similarity in meaning between these complement clauses and the infinitives in sentences 1a–1c (repeated below in 3). Because of this parallelism, the infinitives in these sentences can be called **complement infinitives**.

3 a. Hindus believe cows *to be sacred animals*.   —sentential-complement infinitive
   b. Any hopes for the strike *to end quickly* are fading fast.   —nominal-complement infinitive
   c. Stanley is happy *to have a job*. volunteer   —adjectival-complement infinitive

Infinitives with Raised Subjects

One of our basic principles has been that if two spoken sentences are identical in meaning and similar in form, they are derived from essentially the same underlying structure. If so, we could expect sentences 2a and 3a, for example, both to derive from a structure like the following. (To simplify our presentation, let us temporarily omit the auxiliary category from the verb phrases).

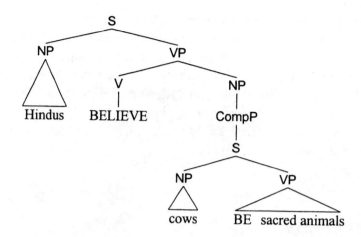

Tree 4 certainly reflects the meaning of both 2a and 3a. To derive the complement clause in spoken sentence 2a from underlying structure 4, we can assume that the T-Infl transformation assigns the inflected form *is* to the verb and perhaps some other transformation supplies the complementizer *that*. (For the latter, we would have to revise our assumption in Chapter 5 that the complementizer is present in the underlying structure).

How then do we derive the infinitive in 3a? One option might be to assume that a transformation simply inserts the infinitive marker into the verb phrase, resulting in the following structure:

5

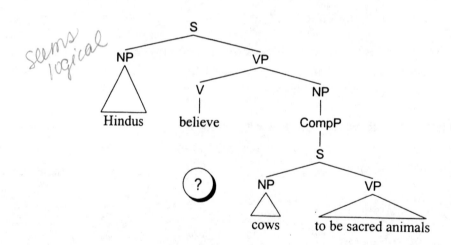

This analysis retains *cows* as the subject of the infinitive phrase *to be sacred animals*, which seems reasonable because that clearly reflects the underlying meaning of the sentence. However, consider what happens if we try to replace *cows* in 5 with a personal pronoun. Because *cows* is the subject of a clause in this analysis, we would expect it to be replaced by the nominative pronoun *they*. Instead, the objective pronoun *them* is the grammatical form in this instance:

6   Hindus believe *them* to be sacred animals.   [not *they*]

Objective-case pronouns, such as *them, her, him, me,* and *us* are used elsewhere only when a noun phrase occurs in an object position, never in a subject position. We can conclude that, if 4 represents the underlying structure of 3a, that structure must somehow be transformed in a way that would move *cows* to an object position in the sentence's spoken structure. That is, we can hypothesize a transformation that would take *cows* out of the lower clause, as in the following:

7

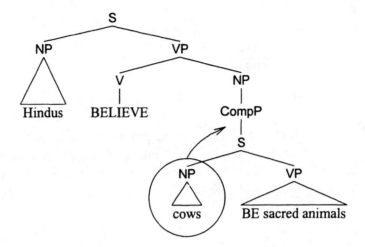

According to this hypothesis, the derivation of **2a** would be this:

8

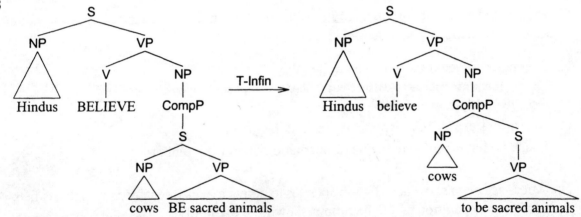

The transformation, which we will call the ***infinitive transformation*** (or **T-Infin**), has raised the noun phrase *cows* from its underlying position as the subject of the lower clause to its spoken-structure position as a constituent of the main clause. Because *cows* follows the main-clause verb *believe*, it is now in an object position, thus allowing its replacement by the personal pronoun *them*. Similar sentences bear out our hypothesis that the underlying subjects of infinitive phrases become objects in the spoken structure:

9 **a.** The mayor expected *her* to head the committee. [not **she*]

    b. Our friends consider *us* to be decent fellows. [not **we*]

    c. Medwick knows *himself* to be conscientious. [not **he*]

The last example, 9c, is especially telling, because it contains a reflexive pronoun, *himself*. According to our hypothesis, its derivation includes the following transformations. (Again, for simplicity, we will ignore T-Infl in showing the derivation.)

10

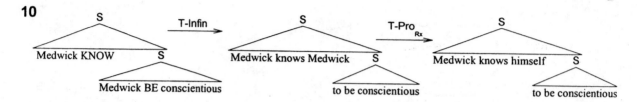

In Chapter 9, we discovered that two identical noun phrases need to occur *within the same clause* for the second of them to become a reflexive pronoun. The two *Medwick*s are in different clauses in the underlying structure of 10, but they become members of the same clause as a result of the T-Infin transformation, making it possible for T-Pro$_{Rx}$ to apply, transforming the second *Medwick* into the reflexive pronoun *himself*.

Exercises 15.1

1. Underline the sentential-complement infinitive phrases in the following sentences. For each, state a corresponding complement-clause sentence.

    a. Sherlock suspected the evidence <u>to be false</u>.
        [Sentence with complement clause: Sherlock suspected *that the evidence was false*.]
    b. George understood cherries to grow on trees.
    c. Authorities expect the suspect to remain at large.
    d. Elaine believes herself to be the reincarnation of an Egyptian priestess.

2. Draw trees as in 8 to show how T-Infin operates to derive exercise sentences 1a–1d. As in 8, you can assume the operation of T-Infl without showing it explicitly.

(3.) Optional discovery exercise: Linguists disagree whether 5 or 8 better represents the spoken structure of sentence 2a. Consider whether the following data lend support to either position.

    a. i. Scientists know that chocolate causes hallucinations.
        ii. That chocolate causes hallucinations is known by scientists.

    b. i.   Scientists know chocolate to cause hallucinations.
        ii. * Chocolate to cause hallucinations is known by scientists.
        iii. Chocolate is known by scientists to cause hallucinations.

All of these sentences presumably derive from the same underlying structure. Sentences *a-i* and *b-i* are active sentences. Sentence *a-ii* is the passive counterpart of *a-i*. However, *b-iii* (not *b-ii*) is the passive counterpart of *b-i*. Use "triangle" trees as in 10 to show the operation of T-Infin and T-Pass in deriving passive sentences *a-ii* and *b-iii*. Do these sentences provide support for the argument that the underlying subject of an infinitive phrase is raised to become the object of the main clause?

Infinitives with Subjects Preceded by "For"

Now consider these additional sentential-complement clauses:

11 **a.** Mom's dream is *that Ruth will become an orthodontist.*   some verbs
   b. The travelers arranged *that the neighbors would feed the dog.*
   c. The spider planned *that the fly would be ensnared.*

Based on the previous sentences we have examined, we would expect corresponding infinitive phrases to be preceded by their underlying subjects. However, these turn out to be ungrammatical:

12 **a.** Mom's dream is **Ruth to become an orthodontist.*
   b. The travelers arranged **the neighbors to feed the dog.*
   c. The spider planned **the fly to be ensnared.*

Instead, in the actual spoken sentences, these noun phrases are preceded by *for*:

13 **a.** Mom's dream is *for Ruth* to become an orthodontist.
   b. The travelers arranged *for the neighbors* to feed the dog.
   c. The spider planned *for the fly* to be ensnared. volunteer

Certain main-clause verbs, such as *be*, *arrange*, and *plan*, seem to take infinitive phrases whose "subjects" are preceded by *for* (as in 13). Certain other verbs, such as *expect*, *consider*, and *know*, take infinitives that are not preceded by *for* (as in 9).

How then are the sentences of 13 formed? Several competing analyses have been proposed. One hypothesis is that T-Infin not only raises the subject noun phrase but also makes it the object of the preposition *for*. Under this hypothesis, sentence 13a would be derived as follows:

14

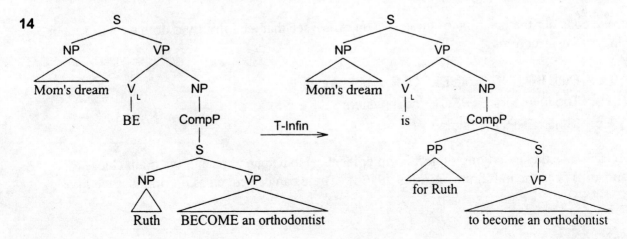

Let us adopt this hypothesis for now. You will have an opportunity to consider alternative hypotheses in an upcoming discovery exercise (beginning on page 226).

Exercises 15.2

1. Underline infinitive phrases in the following sentences. Then draw trees to show their derivations. As in 14, you can draw triangles, and you can assume the operation of T-Infl without showing it explicitly.

    a. Harry's fantasy is for the Cubs to win the World Series.
    b. Benedict prayed for the Visigoths to spare Rome.
    c. One goal of the rehearsals was for all students to sing the same notes.

    An infinitive phrase can also begin a sentence:

    d. For an experiment to work the first time is unprecedented.
    e. For Smalley to have any chance against Biggers will take great luck.

2. With some verbs, the use of *for* seems optional. Show derivations of these two sentences:

    a. We need for everyone to remain calm.
    b. I need you to help me.

Infinitives with Understood Subjects

In some sentences, no noun phrase at all precedes an infinitive:

15 a. Ruth intends *to become a philosopher*.
  b. The investors expect *to make a fortune*.
  c. *To err* is human.

If we consider the meaning of these sentences, we see that the infinitives do have subjects in their underlying structures:

16 a. Ruth INTEND [Ruth BECOME a philosopher]
  b. The investors EXPECT [the investors MAKE a fortune]
  c. [SME ERR] BE human

In each case the underlying subject is either identical to a noun phrase in the main clause (as in 16a and 16b) or is the indefinite *SME* (as in 16c). These can be spoken as pronouns if we like:

17 a. Ruth intends *for herself* to become a philosopher.

   b. The investors expect *themselves* to make a fortune.

   c. *For someone* to err is human.

But we also have the option, as 15 shows, to delete the underlying subjects altogether from the spoken structure. Here is the derivation of 15a:

18

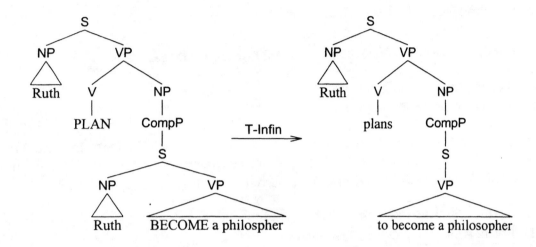

We can now summarize what we have discovered about the infinitive transformation:

19   **Infinitive Transformation (T-Infin)**: When an embedded clause is spoken as an infinitive phrase, its underlying subject is removed from the clause:
   - If the main-clause verb is of the type that includes *believe*, *expect*, and so on, the subject of the embedded clause is raised to become an object of the main clause.
   - If the main-clause verb is of the type that includes *be*, *plan*, and so on, the subject of the embedded clause is raised to become the object of the preposition *for*.
   - With many main-clause verbs, the underlying subject of the embedded clause can be deleted if it is *SME* or if it is identical to a noun phrase in the main clause.

Exercises 15.3

1. Underline the infinitive phrases in the following sentences. Then draw trees to show their derivations. As in 18, you can assume the operation of T-Infl without showing it explicitly.

   a. Dunwiddy tried <u>to join the Marines</u>.
   b. Everybody wants to be a comedian. volunteer
   c. To know Gertrude is to love her.

2. Not all main-clause verbs allow the subject of an infinitive to be deleted. Decide which of the following underlying structures allow the deletion and which do not, and draw trees to show the derivations.

    a. Flanders LIKE [Flanders WEAR loud ties]
    b. Marilyn BELIEVE [Marilyn BE a genius]
    c. The commandos DISCOVER [the commandos BE in a trap]
    d. Axelrod VOLUNTEER [Axelrod GO first]

(3.) Optional discovery exercise: Consider the following sentences:

    a. Portia asked the judge his name.
    b. Portia asked the judge to show mercy.

We recognize *the judge* in sentence *a* to be an indirect object. Is it also true that *the judge* in sentence *b* is an indirect object? That is, is sentence *b* derived from underlying structure *c* using T-IO and T-Infin, or is it derived from underlying structure *d*, using only T-Infin?

    c. Portia ASK [the judge SHOW mercy] of the judge
    d. Portia ASK [the judge SHOW mercy]

Give your reasons for concluding whether *c* or *d* is the underlying structure of *b*, and show the derivation of that sentence.

(4.) Optional discovery exercise: Infinitives have aroused much controversy. Linguists debate about their structure, and the infinitive transformation in 19 is only one of many hypotheses that have been proposed to account for their formation. Let us consider three conflicting analyses of the sentence *Cassie hoped for the skies to clear*. Your task is to jump into the controversy and see if you find reasons to prefer one over the other two. (Derivations in this chapter, such as in 14 above, have been based on analysis *b*.)

    a.

b.

c.

Underlying structure:

- Analyses *a* and *b* assume the same underlying structure as for the complement-clause sentence *Cassie hoped that the skies would clear*. The word *for* is not present in the underlying structure.

- Analysis *c* assumes an underlying structure like that for the sentence *The workers hoped for a raise*. The preposition *for* is present in the underlying structure.

Spoken structure:

- Analysis *a* treats *for* as a complementizer, not a preposition, and *the skies* continues to be the subject of the lower clause in the spoken structure.

  Pro: This is the simplest analysis, requiring the least transformational change. It most closely parallels the spoken structure of *Cassie hoped that the skies would clear*.

Infinitives   227

Con: *For* is used elsewhere as a preposition (*Cassie hoped for good weather*). Also, if *the skies* remains in a subject position, why can't it be replaced by the subject pronoun *they* rather than the object pronoun *them*?

- Analysis *b* makes *the skies* the object of the preposition *for*.

    Pro: Making *the skies* the object of a preposition is consistent with *them* being in the objective case.

    Con: Cassie did not hope "for the skies."

- Analysis *c* treats the entire underlying clause as the object of the preposition *for* in both underlying and spoken structures.

    Pro: It parallels other expressions with "hoped for," such as *Cassie hoped for good weather*. It also accounts for sentences that have no equivalent complement clauses, such as *Cassie waited for the skies to clear*. Third, the infinitive transformation works here exactly as in 8.

    Con: It does not account for the similarity of complement clauses as in *Cassie hoped that the skies would clear*. Also, it is less well motivated in deriving a sentence such as *For the skies to clear would be pleasant*. Finally, it doesn't account for the absence of *for* in *Cassie hoped to work outdoors*.

Nominal and Adjectival Complements

As you would expect, nominal-complement infinitives, such as 20a, and adjectival-complement infinitives, such as 20b, derive in the same way as sentential complements.

20 a. Any hopes *for the strike to end quickly* are fading fast.   —nominal complement

    b. Stanley is happy *to have a job*.   —adjectival complement

A nominal complement follows and modifies a noun:

21

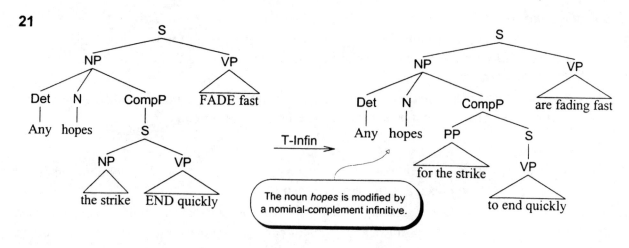

An adjectival complement follows and modifies an adjective:

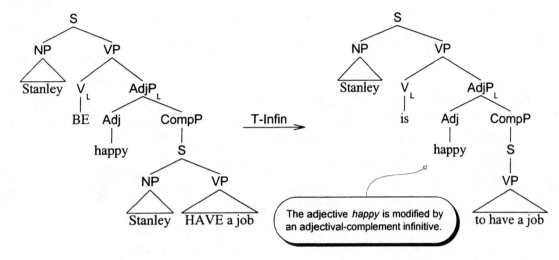

Exercises 15.4

Underline each infinitive phrase in the following sentences, and label it as a sentential complement, a nominal complement, or an adjectival complement. Draw trees to show the derivation of each sentence. You can assume the operation of **T-Infl** without showing it as a separate step.

1. The junta issued an urgent plea for the rebels <u>to surrender</u>.
   [nominal complement: modifies the noun *plea*]
2. Martina is eager <u>to enter the tournament</u>.   [adjectival complement: modifies the adjective *eager*]
3. Dasher was unwilling for Rudolf to join the team.
4. Shy people hate to attract attention.
5. Christina had a notion to get a tattoo.
6. The mechanic was able to fix the car.
7. A reluctance to handle slimy objects was the biologist's undoing.
8. For both sides to apologize would indicate a possibility for the partners to get along.

The Auxiliary Category in Infinitive Phrases

Until now, in looking at infinitive phrases, we have ignored the auxiliary category, with its markers for voice, mood, tense, and auxiliary verbs. We can now give it our attention.

   If we test the possibilities, we discover that infinitives can be either active (*to love*) or passive (*to be loved*), and they can be either positive (*to be*) or negative (*not to be*). We can also have perfect infinitives (*to have eaten*) and progressive infinitives (*to be eating*) but not modal infinitives (**to can eat*). Neither mood nor tense has any effect on the verb's spoken form. We can now revise our rule for the auxiliary category to include the formation of infinitives. Because modals never occur

---

together with infinitives, we can make modals and infinitives alternative choices in the auxiliary. The infinitive marker IM can be used to indicate an infinitive:

23

$$\text{Aux} \rightarrow \text{Voice Mood (Neg) Tense} \left\{ \begin{array}{c} \text{(M)} \\ \text{IM} \end{array} \right\} \text{(Perf) (Prog)}$$

$$\text{IM} \rightarrow \text{to} \; \varnothing$$

In addition to the word *to*, the IM category includes the null sign ∅, which signifies that the first verb in an infinitive is uninflected. We can now show in detail the derivations of infinitives. Here is the derivation of *Dad requires the kids to be working*.

24

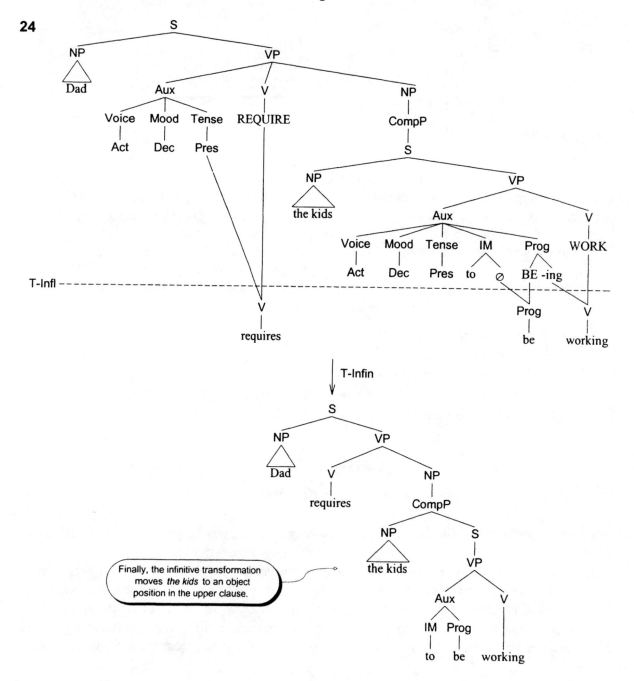

And how are passive infinitives formed? Consider the derivation of this sentence: *For Poirot to be baffled by a case was a rarity.* As always with passives, we assume an active underlying structure:

25   [A case BAFFLE Poirot] BE a rarity

This structure is first transformed by the passive transformation (T-Pass), followed by T-Infl and T-Infin. Here is the detailed derivation:

26

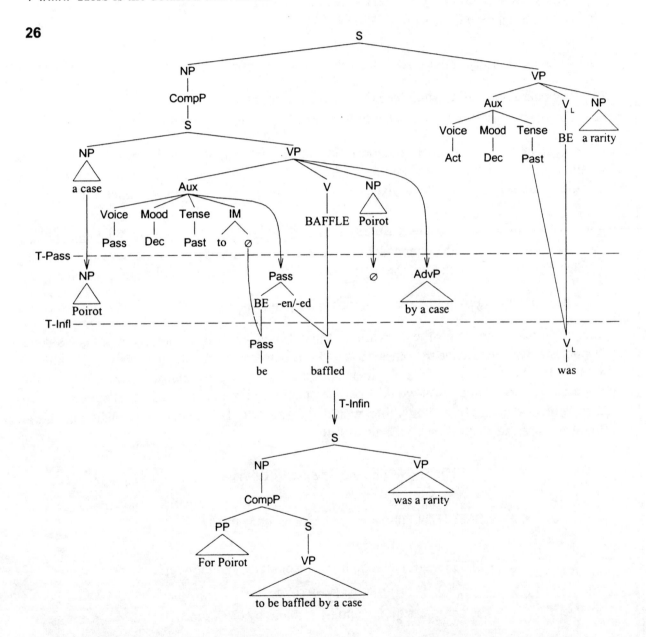

Notice that both the main verb *BE* and the embedded verb *BAFFLE* are marked as being in the past tense in the underlying structure. This tense designation causes the main verb's spoken form to change to the finite form *was*, but it has no effect on the infinitive, which remains nonfinite (*to be*).

Exercises 15.5

1. Show the derivation of each of the following spoken sentences. Use the rules of 23 to generate the auxiliary category for verbs, and show all transformations.

    a. Coworkers suspected Thornbloom to have been taking bribes for years.
    b. To be addressed by the queen is an honor.
    c. Friends were glad for Cyrus to have been promoted.
    d. Dolly has an urge to be sailing.

2. Show the derivations of these sentences with negative infinitives.

    a. The board required the parolee not to leave the country.
    b. The boss hates for customers not to be treated with courtesy by the staff.

    The negative-movement transformation T-Neg appears to be optional with infinitives. Sentences *a* and *b* result if T-Neg is not applied. Alternatively, T-Neg could be applied to move the infinitive marker forward (*to not leave the country, to not be treated with courtesy*).

(3.) Optional discovery exercise: In derivations such as 24 and 26, we assumed that T-Infl operates on the verb phrases in both upper and lower clauses simultaneously. Consider now the following spoken sentence, in which both the main verb and the infinitive are in the passive voice:

   The song was thought to have been inspired by the tragedy.

Can our model account for the derivation of this sentence? If it cannot, we will need a better hypothesis. One alternative hypothesis is that T-rules operate cyclically in a derivation, applying first to the lower clause and only then applying to the upper clause. According to this hypothesis, T-Pass and T-Infl would first operate on the lower clause of our sample sentence, then T-Infin would apply, and only then would T-Pass and T-Infl operate on the upper clause. In other words, its derivation would be as follows:

SME THINK [the tragedy INSPIRE the song]

        ↓ T-Pass, T-Infl (on the lower clause)

SME THINK [the song to be inspired by the tragedy]

        ↓ T-Infin

SME THINK the song [to be inspired by the tragedy]

        ↓ T-Pass, T-Infl (on the upper clause)

The song was thought [to be inspired by the tragedy]

Draw trees to see which hypothesis is better able to account for the derivation of this sentence.

Adverbial Infinitives

The infinitives we have examined so far have all been complements, derived from the same underlying structures as complement clauses. Other classes of infinitives exist as well. Consider the following sentence:

27   The immigrants struggled *to achieve a better life*.

The italicized phrase is an ***adverbial infinitive***, because it modifies the verb *struggled*. Adverbials describe how, when, where, or why a verb's action occurs. In 27, the infinitive tells us *why* the immigrants struggled. We can paraphrase the infinitive phrase in 27 as an adverbial clause:

28   The immigrants struggled *so they could achieve a better life*.

Here is the derivation of 27. Note the adverbial structure in the underlying tree. For simplicity, the derivation again assumes the operation of T-Infl without showing it explicitly.

29

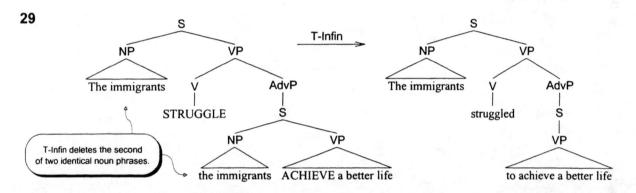

Adverbial infinitives can be derived by the T-Infin transformation (which we formulated in 19 on page 225). One provision of that rule is that "the underlying subject of the embedded clause can be deleted if . . . it is identical to a noun phrase in the main clause." Because *the immigrants* appears in the underlying structure of both clauses, T-Infin deletes that noun phrase from the lower clause.

In grammar, as in life, things are not always what they seem, and the spoken form of a sentence may be quite different from its underlying structure. Consider now the following two spoken sentences, which seem identical in form. Despite these surface similarities, one has a complement infinitive, while the other has an adverbial infinitive:

30 a. Margot expected Les *to welcome the visitors*.   —sentential complement infinitive
   b. Margot selected Les *to welcome the visitors*.   —adverbial infinitive

Notice that 30a can be paraphrased as a complement-clause sentence, while 30b cannot:

31 a. Margot expected that Les would welcome the visitors.
   b. *Margot selected that Les would welcome the visitors.

Conversely, sentence 30b can be paraphrased as an adverbial clause, while 30a cannot:

32 a. *Margot expected Les so he would welcome the visitors.

   b. Margot selected Les so he would welcome the visitors.

Another property of adverbials is that they can be moved to the front of a sentence by the adverbial transformation (T-AdvP). Notice that the complement infinitive in 30a cannot be moved in this way, but the adverbial infinitive in 30b can be moved:

33 a. *To welcome the visitors, Margot expected Les.

   b. To welcome the visitors, Margot selected Les.

Consequently, the two sentences are indeed different and have these underlying structures:

34 a. Margot EXPECT [Les WELCOME the visitors]   — complement structure

   b. Margot SELECT Les [(so) Les WELCOME the visitors]   — adverbial structure

Here is the derivation of 30b, with its adverbial infinitive. T-Infin deletes the second of two occurrences of *Les*:

35

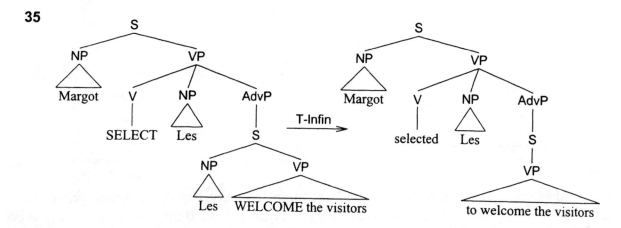

Exercises 15.6

1. Underline the infinitive phrases in these sentences, and state whether each is a complement infinitive or an adverbial infinitive. Then state the sentence's underlying structure, as in 34.

    a. Megan used gum <u>to fix the leak</u>.
        Adverbial. Underlying structure: *Megan USE gum [(so) Megan FIX the leak]*

    b. Friends supposed Marina <u>to be happy</u>.
        Complement. Underlying structure: *Friends SUPPOSE [Marina BE happy]*

    c. Roger needed to lose weight.

    d. Roger dieted to lose weight.

    e. I want you to avoid me.

    f. The mayor appointed Calstrom to be police commissioner.

2. Draw trees to show the derivations of the sentences in exercise 1. As in 29 and 35, you can use triangles and can assume the operation of T-Infl without showing it.

3. Draw trees to show the derivation of the following imperative sentence. For this derivation, include the Aux category and show the operation of T-Infl.

   Draw trees to show the derivation of this sentence.   [yes, this one]

Relative Infinitives

Infinitive phrases are derived from embedded clauses, but not all are derived from complement or adverbial clauses. Consider the infinitives in these sentences:

36 a. The manager *to replace Filsner* is Drimble.
   b. Kathleen recommended a book for the children *to read*.

We can call these ***relative infinitives*** because they derive from underlying relative clauses. That is, their underlying structures are much like those of the following two sentences with relative clauses:

37 a. The manager *who should replace Filsner* is Drimble.
   b. Kathleen recommended a book *that the children might read*.

The sentences of both 36 and 37 have these underlying structures:

38 a. The manager [the manager REPLACE Filsner] BE Drimble
   b. Kathleen RECOMMEND a book [the children READ a book]

To form the relative-clause sentences of 37, T-Pro$_R$ transforms a noun phrase in the embedded clause to a relative pronoun (*who, whom, that,* and so on). To form the infinitive phrases of 36, T-Infin deletes these very same noun phrases. Here is the derivation of 36a:

39

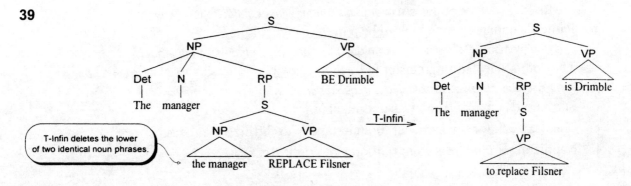

Notice the relative clause structure in the underlying tree of 39.

In all the sentences we have examined so far in this chapter, T-Infin operated either by deleting the lower of two identical noun phrases or else by raising the lower subject to an object position in the main clause. In deriving 36b, it does both:

40

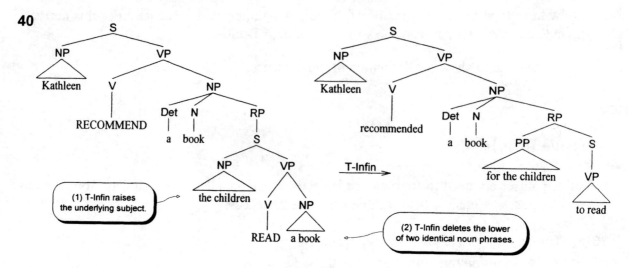

Exercises 15.7

1. Draw trees, as in 39 and 40, to show the derivations of the following sentences with relative infinitives.

   a. Chrissy posed a riddle for Tim to solve.
   b. Corinne knows the very person to represent our interests.
   c. The formulas for the class to memorize for the quiz are in the textbook.

2. Underline each infinitive phrase in the following sentences, and decide if it is a relative infinitive, a complement infinitive, or an adverbial infinitive. For each, state a corresponding spoken sentence with a clause instead of an infinitive phrase.

   a. The delegates discovered the leader <u>to unite the party</u>.
      > Relative. *The delegates discovered the leader who could unite the party.*
   b. Parnell's opponent found her <u>to be a tireless campaigner</u>.
      > Complement. *Parnell's opponent found that she was a tireless campaigner.*
   c. The voters selected Lugmeister <u>to be their mayor</u>.
      > Adverbial. *The voters selected Lugmeister so he would be their mayor.*
   d. For Andie to marry Hugh was unthinkable.
   e. The next task for the gardener to undertake is to fertilize the roses.
   f. Napoleon sent the hussars to reinforce the right flank.

(3.) Optional discovery exercise: Consider this hypothesis:

> <u>Hypothesis</u>: Derivation 40 is in error in claiming that T-Infin performs two operations (deleting and raising) in that sentence. Instead, the deletion of *a book* in that derivation (and the deletion of *the manager* in derivation 39) is actually accomplished by T-Pro$_R$, which in forming a relative infinitive deletes the very same noun phrase that it would transform into a relative pronoun if it were forming a relative clause. The true derivation of 36b should be this:

Kathleen RECOMMEND a book [the children READ <u>a book</u>]

T-Pro$_R$

Kathleen RECOMMEND a book [<u>the children</u> READ ∅]

T-Infin

Kathleen recommended a book for the children [to read]

According to this hypothesis, how would the following sentences be derived?

a.   Rochelle has a report to write.

b.   A man to admire is Rupert.

Do these sentences lend support to the hypothesis?

Extraposed Infinitives

I have saved the most unusual class of infinitives for last. Consider these infinitive phrases:

41 a. *For reporters to find Rex* is easy.

   b. It is easy *for reporters to find Rex*.

   c. Rex is easy *for reporters to find*.

The three spoken sentences of **41** paraphrase each other, and our past experience leads us to hypothesize that they derive from essentially the same underlying structure. We recognize a sentential-complement infinitive in **41a**, which we know to have this underlying structure:

42   [Reporters FIND Rex] BE easy

Consequently, let us assume that all three sentences of **41** derive from underlying structure **42**.

   But wait!, you might say. Sentence **41c** looks like an adjectival-complement infinitive. Compare it with a similar looking adjectival-complement infinitive:

43 a.   Rex is eager *for reporters to interview him*.   — adjectival-complement infinitive

   b.   Rex is easy *for reporters to find*.   — ?

Sentence 43a is indeed a straightforward adjectival-complement infinitive, with an infinitive phrase modifying the adjective *eager*. It also corresponds to a spoken sentence with an adjectival-complement clause:

44   Rex is eager *that reporters interview him.*   —adjectival-complement clause

Note, however, that there is no such corresponding clause for 43a:

45   *Rex is easy that reporters find.

As another point of comparison between 43a and 43b, note that the adjective in 43a directly describes Rex: We can say that Rex is eager. With 43b, however, we cannot say that Rex is easy. That adjective does not directly describe him at all. What is easy is not Rex himself but the action described in the infinitive phrase: for reporters to find Rex. *That* is what is easy.

We have good reason, then, to claim that 43b is not an adjectival-complement infinitive. Let us return to our original hypothesis that all three sentences of 41 derive from underlying structure 42. Let's see if we can discover how they are derived.

We already know that 41a, with its sentential-complement infinitive, is derived as follows:

46

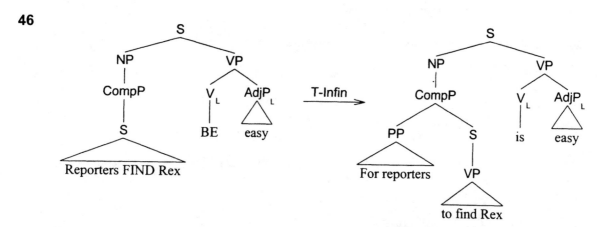

Now let us consider sentence 41b, *It is easy for reporters to find Rex.* In order to derive this sentence from underlying structure 42, two steps seem necessary, and we can describe each as a transformational rule.

First, we must move the complement (*Reporters FIND Rex*) to the end of the sentence. Movement of a complement from one position to another is called **extraposition,** a procedure that we can state formally as the **extraposition transformation:**

47   **Extraposition (T-Extra)**: A sentential-complement clause can be removed from the subject noun phrase and placed in a complement position at the end of the main clause.

T-Extra works as follows:

48   [Reporters FIND Rex] BE easy

Second, we must account for the word *it* in sentence 41b. *It* looks like a personal pronoun, but, if so, what noun phrase does it "stand for"? In fact, *it* appears to have no underlying meaning at all in this sentence, just like the word *it* in such sentences as *It is raining* or *It is wintertime*. In all of these cases, *it* does not seem to be a true pronoun. Instead, it seems to be present for no other purpose than to provide a subject when a sentence lacks one. Let us call such a word an *expletive* (abbreviated **Expl**), a dummy marker inserted as a grammatical place-filler. We can state this operation as a transformational rule:

49 **Expletive Insertion (T-Expl)**: Insert an expletive when one is needed to fill an empty noun phrase.

These two T-rules enable us to derive 41b. A broken-line diagram can show these steps clearly:

50

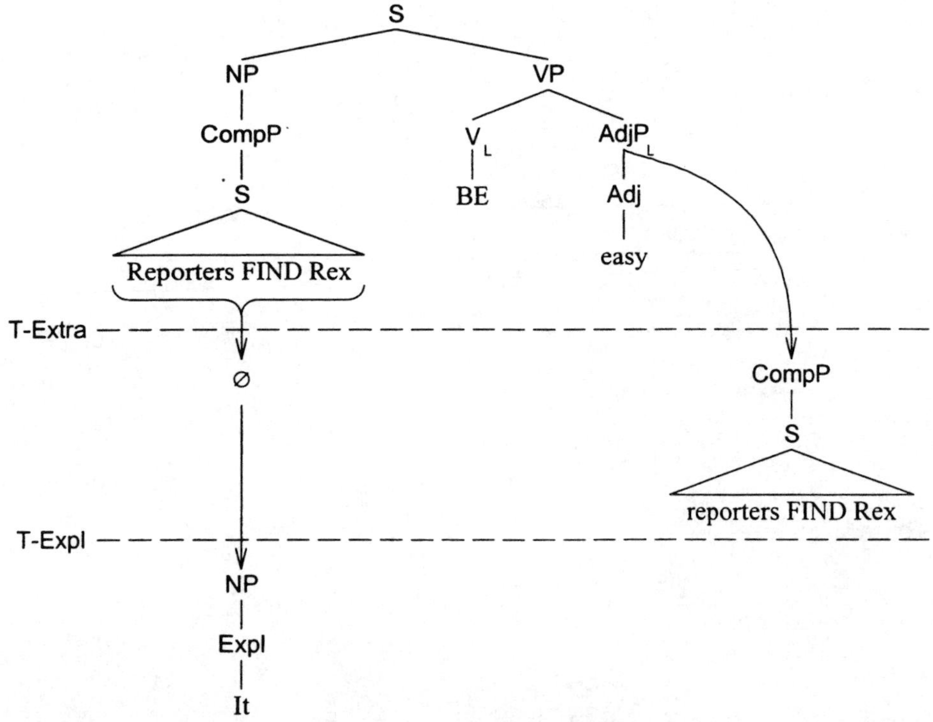

We can now apply T-Infin (and of course T-Infl) to produce spoken sentence 41b:

51

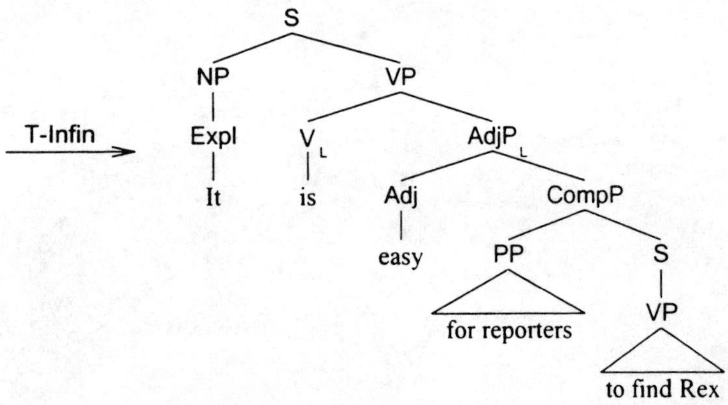

Having accounted for 41a and 41b, it only remains for us to derive 41c, *Rex is easy for reporters to find*. In 50, we filled the empty subject position with an expletive. If, instead, we were to fill that position with the noun phrase *Rex*, the result would be 41c. That is, we need one more transformational rule:

52 **Raising from an Extraposed Infinitive Phrase (T-Raise/Extra)**: After a complement has been extraposed from a subject position, its object noun phrase may be raised to fill the empty subject position in the main clause.

If this transformation is applied, we can derive 41c:

53

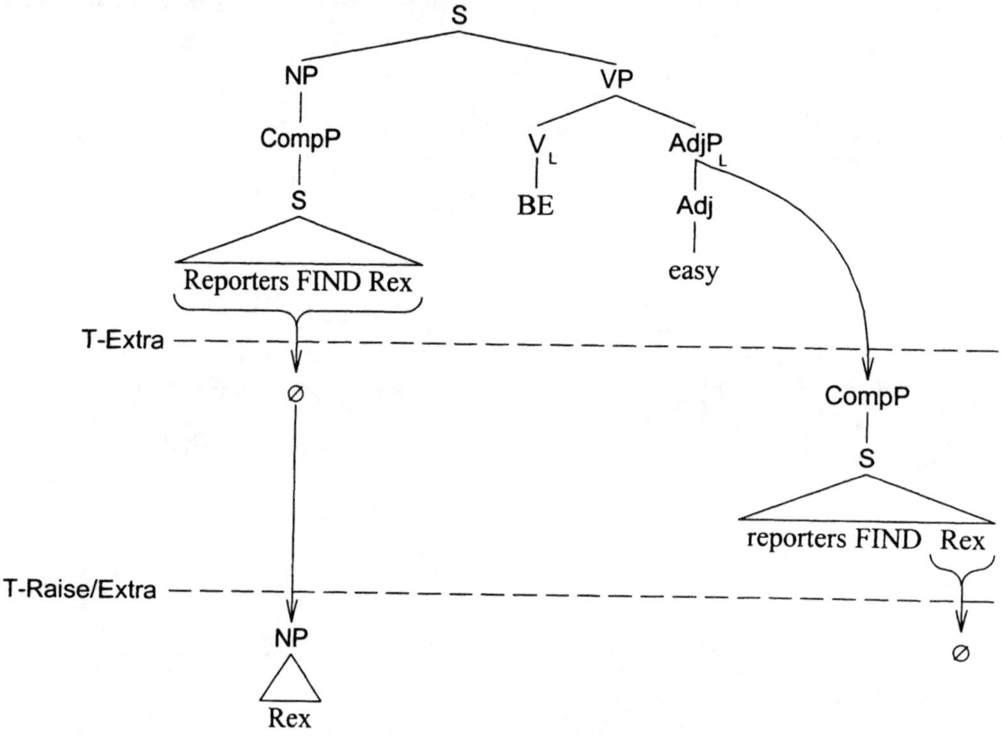

The final step in the derivation is to apply T-Infin (and T-Infl) and so produce spoken sentence 41c:

54

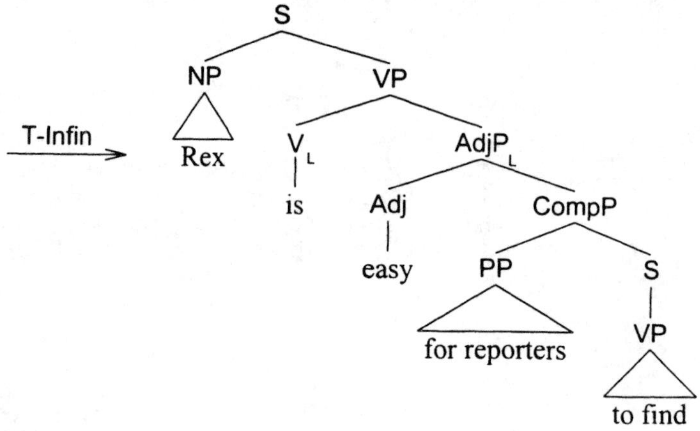

We have now accounted for the sentential-complement infinitive in sentence 41a, as well as the two extraposed infinitives in sentences 41b and 41c. All derive from the same underlying structure.

Exercises 15.8

1. Show the derivations of the following sentences with extraposed infinitives:

   a. It is unusual for Eudora to smile.
   b. It was unfortunate for Placido to have lost his voice.
   c. Virginia was pleasant to talk to.
   d. The lawn is hard for the kids to mow.
   e. It is infuriating to make stupid mistakes.

2. Decide whether the infinitive phrases in the following sentences are true adjectival-complement infinitives or are extraposed infinitives.

   a. These oysters are impossible for us to pry open.
   b. Chauncey is keen for the cricket match to begin.
   c. I will be sad to reach the end of this class.
   d. Derivations can be fun to draw.

(3.) Optional discovery exercise: In addition to extraposed infinitives that resemble adjectival complements, some other extraposed infinitives resemble sentential and nominal complements. Devise derivations to account for the following sentences:

   a. It saddens me to learn of your misfortunes.
   b. It was a pleasure to talk to Virginia.
   c. The lawn is a nightmare for the kids to mow.

(4.) Optional discovery exercise: In addition to *it*, the word *there* can also act as an expletive. Speculate about the derivations of the following three sentences:

   a. There are homemade cookies on the counter.
   b. There is a storm coming.
   c. There should have been more security guards on hand.

The expletive *there* is a different word from the place adverb *there*, as in *There (not here) is where he lives*. Identify each occurrence of *there* in the following sentences as either an expletive or an adverb:

   d. There is a cow over there.
   e. There is some money missing.

f. Eureka! *There* is the missing money!

g. There go the fireworks.

(5.) Optional discovery exercise: Speculate about the derivations of these sentences:

a. It is sad that this chapter is almost over.

b. It was clever of you to bring a spare key.

c. Ebenezer is a hard man to cheat.

[Hint for 5c: Consult the pattern "Relatives with Raised Adjectives" on page 243.]

d. Hopes are fading fast for the strike to end quickly.

Summary of Principal Infinitive Patterns

We have examined infinitives in greater detail than any other construction—and we have found in them far greater variety and complexity. Having a general understanding of how infinitives are formed is probably more important than memorizing every pattern. Nevertheless, at this point you may wish to review the principal infinitive patterns that we have examined. Here are sample sentences in each pattern and their approximate underlying structures:

55

PRINCIPAL INFINITIVE PATTERNS

Complement Infinitives

Sentential Complements without "for"

Ann expected Ray to lead the parade.	Ann EXPECT [Ray LEAD the parade]
Ann expected to lead the parade.	Ann EXPECT [Ann LEAD the parade]

Sentential Complements with "for"

Ann hoped for Ray to lead the parade.	Ann HOPE [Ray LEAD the parade]
Ann hoped to lead the parade.	Ann HOPE [Ann LEAD the parade]
For Ray to lead the parade was important.	[Ray LEAD the parade] BE important
To lead the parade was important.	[SME LEAD the parade] BE important

Nominal Complements

Ann made a wish for Ray to lead the parade.	Ann MAKE a wish [Ray LEAD the parade]
Ann made a wish to lead the parade.	Ann MAKE a wish [Ann LEAD the parade]

Adjectival Complements

Ann was eager for Ray to lead the parade.   Ann BE eager [Ray LEAD the parade]
Ann was eager to lead the parade.   Ann BE eager [Ann LEAD the parade]

Extraposed Complements with Expletives

It was easy for Ann to lead the parade.   [Ann LEAD the parade] BE easy
It was easy to lead the parade.   [SME LEAD the parade] BE easy

Extraposed Complements with Raised Subjects

The parade was easy for Ann to lead.   [Ann LEAD the parade] BE easy
The parade was easy to lead.   [SME LEAD the parade] BE easy

Adverbial Infinitives

Adverbials

Ann paid a bribe for Ray to lead the parade.   Ann PAY a bribe [Ray LEAD the parade]
Ann paid a bribe to lead the parade   Ann PAY a bribe [Ann LEAD the parade]
Ann chose Ray to lead the parade.   Ann CHOOSE Ray [Ray LEAD the parade]
Ann chose herself to lead the parade.   Ann CHOOSE Ann [Ann LEAD the parade]

Relative Infinitives

Relatives

The person to lead the parade was Ray.   The person [the person LEAD the parade] BE Ray
The person for Ann to choose was Ray.   The person [Ann CHOOSE the person] BE Ray
The person to choose was Ray.   The person [SME CHOOSE the person] BE Ray

Relatives with Raised Adjectives

The Tournament of Roses was an easy   The Tournament of Roses BE a parade [[Ann
   parade for Ann to lead.   LEAD the parade] BE easy]
The Tournament of Roses was an easy   The Tournament of Roses BE a parade [[SME
   parade to lead.   LEAD the parade] BE easy]

Exercises 15.9

1. This exercise calls on you to use all the information you have learned in this chapter, as well as your insight and ingenuity. The sentences in each of the following pairs are very similar in their spoken structures, but they may be derived from dissimilar underlying structures. Identify which pattern each infinitive belongs to, and state the sentence's underlying structure.

    a. i. Daphne is happy to please.
        ii. Daphne is hard to please.

b. i. Carla expected Gladys to leave.

   ii. Carla promised Gladys to leave.

c. i. The Warthogs are the team to win.

   ii. The Warthogs are the team to watch.

d. i. We prayed for the song to end.

   ii. We prayed for a song to dance to.

e. i. The denture salesman encountered a difficult person to sell to.

   ii. The denture salesman encountered a toothless person to sell to.

f. i. Aladdin hoped for a genie to appear.

   ii. Aladdin hoped for a bride to marry.

(2.) Optional discovery exercise: This additional pair of sentences calls for original thinking. Speculate how each is derived:

   i. College is a time to remember.

   ii. College is a time to learn.

(3.) Optional discovery exercise: Infinitives, as you have seen, are a complex and fascinating topic—perhaps even a bit too complex and fascinating for some tastes. You may be discouraged—or delighted—to learn that we have not yet exhausted the subject. As one final exercise, speculate on the derivation of this sentence:

   The students lacked the strength to continue.

A Note on Usage: Split Infinitives

In the eighteenth century, certain grammarians decided that then-current English usage was both slipshod and incorrect, and they took it upon themselves to prescribe rules of proper English usage. Many of their rules had no basis in the language as it was actually spoken or written. Over the years, however, some of their rules have entered standard usage, such as their condemnation of double negatives, as in *I don't have none*. Others have been deservedly forgotten, while still others continue to be proclaimed as prescriptive rules by people who consider themselves language purists, even though these rules are ignored in actual practice.

One example of the latter is the prohibition of "split infinitives." This rule holds that it is improper in an infinitive to place an adverbial between an infinitive marker *to* and the verb. Examples of "split" infinitives are shown in 56.

56 a. The company's goal is *to sharply increase* sales next year.

b. *To always speak* properly is Simon's aspiration.

Such sentences are widely spoken, however, and split infinitives are frequently used by literate and well-educated speakers. Most modern stylists object to split infinitives only when they are awkward, as in this example:

57   She tried to as quickly as possible finish her dinner.

Judgments of awkwardness are, of course, subjective, and student writers are best advised to trust their own good sense and their ears for language, rather than relying on any general "rule" about split infinitives.

Exercises 15.10

1. If you are not convinced that split infinitives can ever be acceptable, you might attempt to move the adverb in the following sentence so as to unsplit the infinitive:

    The queen told the page *to quietly enter* the chamber where the king was sleeping.

16 Gerunds, Participles, and Absolutes

Grammatical forms such as infinitives that are derived from verb phrases by a transformational rule are traditionally known as *verbals*. In addition to infinitives, two other types of verbals are *gerunds* and *participles*.

Gerunds

We have already seen that noun phrases can take many different forms. As the italicized phrases in 1 demonstrate, a noun phrase can be (among other options) a simple noun, an entire clause, or an infinitive phrase:

1 **a.** *Exercise* is important.   —noun
   b. *That one gets exercise* is important.   —complement clause
   c. *To get exercise* is important.   —infinitive phrase

We will now consider yet another option that speakers of English have for filling the NP category—namely, a gerund phrase, as in this example:

2   *Getting exercise* is important.   —gerund phrase

A ***gerund phrase***, like an infinitive phrase, can act as a noun phrase. A ***gerund*** is formed by adding the *-ing* inflection to the verb. In 2, *getting* is a gerund; *getting exercise* is a gerund phrase. Like complement clauses and infinitive phrases, gerund phrases are derived from underlying clauses, as, for example, in 3. The underlying structure in 3 is the same structure that underlies both the complement-clause sentence 1b and the infinitive-phrase sentence 1c. The different spoken structures are produced, depending on which transformational rule is applied to the underlying structure. (For simplicity, the operation of T-Infl is assumed but not explicitly shown in derivation 3.)

3

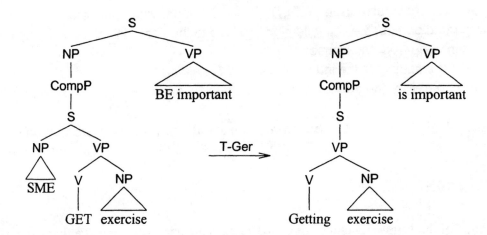

The underlying subject of the complement clause in 3 is the indefinite *SME*, which is then deleted by the transformation. Like infinitive phrases, gerund phrases can also be derived from underlying clauses with specified subjects. Consider the following underlying sentence:

4   [Meg HELP troubled children] BE impressive

Several different spoken sentences can be derived from this structure, including a gerund phrase:

5 **a.** *That Meg helps troubled children* is impressive.   — complement clause
    b. For Meg *to help troubled children* is impressive.   — infinitive phrase
    c. Meg's *helping troubled children* is impressive.   — gerund phrase

As you can see from 5c, the subject of the underlying clause (*Meg*) becomes a possessive noun phrase (*Meg's*) in the spoken sentence, as shown in 6:

6

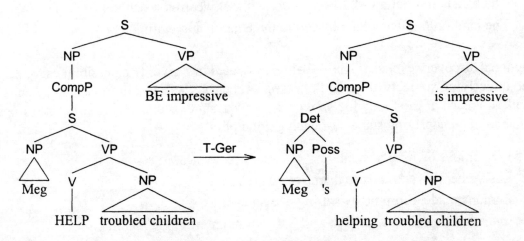

We can summarize our observations about gerunds in a rule:

---

7   Gerund transformation (T-Ger): When an underlying complement clause is spoken as a gerund phrase, the *-ing* inflection is added to the verb. In addition, the underlying subject is removed from the clause:

- If the subject is the indefinite *SME*, it is deleted.
- Otherwise, the subject is made possessive and moved to precede the clause.

Notice the parallels between this transformation and the infinitive transformation on page 225.

Exercises 16.1

1. For each of the following underlying structures, state a spoken sentence that can be derived from it with a complement clause (some of these will be awkward) and another with a gerund phrase:

    a. [SME TAKE vitamins] PREVENT illness
    b. [Viola RECEIVE a scholarship] RELIEVE Mom and Dad
    c. The Elroys RESENT [the Hempels not INVITE the Elroys to the soiree]
    d. The worst crime BE [SME MURDER a fellow human]

2. Draw trees to show the derivations of the following sentences. As in 6, you can assume the operation of T-Infl without showing it explicitly.

    a. Having a hippo for a pet irks the neighbors.
    b. Everett's bursting into the room disrupted the conference.
    c. Taking out a mortgage means getting approval from a bank.
    d. We admired Sonia's doing the right thing.
    e. The legislation outlawed driving a car without wearing a seatbelt.
    f. The landlord's raising the rent led to the tenants' circulating a petition.

(3.) Optional discovery exercise: The T-Ger rule as stated in 7 gives two possibilities for dealing with the underlying subjects of gerund phrases. Actually, there is a third case to be considered as well. For each of the following spoken sentences, state its underlying structure. In particular, consider the underlying subject of each gerund phrase.

    a. Fred enjoys owning a yacht.   [Consider: Who owns the yacht?]
    b. Losing her driver's license dismayed Cornelia.
    c. Ramona made a fortune by selling encyclopedias.
    d. Injuring themselves kept Bob and Sally from entering the marathon.

Now revise rule 7 as necessary to account for these sentences. Do these changes make the T-Ger rule even more parallel with the T-Infin rule on page 225?

Participles

Whereas gerunds are verbals that function much like nouns, *participles* are verbals that function much like adjectives. They are used to modify nouns. *Participial phrases* are italicized in the following sentences:

8 a. The man *walking the dog* witnessed the burglary.   —active participial phrase
   b. The sonnets *written by the poet* describe a cat.   —passive participial phrase

In 8a, *walking* is an ***active participle*** (commonly, but inaccurately, called a "present participle"). The participial phrase *walking the dog* modifies the noun *man*. In 8b, *written* is a ***passive participle*** (commonly, but inaccurately, called a "past participle"). The participial phrase *written by the poet* modifies the noun *sonnets*.

We have already seen that infinitives and gerunds derive from underlying clauses. Is the same also true for participles? In fact, we can find paraphrases of 8a and 8b in sentences with relative clauses:

9 a. The man *who was walking the dog* witnessed a burglary.   —active relative clause
   b. The sonnets *that were written by the poet* describe a cat.   —passive relative clause

Let us assume that the sentences of 8 derive from the same underlying structures as those of 9. That is, we will assume that participles derive from underlying relative clauses.

Notice that we can produce the participial phrases in 8 by deleting words from the relative clauses in 9. That is, we can delete the following words to derive sentence 8a, with its active participial phrase:

10   The man [the man BE walking the dog] WITNESS a burglary

To produce 8b, the passive transformation is performed. Then the following deletion creates the passive participial phrase:

11   The sonnets [the sonnets BE written by the poet] DESCRIBE a cat

In each case, the underlying subject of the relative clause and the verb *BE* are deleted. We can hypothesize a transformation rule that derives participles, which we can call ***relative-clause reduction***:

12   **Relative-Clause Reduction (T-RelRed):** A participial phrase can be formed from a relative clause under these two conditions:
   • the subject of the relative clause is identical to the noun phrase modified by the clause;
   • the first verb in the relative clause is *BE*.
   The subject of the clause and *BE* are deleted to form the participial phrase.

Here is a detailed derivation of the participial phrase in 8a, *The man walking the dog witnessed a burglary*. (For simplicity, let us ignore the operation of T-Infl on the main verb *witnessed*.)

13

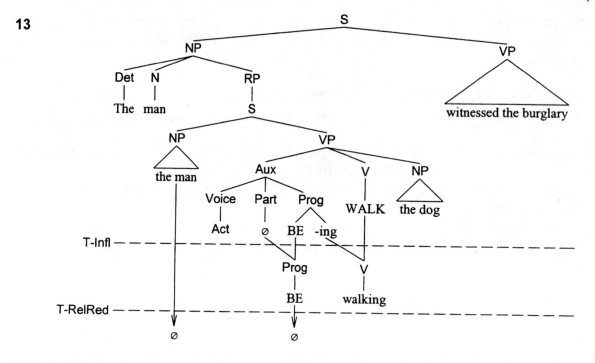

To derive the passive participle in 8b, we must also perform the passive transformation:

14

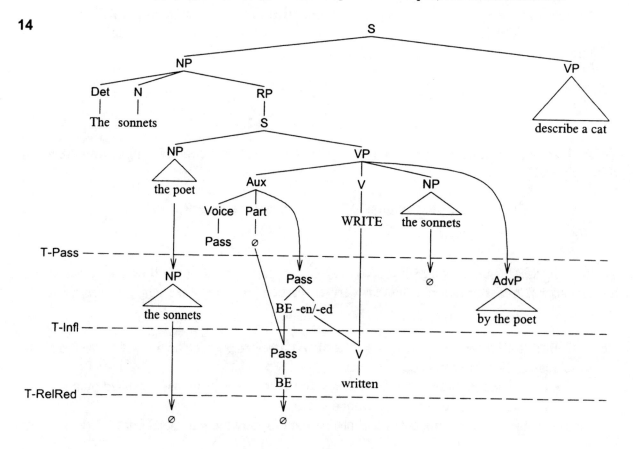

Other Structures Derived from Relative Clauses

An adjectival phrase that follows the noun it modifies is similar to a participial phrase:

15   People *eager for glory* joined the crusade.   —adjectival phrase

It would be reasonable to hypothesize that the italicized adjectival phrase in 15 is also derived by reducing an underlying relative clause (i.e., through T-RelRed):

16   People [<u>people BE</u> eager for glory] JOIN the crusade

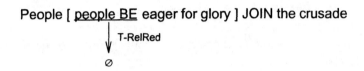

T-RelRed

Ø

Consider also the following sentence with an appositive:

17   My brother *the chef* loves Indonesian food.   —appositive

We might speculate that appositives are derived in the very same way — as reduced relative clauses:

18   My brother [<u>my brother BE</u> the chef] LOVE Indonesian food

T-RelRed

Ø

Exercises 16.2

1. Underline the participial phrases in the following sentences, and identify them as either active or passive:

    a. The box <u>sitting on the desk</u> contains chocolates.   —active
    b. We encountered a man wearing pajamas in public.
    c. The songs played by the station were oldies.
    d. The fish caught by the tourist was a trout weighing three pounds.
    e. The weapon lying near the body was a pistol made in Europe.

2. Draw trees as in 13 and 14 to show the derivations of the sentences in exercise 1.

3. If the adjectival phrase and appositives in the following sentences are derived from relative clauses, what would be their underlying structures?

    a. Eyes red from fatigue need rest.
    b. The terrorist wrote the word *Revenge!* on the wall.
    c. We drove on a road full of potholes and covered with leaves.

Restrictive and Nonrestrictive Participles

The underlying structures of 13, 14, 16, and 18 could also be used to derive relative-clause sentences by applying T-Pro$_R$ instead of T-RelRed:

19 a. The man *who was walking the dog* witnessed the burglary.
   b. The sonnets *that are written by the poet* describe a cat.
   c. People *who were eager for glory* joined the crusade.
   d. My brother *who is the chef* loves Indonesian food.

All four of these sentences have restrictive relative clauses, and so their reduced counterparts can also be called restrictive:

20 a. The man *walking the dog* witnessed the burglary.   — restrictive participial phrase
   b. The sonnets *written by the poet* describe a cat.   — restrictive participial phrase
   c. People *eager for glory* joined the crusade.   — restrictive adjectival phrase
   d. My brother *the chef* loves Indonesian food.   — restrictive appositive

The participles in 20a and 20b can be called ***restrictive participles***. The adjectival phrase in 20c and the appositive in 20d are also restrictive.

Relative clauses, we saw, can be either restrictive or nonrestrictive. Is the same also true of participles and similar phrases? The answer is yes. Nonrestrictive relative clauses also have reduced equivalents:

21 a. Missy, *drawing sketches in her notebook*, passed the time quietly.

                                                         — nonrestrictive participial phrase
   b. Meg's husband, *consumed by jealousy*, spied on her at work.

                                                         — nonrestrictive participial phrase
   c. The children, *happy and carefree*, played in the tree house.

                                                         — nonrestrictive adjectival phrase
   d. Dabney, *a notorious paranoid*, worries constantly about germs.

                                                         — nonrestrictive appositive

The participles in 21a and 21b are ***nonrestrictive participles***. The adjectival phrase in 21c and the appositive in 21d are also nonrestrictive.

Nonrestrictive participles, like nonrestrictive relative clauses, provide supplemental information about the nouns they modify. A nonrestrictive phrase, such as those in 21, is not essential to the meaning of the main clause; if it were removed, the essential meaning of the main clause would remain intact. The main clause of 21a, for example, retains its meaning if the nonrestrictive participial phrase is removed:

22   Missy passed the time quietly.

Chapter 16

In contrast, note how meaning would be affected if the italicized restrictive participial phrase were removed from the following sentence:

23 Only a lunatic would drink water *mixed with turpentine.* — restrictive participial phrase

Another difference is that nonrestrictive phrases, unlike restrictive phrases, are set off from the rest of the sentence by brief pauses in speech, which are represented by commas in writing. Note the difference in punctuation between the sentences of 20 and 21.

Participles in Other Positions

Moving Nonrestrictive Participles

Nonrestrictive phrases can be moved to the beginning of a sentence. For example, the phrases in 21 can be moved as follows:

24 a. *Drawing sketches in her notebook,* Missy passed the time quietly.
   b. *Consumed by jealousy,* Meg's husband spied on her at work.
   c. *Happy and carefree,* the children played in the tree house.
   d. *A notorious paranoid,* Dabney worries constantly about germs.

Frequently nonrestrictive phrases can also be moved to the end of sentences:

25 a. Missy passed the time quietly, *drawing sketches in her notebook.*
   b. Meg's husband spied on her at work, *consumed by jealousy.*
   c. The children played in the tree house, *happy and carefree.*

The rule that moves these phrases was introduced in a discovery exercise on page 169. We can now formulate that rule:

26 **Nonrestrictive-Phrase Movement (T-NRP):** If a nonrestrictive phrase that has been derived by T-RelRed modifies a noun phrase that begins the sentences, the nonrestrictive phrase may be moved to precede that noun phrase. It may also be moved to the end of the sentence.

Although participial phrases can sometimes be moved away from the noun phrases that they modify—as in 25—the resulting spoken sentences can cause confusion if the phrases are moved next to other noun phrases. In such cases, they are known as ***dangling modifiers***, as in these examples:

27 a. (?) *Opening the door,* the sight that I saw shocked me.   — dangling participle
   b. (?) *Distracted by the children,* the steak burnt to a crisp.   — dangling participle

---

Gerunds, Participles, and Absolutes   253

c. (?) Larry accosted Tony, *eager for a fight.* — dangling adjective

d. (?) Dabney worries constantly about germs, *a notorious paranoid.* — dangling appositive

The underlying subject of *opening the door* in 27a is *I*, not *the sight*. While perhaps not ungrammatical, dangling modifiers are criticized by stylists, particularly when they result in ambiguities. Hearing 27c, a listener might well think it was Tony, rather than Larry, who was eager to fight. While no one is likely to interpret 27b to mean that the steak was distracted, such a sentence is likely to be greeted with snickers rather than approval. Fortunately, a simple way to amend such a sentence is to place the modifier next to the noun it modifies: *Distracted by the children, Dad let the steak burn to a crisp.*

Moving Restrictive Participles

Movement of restrictive participles is quite different. A restrictive participle (but not a complete participial phrase) can be moved to a position before the modified noun—that is, it can act as an adjective. Compare the participial phrases in 28 with the single participles in 29:

28 a. A baby *crying for its parents* needs attention.

    b. Schildkraut is an artist *neglected by everyone.*

    c. Hell hath no fury like a woman *scorned.*

29 a. A *crying* baby needs attention.

    b. Schildkraut is a *neglected* artist.

    c. A *scorned* man can also become furious.

A new transformational rule is needed to account for the movement of restrictive participles:

30   **Restrictive-Phrase Movement (T-RP):** If a restrictive phrase that has been derived by T-RelRed contains a single participle or adjective (but not a multiword participial or adjectival phrase), that participle or adjective may be moved to an adjectival position preceding the noun it modifies.

Exercises 16.3

1. Underline the participial phrases in the following sentences, and identify them as restrictive or nonrestrictive. State the approximate underlying structure of each sentence.

    a.   A <u>warbling</u> mockingbird distracted the poet.
                Restrictive.   *A mockingbird [a mockingbird BE warbling] DISTRACT the poet*

    b.   Wallace, miffed by an apparent snub, refused to perform.

    c.   Giggling uncontrollably, the couple ran from the theater.

    d. Burton enjoys a steak cooked over an open fire.

    e. Missed opportunities doomed the struggling business.

2. Which of the participles in exercise 1 were moved by **T-RP** or **T-NRP**? Show the derivations of 1a and 1c.

(3.) Optional discovery exercise: In addition to the active participle *seeing* (derived by T-RelRed from the progressive form (*BE seeing*) and the passive participle *seen* (derived by T-RelRed from the passive form (*BE seen*), there are also perfect participle forms: the active *having seen* and *having been seeing* and the passive *having been seen*. None of these has an equivalent relative clause (**who is having seen* . . . , **who is having been seen* . . .). Perhaps, in order to derive participles from verb phrases with perfect auxiliaries, a supporting auxiliary (*BE + -ing*) is added in such cases. Devise this rule, and draw derivations for the following sentences:

    a. The explorer, having lost the map, asked for directions.

    b. Having been caught in a trap, the rebels surrendered.

    c. Renee, having been patient for hours, rebelled.

    d. Having been planning the breakout for years, the prisoners were ready for anything.

(4.) Optional discovery exercise: Like participles, gerunds can occur in a number of active and passive forms. Is our gerund transformational rule, stated in 7, adequate to account for the following sentence?

    Having lost honorably is no disgrace.

(5.) Optional discovery exercise: The following ambiguous sentence has two interpretations:

    a. The FBI caught the terrorists threatening the embassy.

One of the readings has the corresponding passive sentence *The terrorists threatening the embassy were caught*, while the other reading has this passive equivalent: *The terrorists were caught threatening the embassy*. Can you speculate on the derivations of the two readings? You may also wish to consider the ambiguity of the following sentences:

    b. Visiting relatives can be boring.

    c. Mickey watched the man climbing the ladder.

    d. Dolly found the money missing from the till.

Absolutes

An *absolute* consists of a noun phrase and a modifying phrase. Curiously, it does not fill any of the typical noun-phrase roles we have encountered—subject, direct object, indirect object, object of a preposition—but instead floats apart from the main clause, as in the following italicized examples:

31 a. Werner walked to work, *the weather being beautiful*.
   b. *All attempts at negotiation having failed*, the peasants resorted to violence.
   c. The roller coaster roared down the tracks, *its passengers screaming with terror and delight*.

While seemingly independent of the main clause, an absolute has ties of meaning (and, we can assume, underlying syntactic ties) to that clause. Note the similarity of the sentences in 31 to the following sentences with adverbial clauses:

32 a. Werner walked to work *because the weather was beautiful*.
   b. *After all attempts at negotiation had failed*, the peasants resorted to violence.
   c. The roller coaster roared down the tracks, *while its passengers screamed with terror and delight*.

We can assume that the sentences of 31 and 32 derive from similar underlying structures. Adjectival phrases and appositives are also possible in absolute constrictions, as in the following:

33 a. *Her hands blue from the cold*, Morgan fumbled with her mittens.
   b. *His unexpected sortie a complete success*, the general pressed his advantage.

Having made it this far, you are well skilled in grammatical analysis. I will leave it to you, in the discovery exercise that follows, to devise the rules necessary to derive absolute constructions.

Exercises 16.4

1. For each of the following sentences, invent an appropriate absolute construction to fill the position indicated.

   a. . . . , the pirates boarded the captured vessel.
   b. The runner, . . . , crossed the finish line and collapsed.
   c. The motorcycle sped down the hill out of control, ...

(2.) Optional discovery exercise: Explore in greater detail the derivations of sentences with absolute constructions, such as those in 31. Formulate any revisions of existing T-rules (or entirely new T-rules) that are needed to derive those sentences.

17 Abbreviating Sentences: Ellipsis and Pro-Forms

In several of the constructions we have examined, an element that is present in the underlying structure of a sentence is deleted from the spoken structure. For example, the spoken command *Open the door* has the understood meaning *HEARER OPEN the door*. The underlying subject *HEARER* is eliminated by T-Imp, the imperative transformation. In other sentences the indefinite element *SME* is eliminated. For example, the passive sentence *Smoking is forbidden* derives from the underlying structure *SME FORBID SME SMOKE*. The *SME*s are omitted when the transformational rules T-Ger and T-Pass are applied. The elimination of an underlying element from a spoken sentence by a transformation is called *ellipsis*.

Ellipsis

Ellipsis can occur in other circumstances as well. When elements occur more than once in a sentence or in adjacent sentences, all but one occurrence of the identical elements can sometimes be omitted from the spoken sentence. In each of the following examples, a sentence with an ellipsis is followed by the same sentence in which the missing elements have been retained:

1 **a.** Travis votes Democratic; Olivia Republican.   — sentence with ellipsis

   b. Travis votes Democratic; Olivia *votes* Republican.   — sentence without ellipsis

2 **a.** If we get the breaks, we will win; if not, we will lose.

   b. If we get the breaks, we will win; if *we do* not *get the breaks*, we will lose.

3 **a.** First we noticed Pamela's gloves on a chair and then Christine's on the floor.

   b. First we noticed Pamela's gloves on a chair and then *we noticed* Christine's *gloves* on the floor.

Ellipsis can also occur in conversation, when one speaker omits elements spoken by a previous speaker:

4 **a.** "Who made this mess?" "Julie."   — sentence with ellipsis

   b. "Who made this mess?" "Julie *made this mess*."   — sentence without ellipsis

In examples 1–4, ellipsis occurs when an element appears twice or more in the underlying structure. Ellipsis can also occur when the missing element is obvious, even though it occurs only once in the underlying structure, as in this example:

5 a. I am expected for dinner at my parents'.   —sentence with ellipsis
   b. I am expected for dinner at my parents' *house*.   —sentence without ellipsis

The concept *house* is understood by the hearer without its being spoken; the hearer has no difficulty reconstructing the underlying meaning.

The omission of obvious elements also occurs frequently in posted notices (*Smoking strictly forbidden on assembly line*) and in newspaper headlines (*UFO Sighted by Beauty Queen*).

We can state the principle behind these ellipses, in very general terms, as a transformational rule:

6 **Ellipsis (T-Ell):** When an element occurs twice or more in an underlying structure (either in one sentence or in adjacent sentences), the latter occurrences of that element can be omitted in the spoken structure. Similarly, when an element is obvious to the hearers, it can be omitted.

Of course, this rule has many restrictions and exceptions (for example: In the sentence *The cat chased the mouse*, the second occurrence of the article *the* cannot be omitted). Rule 6 is a general rather than a precise statement of the principle of ellipsis.

Exercises 17.1

1. Each of the following sentences has an ellipsis. Supply the missing but understood element(s):

   a. Although sick of traveling, we packed our bags one more time.
   b. Mildred enjoys shrimp whether boiled or fried.
   c. The tourists have seen all the sights they could.
   d. Fergus became a lawyer and Vladimir a journalist.
   e. We admire Trollope's novels as well as Smollett's.
   f. I have my favorite pastimes; you yours.
   g. If ready, begin; if not, hold you fire.
   h. When in doubt, get advice.
   i. The children were preparing for bedtime, and the adults for a long night of work.
   j. Although we should have, we did not pay our taxes on time.
   k. "Has the concert started?" "Not yet."
   l. See you after New Year's.

Decide what causes the ambiguity of the following actual headline, and state the non-elliptical versions of both interpretations:

m. "California Sheriff Wants Man Shot by Patrolman"

2. Consider the hypothesis that the italicized verb phrase in each of the following sentences is an infinitive phrase, even though the infinitive marker *to* is not present.

   a. Chuck's storytelling made the time *fly by*.
   b. Patrick heard the car *backfire*.
   c. The family saw the building *burn*.
   d. What Tricia did was *take a vacation*.

According to this hypothesis, the infinitive marker *to* has been deleted from the spoken structure. Do you agree that these phrases are infinitive phrases? As data to consider in making your decision, state the passive versions of sentences 2a–2c (*The time was made . . .*).

Objective Complements

Sentences with ***objective complements*** can also be assumed to derive through ellipsis. In such sentences, the object noun phrase is followed (i.e., complemented) by another phrase: usually a noun phrase, an adjectival phrase, or a participial phrase. Objective complements are italicized in these examples:

7 **a.** The Lodge considered Humphrey *a loyal Moose*. —noun phrase as objective complement
    b. Real men prefer their milk *ice cold*. —adjectival phrase as objective complement
    c. The judge ordered the suspect *released on bail*. —participial phrase as objective complement

In analyzing such sentences, we can note the existence of similar sentences in which those same complement phrases occur within infinitive phrases:

8 **a.** The Lodge considered Humphrey *to be a loyal Moose*.
    b. Real men prefer their milk *to be ice cold*.
    c. The judge ordered the suspect *to be released on bail*.

Because we recognize the sentences of 7 and 8 to be paraphrases of each other, we can assume they derive from the same underlying structures.

In Chapter 15, we classified infinitives like those in 8 as sentential-complement infinitives. That is, they derive from the underlying complement clauses in 9:

9 **a.** The Lodge CONSIDER [Humphrey BE a loyal Moose]
    b. Real men PREFER [their milk BE ice cold]
    c. [Following T-Pass:] The judge ORDER [the suspect BE released on bail]

Here, in a somewhat abbreviated version, is the derivation of sentence 7a:

10

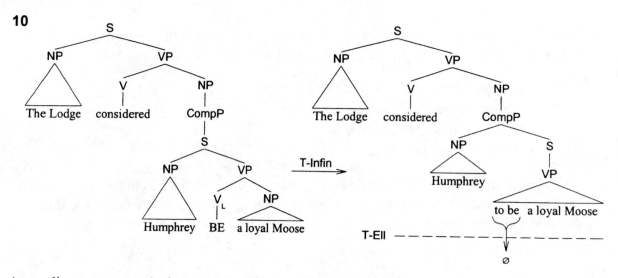

According to our analysis, an objective complement is derived from a sentential-complement infinitive phrase with a linking verb. The infinitive *to be* is then deleted by the ellipsis transformation.

Exercises 17.2

1. Using derivation 10 as a model, show the derivations of sentences 7b and 7c.

2. State the underlying structures of the following sentences, and show their derivations:

    a. Leon fancied himself an astute investor.
    b. New circumstances rendered the plan useless.
    c. The examiners believed the program without merit.
    d. A cheerful attitude made the job easy.
    e. The directive was declared inoperative by the bureaucrats.
    f. The boss wanted the product delivered on time.

(3.) Optional discovery exercise: The objective complements in exercises 1 and 2 above are derived from sentential-complement infinitive phrases. The objective complements in the following sentences are derived from adverbial infinitives (adverbial infinitives were discussed beginning on page 233). Show their derivations.

    a. The Dickinsons named the baby Emily.
    b. The Lodge elected Humphrey the new Grand Exalted Moose.
    c. Winston scrubbed the floor clean.

Ellipsis in Comparisons

Another circumstance in which ellipsis can occur is in a comparison, where an element in one clause is compared to an element in another clause. Each of the following is a comparative sentence with an ellipsis (followed in each case by the same sentence with the elliptical elements restored). In sentences 11–13, the adjectives *nervous*, *older*, and *angry* are the bases for the comparisons:

11 a. Yvette was less nervous than Lawrence. — comparison with ellipsis
   b. Yvette was less nervous than Lawrence *was nervous*. — comparison without ellipsis

12 a. Lee is older than Duane.
   b. Lee is older than Duane *is old*.

13 a. Adrian is as angry as I am.
   b. Adrian is as angry as I am *angry*.

In sentences 14 and 15, the adverbs *better* and *loudly* are the basis for the comparisons:

14 a. Nan likes fiction better than nonfiction.
   b. Nan likes fiction better than *Nan likes* nonfiction.

15 a. Jerry snores less loudly than Artie.
   b. Jerry snores less loudly than Artie *snores*.

T-Ell has applied to produce the ellipsis in each of these five sentences.

A Closer Examination of Comparison

Because we have not yet studied constructions involving comparison, a closer examination of them is in order.

Comparison of adjectives and adverbs is expressed through sequences such as *more . . . than*, *less . . . than*, *as . . . as*, and *(not) so . . . as*. The introductory elements *more, less, as,* and *so* can be classified as degree modifiers (you may wish to review our discussion of degree modifiers beginning on page 86). The elements *than* and *as* that follow the adjective or adverb can be classified as a type of subordinating conjunction. More specifically, we will call them **comparative conjunctions** (abbreviated C_{Cp}).

When a compared adjective or adverb is a short word—usually one or two syllables—the degree modifier can be replaced by the comparative inflectional ending *-er*. Thus in the sentences of 12 and 14 we have the forms *older* and *better* instead of *more old* and *more well*. In fact, the former expressions can be said to derive from the latter ones by a transformation, as in 16.

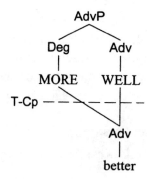

We can call the transformation that derives *better* from *MORE WELL* the ***Comparative-Inflection Transformation*** or **T-Cp**. Adjectives and adverbs are traditionally classified as having three forms: the ***positive*** or uncompared form (*pretty, beautiful, well*), the ***comparative*** form (*prettier, more beautiful, better*), and the ***superlative*** form (*prettiest, most beautiful, best*). T-Cp is also used to derive superlative forms such as *prettiest* and *best* from *MOST PRETTY* and *MOST WELL*.

According to our analysis, sentence 11a, *Yvette was less nervous than Lawrence*, is derived as follows. (For simplicity, the inflection of verbs is assumed rather than shown.)

17

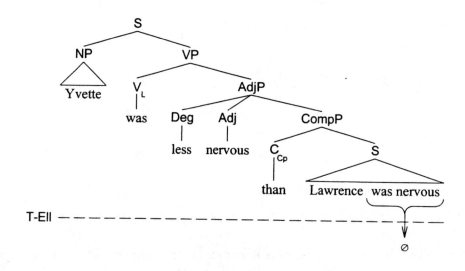

The derivations of 13a, *Adrian is as angry as I am*, and of 14a, *Nan likes fiction better than nonfiction*, are shown in 18 and 19.

18

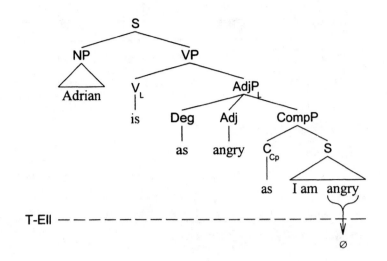

19

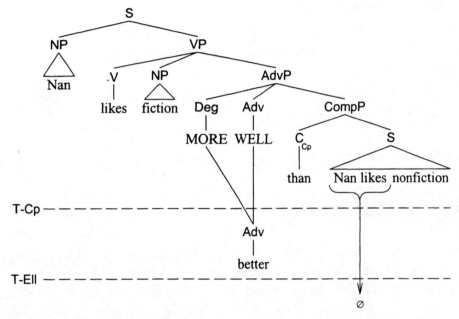

Derivation 19 makes the claim that adverbial phrases, as well as adjectival phrases, can take complements. This is in fact the case, as sentences 20a and 20b demonstrate:

20 a. The jogger is so fanatical *that she runs even during blizzards.*

— adjectival-complement clause

   b. The jogger trains so fanatically *that she runs even during blizzards.*

— adverbial-complement clause

Our transformation rules for adjectives and adverbs can be modified to account for comparatives and for ***adverbial-complement clauses,*** as shown in 21.

21

$$AdjP_L \rightarrow (Deg) \; Adj \; (CompP)$$

$$AdvP \rightarrow (Deg) \; Adv \; (CompP)$$

$$CompP \rightarrow \left\{ \begin{array}{c} C_{Cl} \\ C_{Cp} \end{array} \right\} S$$

Exercises 17.3

1. Show the derivations of the following comparative sentences. As in 17–19, you can assume the inflection of verbs without showing it directly.

   a. Gretel is smarter than Hansel.
   b. Raymond plays the saxophone more expertly than Gene.
   c. Raymond plays the saxophone more expertly than the tuba.
   d. You are as pretty as a picture.
   e. More than ever, Abraham likes peace and quiet.
   f. Spenser will try harder than Marlowe will.

2. Account for the ambiguity of the following sentence, and show the derivations for both interpretations.

   Michele likes Fran better than Dean.

(3.) Optional discovery exercise: In exercise sentence 1f, the auxiliary *will* was retained in the spoken structure of the comparative clause, even though T-Ell deleted the rest of the verb phrase. Notice that when a comparative clause lacks an auxiliary, the supporting auxiliary *DO* can be supplied:

   Spenser tries harder than Marlowe does.

Revise the transformation T-Supp on page 188 to account for sentences such as this one.

(4.) Optional discovery exercise: An adjectival phrase that contains a comparative clause, such as *less nervous than Lawrence* in 11a, occurs following a linking verb. When a comparative adjectival phrase precedes a noun, that noun may also be followed by a comparative clause, as in this example:

   Yvette was a less nervous person than Lawrence.

Moreover, in addition to acting as degree modifiers before adjectives and adverbs, *more* and *less* can also act as quantifiers before nouns (*more people, less room*). A noun preceded by these quantifiers can be followed by a comparative clause, as in the following example.

Lawrence experienced more anxiety than Yvette.

How might our grammar account for such sentences?

(5.) Optional discovery exercise: Can we compare prepositional phrases that act as adjectival or adverbial phrases? Consider such prepositional phrases as *in love*, *on time*, *in tune*, and *like a professional*. What about such prepositional phrases as *with enthusiasm* and *in a good mood*? Can adverbial clauses also be compared? Consider the following sentence:

He made a contribution more because he felt guilty than because he felt generous.

Revise the rules of 21 to account for these data.

(6.) Optional discovery exercise: In addition to the determiner (or "attributive") possessive pronouns (*my*, *your*, *her*, and so on) that can replace possessive noun-phrase modifiers (*Mary's old car* → *her old car*), there also exist **nominal** (or "substantive") **possessive pronouns** (*mine*, *yours*, *hers*, and so on) that can replace not just the possessive modifiers but entire noun phrases (*Mary's old car* → *hers*). How might our grammar account for a sentence such as the following with a nominal possessive pronoun?

Mary's car has less rust on its body than mine has.

Pro-Forms

Determiner Pronouns

In discovery exercise 6, immediately above, we observed that for each possessive pronoun that acts as a determiner (such as *my*, *our*, and *their*), there also exists a corresponding possessive pronoun that acts as a noun phrase (*mine*, *ours*, *theirs*). Other types of determiners also have corresponding forms that act as noun phrases and so can be called pronouns (the "pro" in *pronoun* is the Latin word meaning "for"; pronouns stand *for* noun phrases). These determiners include demonstratives (*this*, *that*, *these*, *those*), quantifiers (*many*, *some*, *no*, *every*), and possessive noun phrases (*Anne's*, *the king's*). Here are examples of corresponding pronominal forms:

22 **a.** I like *this*. —demonstrative as pronoun
   b. *That* surprised me.
   c. *These* outperform *those*.

23 **a.** I want *some*. —quantifier as pronoun
   b. I don't need *any*.
   c. *None* look interesting.
   d. *Everyone* came.

---

24   The yacht is *Nelson's.*   —possessive NP as pronoun

You may wish to consider whether these examples are true pronouns—that is, whether they *replace* underlying noun phrases—or whether they are really examples of ellipsis—that is, whether T-Ell eliminated all constituents of underlying noun phrases except for the determiners. Under either hypothesis, the underlying concepts represented by sentences 22a, 23a, and 24 might be the following:

25 a. I like THIS WORK

  b. I want SOME CORNFLAKES

  c. The yacht is NELSON'S YACHT

The question we are considering is whether in sentence 22a, *I like this*, the word *this* is a pronoun that replaces (by some form of T-Pro) the concept *THIS WORK*, or whether it is a determiner that is left behind after *WORK* has been eliminated (by T-Ell).

One factor to consider in choosing between hypotheses is the fact that the pronominal words are not always identical with their determiner equivalents. The determiners *my* and *your*, for example, are different from the corresponding pronouns *mine* and *yours*, and the quantifiers *no* and *every* differ from their corresponding pronoun forms *none/no-one/nobody/nothing* and *everyone/everybody/everything*.

Exercises 17.4

1. What other factors, including your intuitions, can help you choose between these two hypotheses? What causes you to prefer one of these hypotheses over the other? Do you have another hypothesis of your own?

2. Of all the determiners discussed in Chapter 6, we have noted pronominal equivalents for all types except for the articles (*a, an, the*). Noun phrases with definite articles can be replaced by personal pronouns:

$$I \text{ met } the \ actress \rightarrow I \text{ met } her.$$
$$I \text{ ate } the \ apple \rightarrow I \text{ ate } it.$$
$$I \text{ found } the \ keys \rightarrow I \text{ found } them.$$

What pronoun(s), if any, can replace noun phrases with indefinite articles?

a. They had sports cars, and I wanted *a sports car* → . . . and I wanted _____.

b. He admired women from Minnesota, and he wanted to meet *some women from Minnesota*   → . . . and he wanted to meet _____.

c. She disliked men from Long Island, and she didn't want to meet *any men from Long Island*   → . . . and she didn't want to meet _____.

Other Pro-Forms

The Pro-Form So

We use pronouns as handy substitutes for longer noun phrases. In addition, other convenient substitutes (or ***pro-forms***) are used to take the place of other types of underlying phrases or concepts. Consider how the pro-form *so* is used in these examples. In each case, what element(s) does *so* replace?

26 a. I doubt Bartleby will be our new boss, but, if *so*, we will make the most of it.
  b. She will believe that goblins exist if you say *so*.
  c. She will go to college if you say *so*.
  d. He wasn't fat before, but he has become *so* now.
  e. She acted cheerfully then but less *so* now.
  f. Charlotte stormed out. *So* ended the conversation.
  g. Phillip picked up the money before Rose could *do so*.
  h. Sean played James Bond in the movies, and Pierce *did so* too.

In sentences 26a–26c, *so* substitutes for an entire clause. Those sentences have underlying structures that correspond to the following:

27 a. I doubt Bartleby will be our new boss, but, if *Bartleby will be our new boss*, we will make the most of it.
  b. She will believe that goblins exist if you say *that goblins exist*.
  c. She will go to college if you say *that she should go to college*.

In sentences 26d and 26e, *so* takes the place of an adjectival phrase and of an adverbial phrase, respectively:

28 a. He wasn't fat before, but he has become *fat* now.
  b. She acted cheerfully then but less *cheerfully* now.

The pro-form *so* does not always take the place of a clearly specified phrase, however. In 26f, for example, *so* replaces an understood but unspecified concept—an underlying adverbial phrase that may be represented as *IN-THE-AFOREMENTIONED-MANNER* or *UNDER-THE-AFORE-MENTIONED-CIRCUMSTANCES*. The underlying concept of 26f is the following:

29 Charlotte stormed out. The conversation ended *UNDER-THE-AFOREMENTIONED-CIRCUMSTANCES*.

In 26g and 26h, *so* is used with the supporting auxiliary verb *DO* as a substitute for the verb phrase:

30 a. Phillip picked up the money before Ross could *pick up the money*.
  b. Sean played James Bond in the movies, and Pierce *played James Bond in the movies* too.

The various pronouns and *so* are not the only pro-forms. Two other words that we have previously treated as adverbs, *then* and *there*, can also be regarded as pro-forms. In the following sentences, it is clear they are used as shorthand for adverbials of time and place respectively:

31 a. She will leave on Saturday, and I will leave *then* too.

   b. He flew to Bombay, and I too will fly *there*.

Because *then* in 31a clearly stands for the time adverbial "on Saturday," and *there* in 31b stands for the place adverbial "to Bombay," we can call these words ***pro-adverbials***.

Although we have not considered all possible pro-forms, we can summarize our observations in a very generalized transformational rule:

32   Pro-Form Substitution (T-ProForm): Certain phrases whose meaning is understood by the hearer may be replaced by a pro-form. A phrase following a linking verb or an entire clause may be replaced by *so*. Other verb phrases may be replaced by *do so*. Adverbial phrases may be replaced by *so* when they describe manner, by *then* when they describe time, and by *there* when they describe place.

Exercises 17.5

1. The following sentences contain pro-forms. For each, state the underlying phrase or concept that the pro-form replaces.

   a. They predict that spring will arrive soon, and I certainly hope so.
   b. I had heard that Korean food was spicy, and it is indeed so.
   c. "The check is in the mail." "So you say, but you've said so at least a dozen times."
   d. I heard that he played the trumpet like an angel, but I did not find that he played so.
   e. They told me to fake tears, but I wasn't able to do so.
   f. I liked New Orleans when I was there during my junior year, although it was very rainy then.

   In the following sentence, speculate on the origin of the pro-form *such*:

   g. I doubt that Winnie gave in, and I'd be surprised if such were the case.

(2.) Optional discovery exercise: Expressions such as *however*, *therefore*, and *for example* are sometimes regarded as conjunctions, because they are used to join sentences. However, they may also be regarded as pro-forms—perhaps as pro-adverbials, like *then* and *there*. Speculate, therefore, on how such words (for example, when they occur within this very paragraph) are derived. What might be the underlying phrases or concepts that they represent?

(3.) Optional discovery exercise: In the following sentences, *each other* and *one another* are **reciprocal pronouns**. What functions do reciprocal pronouns serve? How do they differ in meaning from reflexive pronouns?

    a. Benedick and Beatrice love each other.

    b. The brothers assist one another with their chores.

    c. The cousins borrowed each other's class notes.

(4.) Optional discovery exercise: The word order in some sentences seems to be reversed. Consider, for example, the second sentence of 26f: *So ended the conversation*. Here the subject *the conversation* follows the verb, and the adverbial *so* precedes it. Consider too the following data:

    a. Up popped the toast.

    b. Cold were the nights we spent in Maine.

    c. Silently advanced the stalking adversary.

    d. A jolly old soul was he.

    e. To the victor belong the spoils.

Such sentences have a "literary" feel, and they are more likely to occur in formal writing than in conversation. Still, they do occur. Devise a transformational rule that can account for them. Be sure the rule does not also allow the transposition of subjects and objects (note: Word order makes a difference in a sentence like *Bubba fried the chicken*).

Retrospective

In the course of these seventeen chapters, we have examined a great many English syntactic constructions. In doing so, we have created a model of the internal grammar in our minds that enables us to produce the sentences we speak. It is time to bring together our discoveries in a final update of our grammar. Here is the latest version of the phrase-structure rules that we have formulated:

33

PS RULES: A Final Update

$$S \rightarrow NP \; VP$$

$$NP \rightarrow \begin{cases} (Det) \; (AdjP)^+ \; (Mod_{NP}) \; N \; (PP) \; (CompP) \; (RP) \\ CompP \\ NP \; NRP \end{cases}$$

$$Det \rightarrow \begin{cases} Art \\ Dem \\ Quant \\ NP \; Poss \end{cases}$$

$$Mod_{NP} \rightarrow (AdjP)^+ \; (Mod_{NP}) \; N \; (PP)$$

$$AdjP \rightarrow (Deg)\ Adj$$

$$AdjP_L \rightarrow (Deg)\ Adj\ (CompP)$$

$$AdvP \rightarrow (Deg) \left\{ \begin{array}{l} Adv \\ PP \\ C_S\ S \end{array} \right\} (CompP)$$

$$AdvP_L \rightarrow (Deg) \left\{ \begin{array}{l} Adv_{(Time/Place)} \\ PP_{(Time/Place)} \end{array} \right\}$$

$$CompP \rightarrow \left\{ \begin{array}{l} \left\{ \begin{array}{l} C_{Cl} \\ C_{Cp} \end{array} \right\} S \\ PP \end{array} \right\}$$

$$PP \rightarrow P\ NP$$

$$XP \rightarrow XP\ C_{Co}\ XP$$

$$RP \rightarrow S$$

$$NRP \rightarrow S$$

$$VP \rightarrow \left\{ \begin{array}{l} V\ (NP) \\ V_L \left\{ \begin{array}{l} NP \\ AdjP_L \\ AdvP_L \end{array} \right\} \end{array} \right\} (AdvP)^+$$

$$(V \rightarrow V_P\ Prt)$$

$$Aux \rightarrow Voice\ Mood\ (Neg)\ Tense \left\{ \begin{array}{l} (M) \\ IM \\ Part \end{array} \right\} (Perf)\ (Prog)$$

$$Voice \rightarrow \left\{ \begin{array}{l} Act \\ Pass \end{array} \right\}$$

$$Mood \rightarrow \left\{ \begin{array}{l} Dec \\ Q \\ Imp \\ Sbj \end{array} \right\}$$

$$Neg \rightarrow not$$

$$IM \rightarrow to\ \oslash$$

$$Part \rightarrow \oslash$$

$$Tense \rightarrow \left\{ \begin{array}{l} Pres \\ Past \end{array} \right\}$$

$$M \rightarrow \left\{ \begin{array}{l} WILL \\ SHALL \\ CAN \\ MAY \\ MUST \end{array} \right\} \oslash$$

$$Perf \rightarrow HAVE\ -en/-ed$$

$$Prog \rightarrow BE\ -ing$$

Here is the second part of our model, a list of the transformational rules we have formulated:

34

	T-Rules
T-AdvP	Adverbial movement
T-AuxFront	Auxiliary fronting
T-Cont	Contraction transformation
T-Cp	Comparative-inflection transformation
T-Ell	Ellipsis transformation
T-Expl	Expletive insertion
T-Extra	Extraposition
T-Ger	Gerund transformation
T-Imp	Imperative transformation
T-Infin	Infinitive transformation
T-Infl	Inflection assignment
T-IO	Indirect-object transformation
T-Neg	Negative transformation
T-NRP	Nonrestrictive-phrase movement
T-Pass	Passive transformation
T-Pro$_P$	Personal-pronoun transformation
T-Pro$_Q$	Interrogative-pronoun transformation
T-Pro$_R$	Relative-pronoun transformation
T-Pro$_{Rx}$	Reflexive-pronoun transformation
T-ProForm	Pro-form substitution
T-Prt	Particle movement
T-Raise/Extra	Raising from an extraposed infinitive phrase
T-RelRed	Relative-clause reduction
T-RP	Restrictive-phrase movement
T-Supp	Supporting-auxiliary insertion
T-WH	*Wh* fronting

You may wonder why the T-rules in 34 are presented alphabetically, rather than in the order of their relative application. As we have proceeded, the notion of ordering transformations (that is, specifying which T-rules are performed before which others) has become complicated. For example, in accounting for some derivations, we considered the possibility that T-Rules may apply cyclically, with several rules operating in succession on a lower clause before any of those same rules can apply to an upper clause. We would need to do considerably more exploration before arriving at a definitive account of transformations.

The model of grammar shown in 33 and 34, which we have constructed through trial and error, is capable of generating an enormous range of grammatical English sentences. Still, it is by no means a perfect model. The many discovery exercises throughout the book have raised the possibility of additions or revisions to the model, and you may have encountered still other constructions that we have not taken into account. The English language, as you are now fully aware, is an instrument of such remarkable complexity (and interest!) that our study in this book can only be called introductory.

But the incompleteness of our investigation need not dismay us. You have learned much about the structure of English, and—more important—you are prepared to explore the language further and to construct hypotheses to account for almost any new data you encounter. The English language and the human mental processes that allow us to create it are so intriguing that we can regard the unexplored territories before us as holding promise of ongoing adventure.

The following chapter will provide you with a taste of what lies in store for you if you continue your study of syntax.

Exercises 17.6

1. Test our grammar in 33 and 34 by seeing if it can generate any English sentence that you can suggest. As a procedure for testing the grammar, you may wish to open a book or magazine at random, place your finger anywhere on the page, and see if the grammar is adequate to generate the sentence you encounter. Repeat the procedure several times. If you find gaps or problems with our grammar, test you own skill as a grammarian by seeing if you can adapt our grammar to account for the new data.

(2.) Optional discovery exercise: Good golly! I just thought of a gap. In this book we seem to have overlooked *interjections* such as *Bravo!* and *Phooey!* and *Gesundheit!* Should we regard such exclamations as sentences in their own right? If so, how might we adjust our grammar to account for them?

(3.) Optional discovery exercise: Finally, gentle reader, please speculate about how we might account for terms used in *direct address*, as when we speak the names of persons we are addressing. Examples include the italicized terms in the following sentences:

   a. *Buddy*, can you spare a dime?
   b. Yes, *Virginia*, there is a Santa Claus.
   c. Here's looking at you, *kid*.

18 A Taste of Theoretical Syntax

The preceding chapters have taken more of a ***pragmatic*** than a ***theoretical*** approach to the study of English grammar. That is, I had a practical goal in writing them—to enable readers to gain a broad understanding of how the English language is put together. As a consequence, I focused on the particulars of our language in all its varied constructions (verb phrases, complement clauses, appositives, infinitives, and so on) and paid less attention to the theory of how human languages work in general. I also tried to construct a model of grammar that is as accessible and as teachable as possible, accompanied of course by the consumer advisory that students who go on to more advanced courses in syntax will encounter models of grammar that differ in some or many ways from the model in this book. Advanced courses are also likely to focus more on grammatical theory itself than on the construction of a comprehensive grammar of English or any other particular language. In this chapter, I will give you a taste of some recent ideas in syntactic theory.

Some Claims of Syntactic Theory

By far the leading modern figure in the study of syntax has been Noam Chomsky. As the principal architect of the school known as transformational grammar (beginning with his groundbreaking book *Syntactic Structures* in 1957), Chomsky revolutionized the way we examine language. Since then, he has never ceased to innovate, constantly leading the field in new directions.

The study of syntax has developed rapidly in recent years, with much speculation and many competing theories about how our minds produce language structures. Consequently, among linguists there is great diversity of thought and by no means full agreement. Following is a brief introduction to some principles associated with recent work by Chomsky and others. Some of these claims are more controversial than others, and many linguists subscribe to some but not all of them.

  • **Claim A**: *Humans everywhere are born with a special gift for learning language.*

As the previous chapters have amply demonstrated, a language such as English is devilishly complex. If you are like most students, it took you considerable study and frequent practice with the exercises in this book to gain a conscious understanding (and an introductory one at that) of English syntax. How can we reconcile this complexity with the fact that, as a young child, you achieved a working mastery of your native language with astonishing speed and without apparent effort? How is it that, at an early age, you were able to unconsciously apply the rules of grammar that we have been at such pains to discover with our conscious minds? The conclusion drawn by Chomsky is that the minds of human children are hard-wired (to use a computer analogy) to learn language. That is, we were born with brains that have a special knack for language-learning.

- **Claim B**: *All human languages share a universal grammar.*

You learned your native language with ease, but if by chance you had been born into a household where Spanish was spoken (or Korean or Navajo or Zulu, for that matter), you would have learned that language instead with the same ease. These languages differ not just in vocabulary but in many other particulars. For example, no two languages have identical word order. Without considerable modification, the phrase-structure rules of English would not consistently generate grammatical sentences in any other language.

Because languages are all so different, how is it possible that a child could learn any one language just as quickly and easily as any other? The answer given by Chomsky is that human languages are less different than we might suppose. On the contrary, they must all be alike in some basic way. Despite many superficial differences, they all share fundamental syntactic principles. These principles are commonly referred to as ***Universal Grammar***.

- **Claim C**: *The difficult parts of language are universal and innate; the traits of a particular language that a child must learn are relatively simple.*

According to this hypothesis, humans do not have to learn the principles of Universal Grammar, because these principles are already part of the makeup of the mind. We are born knowing them. A child has only to learn the particulars of its native language. What is more, all the really complex parts of language are part of Universal Grammar and do not need to be learned. Only a series of simple differences separates one language from another. This helps to explain why a child is able to learn its native language so quickly and easily.

- **Claim D**: *Languages differ only in certain either/or traits.*

Not only are the differences between languages simple, but they are either/or choices. According to this interesting and controversial claim, there are never unlimited options for how a certain matter of syntax can be handled by a language. In fact, there cannot even be three or four options, but only two. As a rough analogy, imagine that the mind has a number of switches for language that can be set either "up" or "down." Each switch represents the two options for a particular syntactic choice available to each language. In some languages a particular switch is set to "up," while in some other languages that same switch is set to "down." In learning the grammar of its native language, all a child has to do, in effect, is to figure out which position the language sets for each switch.

As an example, we might assume that children are born knowing (unconsciously, as part of Universal Grammar) that verb phrases can consist of verbs and objects. The child has then the relatively simple task of discovering whether its native language is verb-first (like English: *Eat sushi!*) or verb-last (like Japanese: *Sushi eat!*) and then setting a mental switch accordingly.

- **Claim E**: *Every language has either a head-first or a head-last order.*

Not only are certain either/or decisions made by a language, but some decisions are very general, with far-reaching implications. For example, it has been claimed that every language orders all of its phrases in a similar way.

The principal element in any phrase is called its **head**. In a verb phrase, for example, the verb is the head of the phrase, and in a prepositional phrase, the preposition is the head. According to the claim, every language orders all of its phrases in the same way. English is an example of a head-first language, while Japanese is an example of a head-last language.

1

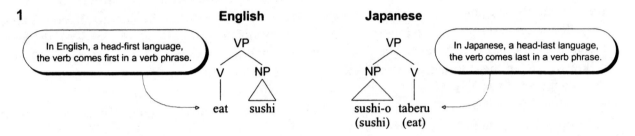

Head-order, it is claimed, is not just a tendency but an invariable rule. In a head-first language *every* phrase begins with a head. If we accept this premise, then we would have to revise some of our analyses in the preceding chapters. For example, we have labeled phrases such as *the sandwich* as noun phrases. Perhaps instead we should regard such phrases as "determiner phrases," with the determiner being the head component:

2

This may strike you as odd, because the noun *sandwich* would seem to be the key word in the phrase. I will provide an explanation, but let's wait until we first consider another hypothesis:

- **Claim F**: *Every phrase is limited to two constituents.*

According to this claim, the nature of language structure is uniformly **binary**, meaning "composed of two parts." Any phrase, whether a verb phrase, a prepositional phrase, or the sentence (S) itself, will never have more than two constituents. If we accept this hypothesis, we would have to reconsider the structure of phrases that we have diagramed with multiple branches. For example, we have assumed that a phrase such as *the best inexpensive Italian restaurant* has five constituents:

3

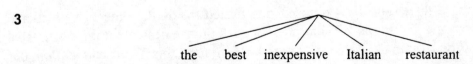

The binary principle would cause us to rethink the structure of this phrase. If no more than two branches can come off a tree at any node, the phrase might instead have the following structure:

4

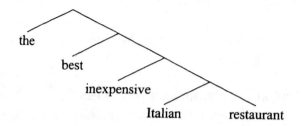

Does this structure make any sense? Well, actually it does. Consider how the adjective *best* works in the phrase. In tree 3, it appears to be merely one of four independent modifiers of the noun *restaurant*. But the phrase does not describe the best *restaurant*—of all restaurants, the one that is best. Rather, it describes the best *inexpensive Italian restaurant*—that is, of all inexpensive Italian restaurants, the one that is best. The word *best* must take into account all three of the words that follow it. To put this another way, *inexpensive Italian restaurant* is a phrase that is modified, as a unit, by the adjective *best*. And to put it still another way, the adjective *best* has within its **scope** the entire phrase *inexpensive Italian restaurant*. Unlike tree 3, tree 4 clearly shows that *best* is in a head position with respect to those other three words.

We can analyze the adjective *inexpensive* in a similar way. The phrase is not comparing inexpensive *restaurants* but inexpensive *Italian restaurants*. Both of those two words fall within its scope. Even the determiner *the* takes into account all four words that follow it: *The* does not just modify *restaurant* but *best inexpensive Italian restaurant*. This explains why it is not unreasonable to claim, as a number of linguists do, that the determiner *the* is the head of the phrase as a whole and to label the uppermost node as a determiner phrase.

In tree 4, the category labels were omitted. Following the principles introduced so far in this chapter, we might supply labels as follows:

5

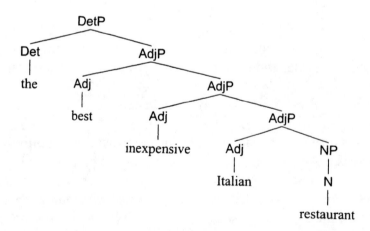

Notice that the tree contains three adjectival phrases, one nested inside the other. A notational convention in wide use when a phrase (an XP) has another such phrase nested within it is to label the lower occurrence as X′ or X̄ (both pronounced "X-bar"). If we used this *X-bar convention*, our tree would be labeled as follows:

6

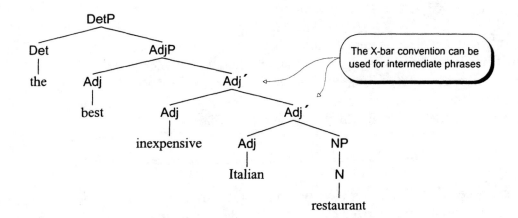

The X-bar convention can be used for intermediate phrases

The binary principle also allows the grammar to account for certain ambiguities—for example, between the two interpretations of the phrase *a sad movie maker*:

7

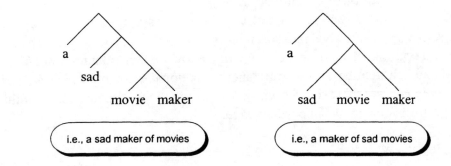

i.e., a sad maker of movies

i.e., a maker of sad movies

While the binary principle is helpful in clarifying the scope of some modifiers, it is less clear how it would accommodate certain other modifiers. Consider, for example, the following phrase:

8   my generous, smart, comical cousin

The noun *cousin* is modified by three adjectives, none of which seems to include the others within its scope. It describes a cousin who happens to be generous, also happens to be smart, and also happens to be comical. These are independent qualities, and the order in which the three adjectives are spoken is arbitrary. How binary branching would capture multiple modifiers that are seemingly independent of each other is not clear.

Whether binary branching is a general tendency of language structure or an invariable rule, claim F is the kind of general statement about language that practitioners of syntax consider worthy of examination. It is in keeping with another principle of syntactic theory:

• **Claim G**: *Rules should be as general and as simple as possible.*

If languages are fundamentally similar, differing only in ways that are simple enough for small children to master, then the rules of particular languages also must be relatively simple. In constructing a model of those rules, we should seek maximum generalizations. We did this to some extent in the preceding chapters, as when we formulated our coordination rule:

9   XP → XP C_{Co} XP

This rule is generalized in that it claims that *all* phrases are coordinated in exactly the same way. Apart from such cases, however, the grammar that we created (in 33 on page 269, for example) includes a great many different, and highly specific, rules. Perhaps there are additional generalizations that we overlooked. In fact, linguists seek the most *sweeping* generalizations possible. Consider, for example, the following hypothesis:

- **Claim H**: *All phrases in a language have the same general structure.*

This is a sweeping claim if ever there was one. If it is true, then not just coordinate phrases but *all* English phrases can be generated by a single XP rule. Let us see what arguments can be formulated to support the hypothesis. (To simplify the following discussion, let us temporarily ignore the binary hypothesis, although we will return to it later. We may also wish to revisit the question of whether a phrase like *the sandwich* should be considered a noun phrase or a determiner phrase. For now, let us revert to using the traditional NP category label.)

One similarity we have observed is that each phrase has a head element: the verb in a verb phrase, the adjective in an adjectival phrase, and so on. In addition, each of these head elements can be preceded by an optional element, which we will call by the general name *specifier* (abbreviated **spec**). Each head can also be followed by another optional element, which we will call by the general name *complement* (abbreviated **comp**). According to this hypothesis, the following general rule can account for every phrase in our language:

10   XP → (spec) X (comp)

As examples of this structure, consider the following phrases, in which the head components are italicized:

11 a. a *bolt* from the blue   —NP
     b. very *surprised* by the news   —AdjP
     c. totally *without* a clue   ·   —PP

The head in each of these phrases is preceded by a specifier and followed by a complement. Specifiers include both determiners (such as *a* in 11a) and degree modifiers (*very* in 11b and *totally* in 11c). These specifiers have roughly similar functions, allowing us to define specifiers as components that specify the identity or extent of the head of the phrase.

Complements include prepositional phrases and noun phrases. A prepositional phrase can be the complement of a noun phrase (*from the blue* in 11a) and of an adjectival phrase (*by the news* in 11b). The complement of a prepositional phrase is its object noun phrase (*a clue* in 11c). Complements can be defined as phrases that in some way complete the meaning or purpose of the head element.

The phrases in 11 conform to the structure of our universal rule 10 and give some support to hypothesis H. However, three phrases is a long way from *all* phrases. Let us look at some less obvious cases. Do verb phrases also have the structure of rule 10? Consider the following verb phrases:

12 a. seldom *causes* any problem

  b. always *raises* the flag

  c. genuinely *likes* opera

Object noun phrases act as complements of the verbs in these sentences (*any problem*, *the flag*, *opera*). The words *seldom*, *always*, and *genuinely* precede the verb and, let us claim, act as specifiers. This would require a change in our thinking, because we have hitherto regarded these words as adverbs (whose underlying position is at the end, not the beginning, of the verb phrase). Nevertheless, a good case can be made for seeing them as specifiers. For one thing, these same words can act as degree modifiers (specifiers) when they precede adjectives or prepositional phrases (as in *seldom late*, *always in a good mood*, and *genuinely fearful*). Second, unlike typical adverbs, these words are far more likely to come right before a verb (*Francis seldom raises the flag*) than at the end of a sentence (?*Francis raises the flag seldom*) or at the beginning (**Seldom Francis raises the flag*). Consequently, we have defensible grounds for claiming they are specifiers of verbs.

If the hypothesis that rule 10 describes *every* English phrase is correct, then it should also describe the sentence itself. The sentence rule that we have used throughout this book (S → NP VP) clearly does not reflect the structure of 10. Some linguists, however, have made the interesting claim that the auxiliary element (Aux) that we have regarded as a component of the verb phrase is actually a direct component of the sentence itself. What is more, they argue, it is the head element of the sentence, making the sentence in effect an "auxiliary phrase" or AuxP. The subject NP of the sentence is then its specifier, and the predicate VP is the complement. If so, all of the following phrases have the specifier-head-complement structure of rule 10:

13

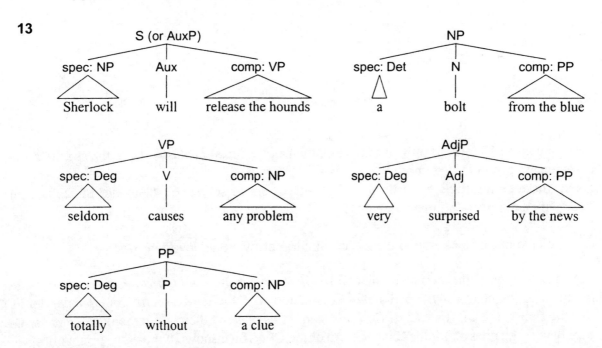

To accept rule 10, we would have to abandon two earlier claims: that all phrases are binary and that English is a head-first (rather than head-middle) language. But wait! By using the X-bar convention that we discussed earlier, we can recast rule 10 as the following two rules:

14   XP → (spec) X′

X′ → X (comp)

Using these rules, the grammar generates phrases like the following:

15 a.

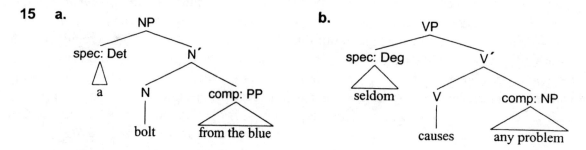

b.

Now binary branching is restored, and the head elements occupy a left (head-first) position. Because we have analyzed the determiner in 15a as a specifier rather than a head element, we can find support for labeling such a phrase as NP rather than DetP (although both terms are in use among linguists).

In any phrase, both the specifier and the complement are optional elements. We can show the positions of these elements in our diagrams, even when they are not filled by any word or phrase:

16

```
            NP
          /    \
       spec     N′
              /    \
             N     comp
             |
        enthusiasm
```

The noun phrase in 16 consists only of one word, the head noun *enthusiasm*. Both the specifier and the complement positions are empty.

Using these conventions, we can now diagram an entire sentence. Consider the following sentence with a nominal-complement clause:

17   The king of Slobovia issued a warning that the army would invade Fredonia.

As you might expect, the complement clause (*that the army would invade Fredonia*) is the complement of the noun *warning*. To avoid confusion with the general term *complement*, let us re-label the clause as a **CP** (instead of CompP), and let us re-label the complementizer (*that*) as **C**. In keeping with the rules of **14**, the C is the head of the CP. If we show all the empty categories, we would draw this diagram:

18

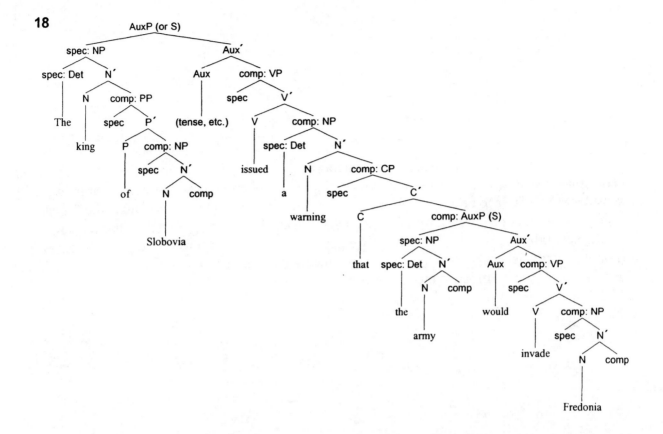

For simplicity, I have ignored the derivation of verb tenses in this diagram. Even so, the tree is not very simple. On the contrary, it illustrates one of the great ironies associated with syntactic theory: The more the rules of grammar get simplified, the more complex the trees become.

What is the reason, you may ask, for showing empty categories in a diagram such as 16 or 18? The answer has to do with another claim of syntactic theory:

- **Claim I**: *Transformations do not change the underlying structure of a sentence.*

The T-rules that we formulated in previous chapters have not observed this principle. For example, when we derived *wh*-questions in Chapter 13, we moved both the *wh*-phrase and the auxiliary, tacking them on to the front of the sentence, as when we derived *Which car should Bernie wash?*

19   Bernie <u>should</u> wash <u>which car</u>

As a consequence, the spoken structure has a very different shape from the underlying structure. However, hypothesis I, the structure-preserving principle, states that an element can only be moved to an existing (empty) position. In **19**, this principle would prevent us from moving *which car* and *should* to the front of the sentence unless unfilled categories were there to accommodate them.

Now take a look at the beginning of the complement clause (*that the army . . .*) in tree **18**. Notice that the clause is preceded by this structure:

20

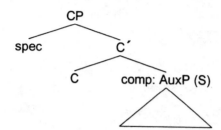

In the interests of achieving the greatest generalization, as required by principles G and H, let us claim that this structure precedes *all clauses*, including main clauses. In other words, we will consider *every* clause to be a complement clause of sorts, except that in main clauses the C position is empty instead of being filled by a complementizer such as *that* or *if*. With this change, derivation 19 can now proceed, because there are now empty categories that can receive the moved elements. (For simplicity, let us omit from the following diagram the assignment of verb inflections and the derivation of the interrogative pronoun *which*.)

21

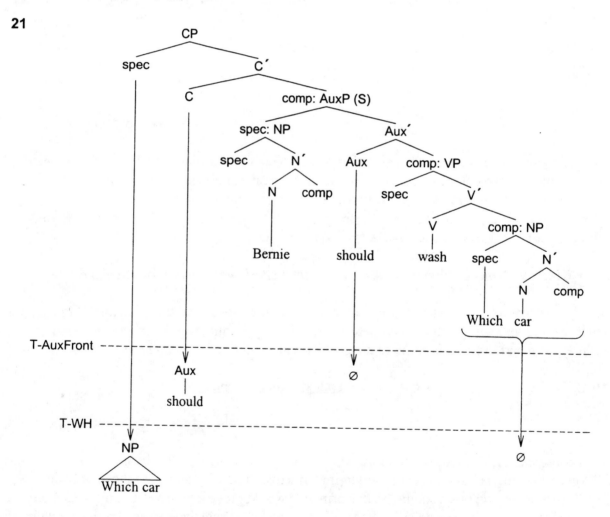

The auxiliary-fronting transformation moves the auxiliary *should* to the formerly empty C position, and the *wh*-fronting transformation moves the noun phrase *which car* to the initial specifier position.

Although elements have been moved from one position to another, the structure of the tree is not changed, just as hypothesis I requires.

A broken-line diagram such as 21 shows the underlying structure of the sentence and then records transformational changes below broken lines. A somewhat different, but equivalent, diagraming convention is in common use among linguists. It shows the final *spoken* structure of a sentence and uses arrows to record the underlying locations from which elements have been moved. The original site of the moved element is marked by the symbol ***t*** (short for ***trace***) to signify that the position is now empty.

Here is what diagram 21 would look like using this convention:

22

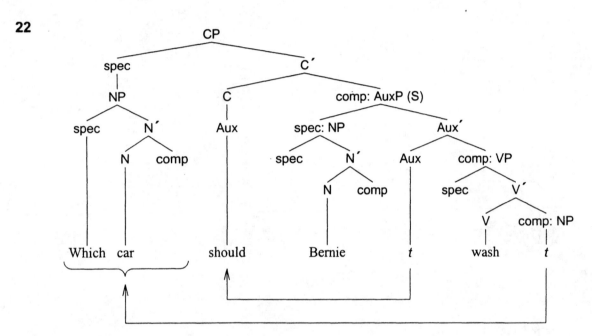

In 22 it is not necessary to show more than one tree because the structure of the underlying and spoken structures are the same. Note also that diagrams 21 and 22 are equivalent and make the same claims about how the sentence is derived.

In proposing phrase-structure rules such as 14, and also in formulating transformational rules, linguists seek the most general principles that may operate in a language. The result could be called a "theoretical grammar," which is likely to differ in many respects and to serve different purposes from the "teaching grammar" presented in this book. Unfortunately, space does not permit me to give you more than a taste of the exciting developments now ongoing in the field of syntax. I hope that you have found it a tantalizing taste and that you are hungry to continue your discovery of English grammar and of the many other pleasures and mysteries involved in the study of human language.

For Further Reading

Borsley, Robert. *Syntactic Theory: A Unified Approach.* London: Edward Arnold, 1991.

Haegeman, Liliane. *Introduction to Government and Binding Theory.* 2nd ed. Cambridge, MA: Blackwell, 1994.

Radford, Andrew. *Syntax: A Minimalist Introduction.* New York: Cambridge University Press, 1997.

19   Grammar in the Schools

Few topics in education have been the subject of as much controversy in recent years as the teaching of grammar. Although grammar was once a central and unquestioned part of the curriculum (the elementary grades are still known as "grammar school"), its role is now very much debated. Past assumptions about the effectiveness of grammar-teaching in the development of speaking, writing, and thinking skills have been called into question. Moreover, the introduction of modern scientific approaches to language study (most notably, transformational grammar) have challenged the validity of the grammar systems traditionally taught in the schools, while at the same time the complexity of those modern systems has raised questions about their own applicability and teachability in elementary and secondary classrooms. More than ever before, teachers and parents are uncertain and confused about how — and even *whether* — grammar should be taught.

A Brief History of Grammar Instruction

Although we think of instruction in English grammar as a traditional part of education, it is in fact a relatively recent phenomenon, and it has occupied a central place within the curriculum for only about the last hundred years. The changing role of grammar is in large part due to changing attitudes toward the language itself.

In the Middle Ages and in succeeding centuries, English and other vernacular languages (the national languages spoken in everyday life) were held in lower regard than the classical languages of Latin, Greek, and Hebrew. The modern notion of "progress" was an attitude quite alien to the time. Rather than progressing, knowledge and culture were thought to have declined from the days of classical antiquity. It was believed that the highest pinnacle of science, literature, and the arts had been achieved in that earlier age, and consequently the focus of education was on classical, not contemporary, studies. Latin retained its high status in Europe as the language of religion, law, and scholarship.

In English schools, the central subjects within the curriculum were Latin and Latin literature. From the earliest grades, students studied Latin grammar intensively, while English grammar was not studied simply because it was not thought worthy of study. Until very recent centuries, it was even questioned whether English had a grammar. (If that seems preposterous, remember that the same false attitude is widely held today about African American English and other dialects.)

the model for English was contrived to resemble the Latin model as closely as possible. This unscientific, Latin-based model became the basis for school instruction, and its influence is still felt today. For generations, school children were taught many inexact notions: English, for example, was said to have eight parts of speech and a classification of verb tenses and noun cases akin to those of Latin. None of these notions has a basis in the actual structure of English.

The growth of the British Empire and the gaining of independence by the American colonies led to increased national pride within both the British Isles and the United States. One consequence was an increasing pride in the language. In America, the stature of English—and consequently of English studies in the schools—was unquestioned, and from the end of the nineteenth century the study of grammar occupied the central place in the language-arts curriculum. The term "grammar" has been used in a very broad sense, encompassing Latin-based descriptions of syntax, prescriptive rather than descriptive rules based on logic (for example, "double negatives are ungrammatical because two negatives make a positive"), rules of style ("awkward and unnecessary repetition of words and sounds should be avoided"), and rules of punctuation ("the semicolon is used to separate items in a series when one of those items contains a comma within it"). The latter two topics, stylistic conventions and punctuation, are usually referred to as the study of *usage*, which is different from syntax, the study of how language is structured. As practiced in many classrooms, language study was quite narrow, going little beyond "skill and drill" exercises.

In the twentieth century, while "traditional" grammar continued to hold sway in the schools, linguists in academia were developing more scientific approaches that attempted to describe the actual structure of English, not the structure it might have if it were more like Latin or if it conformed to the wishes of the describers. *Structural linguistics*, the dominant school of descriptive linguistics in the middle decades of the twentieth century, held that the syntax of a sentence should be studied without regard to the sentence's meaning. (What constitutes a noun is determined by structural characteristics, such as where it can occur within a sentence, rather than by a definition based on meaning: "A noun is the name of a person, place, or thing.")

Since the late 1950s, when it was developed by Noam Chomsky, *transformational grammar* has replaced structuralism as the principal school of modern linguistic thought. Transformational syntax is interested in creating a model not just of sentences as they are actually produced (which we have called *spoken structures*) but also of how speakers produce them. An important claim of transformational grammar is that sentences have a sort of history: spoken sentences are the products of changes (or *transformations*) from more abstract forms (*underlying structures*). Because underlying structures are related to the concepts or ideas being communicated by sentences, transformational grammar is also more interested in meaning than is structural grammar.

Structural and transformational grammar have had an impact on grammar teaching in the schools. It is now widely recognized, for example, that English and all other languages constantly change and that correctness is determined not by logical or traditional rules but by the actual practice of those who speak and write the language. What is correct in formal written English is determined by the usage of literate writers. If they routinely begin sentences with conjunctions and end them with prepositions (as indeed they do), then such practices are part of standard English.

Not every attempt to introduce scientific concepts into the curriculum, however, has been successful. Part of the reason is the complexity of modern systems, which can make them inappropriate as teaching models, at least without modification.

Another cause of difficulty with introducing scientific grammar study into the schools has been the attempt to put it to uses for which it was never intended. Transformational grammar attempts to provide accurate descriptions of our unconscious knowledge about language. It assumes that conscious knowledge about language is quite separate from the unconscious knowledge that enables us to produce and understand language. Grammar instruction in the schools, however, has traditionally been based on a very different theory—namely, that better speaking and writing abilities will automatically follow from increased conscious knowledge about language. In recent years, this theory has been called into question.

Since the 1970s, the educational pendulum has swung away from the emphasis of earlier decades on traditional grammar. As a result, many of today's students—and their teachers—have had little formal instruction in grammar of any kind. Is this development appropriate, we may now ask, or is it time for an informed reexamination of the role grammar can and should play in the curriculum?

Some Limitations of Grammar Instruction

If a case is to be made for grammar study in the schools, it must avoid unsupported claims and must take into account not only the benefits but also the limitations of grammar study. The arguments traditionally given for the kind of grammar instruction that dominated English studies for most of the twentieth century were based on claims for grammar's utility. It was argued that by studying grammar, students would learn the makeup of the language and so be able to apply what they learned as better speakers, writers, and readers. Recent linguistic theory, however, argues for a considerably more complex reality, and numerous research studies have suggested that the link between grammar study and improved language skills is neither simple nor direct.

Any claim that the study of grammar does not automatically results in better reading and writing may strike you as surprising and suspect. Like many who have gone into language-arts teaching, you may have always loved studying grammar. It may seem reasonable or even obvious to attribute your own success in reading and writing to the instruction you received in grammar. Nevertheless, evidence is strong that the connection between the two is indirect at best. To see why, we must consider the difference between our conscious and our unconscious knowledge of language. The unconscious faculty of the mind that directs our production and understanding of language is separate from the conscious faculty that is affected by grammar study. Conscious knowledge is not automatically transformed into unconscious knowledge. When we learn about language consciously, our ability to produce language is not necessarily improved. Learning about grammar (by itself) has about the same effect on the ability to read and write as learning about leg muscles has on the ability to run.

What linguists have learned about *child language acquisition* (the way in which infants and children learn to use language) also supports this argument. Whenever you or I produce a sentence, we are following unconscious principles or rules. Most of them we acquired very early, since we were speaking grammatical English long before we were old enough to attend school. Obviously we did not learn these rules directly. Our parents did not tell us, for example, that a sentence must consist of a subject (a noun phrase) and a predicate (a verb phrase), and yet we were applying this rule before we were out of diapers. Nor did we learn by simple imitation: The speech of children is different in significant ways from the speech of adults. Rather, we were exposed to language, and from that exposure, we figured out the rules on our own.

Linguists believe that children are born with a capacity (we can call it an instinct if we like) for learning language. Children's minds are innately prepared to discover and then apply the rules of whatever language is spoken around them. Children learn these rules without specific instruction (making mistakes at first and overgeneralizing—saying, for example, "I eated" and "she gots," but with further experience learning to refine their rules and to allow for exceptions). Direct teaching by parents *about* language does the child little if any good. Children learn language very much on their own, and while parents can provide a rich language environment that can aid children in learning, even children who are ignored still learn language, provided they are at least exposed to language spoken around them. Given the extraordinary complexity of the rules of language (as our analysis in this book has amply demonstrated), we must truly be impressed by the innate capacity of human children to learn language.

School children learn to read and write in similar ways. Most of what they learn about reading, for example, comes from their own experiences. Direct instruction plays a relatively minor part; exposure to the written word is far more important. Children who since infancy have been read to on their parents' laps become early readers. Schools that make frequent reading for study and pleasure (rather than isolated phonics drills) the primary focus of their reading program have the best results.

Writing, too, is largely self-taught. The best predictor of the writing abilities of college students is the amount of reading and writing they have previously done—not the amount of instruction they have had in the rules of grammar or usage. To foster literacy, schools can offer an environment in which language skills can flourish; they can provide experiences which aid development; and they can promote attitudes that encourage learning—but they cannot teach those skills directly.

Modern composition theory is in accord with linguistic theory about the ineffectiveness of *isolated* grammar instruction in promoting writing ability. It rejects traditional arguments for a building-block model of acquiring writing skills: As a first step in learning to write (according to the building-block model) children are introduced to grammar so that they can understand the language. They are then drilled in small units of language such as words and spelling. They next progress to sentences, then to paragraphs, and only then are they ready to tackle an essay. Modern theory rejects this approach, holding that students learn to write by writing. They should begin writing from the earliest grades, and they should write and read as often as possible. Any attempts to teach writing skills apart from actual writing will fail. Improvements in grammatical sophistication come from exposure and practice in using new grammatical forms, not from isolated learning *about* grammar.

The findings of experimental research have also disappointed those who hoped to prove the traditional arguments for grammar teaching. Dozens of carefully conducted experiments dating back to the beginning of this century have shown little connection between traditional grammar study and either improved control over surface features such as style and mechanics or improved expression. The old arguments based on utility do not by themselves provide a strong case for grammar instruction.

Studying Grammar Is Valuable and Important

If we can rid ourselves of some of the old assumptions about goals and methods, however, we can make a case for teaching grammar—properly defined—that is unassailable.

Grammar Instruction as a Means to Better Language Skills

Whatever the controversy about teaching conscious grammatical knowledge, there is certainly no controversy about the value of students' increasing their unconscious grammatical knowledge. Teachers who disagree about methods of teaching grammar fully agree that students should gain a working command of grammar. All teachers want their students to speak and write fluent, effective, and grammatical English. Moreover, they want them to extend their grammatical sophistication, to have at their disposal a wide range of grammatical constructions. How, we may ask, can this knowledge best be achieved? What should teachers and parents do?

In the terms that we have studied, increased grammatical sophistication means acquiring more unconscious syntactic rules and applying them in productive ways. As student writers mature, for example, their syntactic repertoires grow to include adverbial clauses, participial phrases, and appositives. They learn to make choices about moving adverbials and selecting active or passive voice for reasons of emphasis and style. Much of this increased grammatical knowledge comes from exposure and practice: They learn through reading, and they refine what they learn through writing. Parents and teachers play an important role by fostering that experience. Competent writing will come naturally and fluently to children if they write frequently in school, as a part of their daily work in all subjects, not just in order to produce occasional English "essays."

More direct methods can also be useful, provided they are tied to actual writing. While isolated teaching about grammar has little direct impact on writing skills, teaching that is intimately tied with writing can produce results. As the following pages demonstrate, new grammatical constructions can be modeled and imitated in various ways so as to extend students' grammatical repertoires. Some instructional methods, it seems, can indeed lead to wider unconscious knowledge of grammar.

Unconscious knowledge, however, is not the only target of our instruction. Conscious knowledge does have a place in at least certain usage skills, and these can be affected by direct instruction. Whereas most spelling and punctuation decisions are automatic (unconscious) matters to us, ingrained as a result of our reading and writing experience, we all make certain other decisions about our writing in a deliberate (conscious) way. In examining my own writing practice, for example, I can easily think of several examples. When I write an *i-t-s*, I consciously remember a rule about which one gets the apostrophe (*it's* is the contraction for *it is*; *its* is the possessive of *it*). In punctuating a relative clause, I sometimes need to consider whether the clause is restrictive or nonrestrictive (the latter is separated from the main clause by commas). When I write *affect* and *effect* I have to think consciously about which one is which (you can have an *effect, affect* the outcome, or *effect* a change).

Like all other writers, I have a whole fund of conscious stylistic notions that I apply whenever I write or edit my writing. When I write a series of phrases, I check that they are in parallel form (for instance, not mixing noun phrases with verb phrases or clauses, as in: *She likes sports, science, does crossword puzzles, and she reads mysteries*). I consciously avoid words I consider pretentious (*utilize* instead of *use*), and I try to delete unnecessary phrases to make my writing more direct. I am sure I acquired these conscious principles about writing not just from experience but also from direct school instruction and from reading articles and books about writing.

Schools can and should teach those elements of mechanics and style that are matters of conscious knowledge. Such teaching is ineffective, however, if it is conducted apart from a writing context. A lesson on punctuating relative clauses, taught by itself to a middle-school class, in most cases simply will not work. On the other hand, if that class is engaged in a large-group editing session, discussing ways to help a student improve a draft of an essay, questions about punctuation will arise naturally. Students will retain information about usage only when they are motivated—when they feel a need to learn that information and believe it will benefit them. Creating a receptive attitude and a commitment to writing is perhaps the most important task of the writing teacher.

Inasmuch as a case can be made for certain teaching about usage, is there anything to be said in favor of teaching syntax itself? Is conscious grammatical knowledge of any value? Is it desirable for students to be able to recognize nouns and verbs, or to know a gerund when they write one?

One quite common argument for learning grammar is that it gives students a means for talking about their writing. Developing an analytical attitude about writing is a worthwhile goal, and we surely want students to understand how they have written, to think critically about what they have done, and to consider other choices that might have presented themselves. Conscious grammatical knowledge allows for this analysis and provides a vocabulary for communicating about it. This benefit seems reasonable, although it is not universally accepted. A far more compelling practical argument for grammar study, or for any study of language, is a less direct one. Good writers have a passion for language, and those who have such a passion are equipped to become good writers. Language can be a fascinating subject, and the more students know and care about their language, the greater will be their concern for their own writing. Teachers owe it to their students to communicate both the fascination of language study and their own enthusiasm for the subject.

Grammar Instruction for Its Own Sake

Even if one were to reject practical considerations (such as the impact of grammar on other skills), a strong argument can still be made for teaching grammar for its own sake. According to this important argument, grammar is worth learning because it has a value in and of itself.

To argue that a subject has an intrinsic value is a curious type of argument, since it is not subject to outside proof. It is impossible, for example, to prove or disprove the merits of studying the fine arts or higher mathematics. Most students will not become artists or musicians nor will many ever encounter practical applications for trigonometry or Boolean algebra, and yet most of us believe in the value of these studies. Our arguments are based on notions of value that have nothing to do with immediate utility, nothing to do with developing marketable skills or increasing our incomes. Instead we see these subjects as important areas of knowledge, connected in important ways with the meaning of being human, with beauty, and even with the nature of truth itself. Our minds, we feel, are more fully developed, our knowledge more richly completed, through our contact with these studies. It is an argument based on insight, subjective experience, aesthetics, and certain philosophical assumptions, rather than on practical consequences. Nonetheless it is an argument that is not to be dismissed out of hand.

The same arguments support the teaching of grammar. I hope that, having completed the study of this book, you now *know* the value of grammar. I hope you have found a beauty and even a pleasure, perhaps a deeply satisfying one, in understanding the remarkably elegant structure of our language. I hope you have found it a revelation as the operating principles of the English language unfolded before you and as you were struck by the clarity of what was at first quite unclear. Many millions of people have known these experiences and remain convinced of grammar's importance. They love the language, and their study of grammar has played an important role in fostering that love.

Besides conferring aesthetic rewards, the study of grammar also provides important knowledge about ourselves. The use of language is the most central of all the faculties of the human mind. All mental activity that makes us distinctly human presupposes language. Human minds are uniquely adapted to learning language, and the structures of language and of our minds are attuned. Because language is so complex and because such large areas of our brains are devoted to language (as neurological studies show), no other field of study can give us equivalent insight into the nature and structure of our minds. Like the study of philosophy, history, biology, sociology, and psychology, the study of grammar teaches us important lessons about ourselves. Self-knowledge is the central concern of a liberal and humanistic education. It is its own reward. We need look no further to justify its existence.

Methods of Teaching Grammar

Assuming we want to teach grammar, how then do we do so? The methods for teaching grammar to a class of college students are not those most appropriate for primary and secondary students, and teachers must use wisdom and discretion in formulating their plans of instruction. They must also consider their goals carefully. Different methods are appropriate when teaching *applied grammar* (grammatical knowledge that students apply in their reading and writing) and when teaching grammar as a self-contained subject.

Instruction in Applied Grammar

Applied grammar is best taught by teaching reading and writing. As students become more experienced and fluent readers and writers, their unconscious grammatical knowledge improves as well. Consequently, it is important for language-arts instructors on all levels to be trained in methods of teaching reading and writing. It is to those fields that we must look for information about methods for developing applied grammatical skills.

While these methods are largely indirect, they can also include some more direct methods for increasing grammatical sophistication. *Modeling exercises* can introduce students to new syntactic constructions, and they can teach stylistic lessons as well. As an example, the following activities can successfully introduce high school students to the use of participial modifiers.

A TYPICAL MODELING EXERCISE

In each blank space, supply a present participle (*-ing* phrase) to modify the preceding noun, as in these examples:

    a. The angry demonstrators, *shaking their fists at the police,* advanced on the courthouse.
    b. *Stuffing their faces with mangos and rice,* the children ate greedily.

Now use your imagination to invent similar modifiers for these sentences:

    1. The pirates, _____[insert *-ing* phrase here]_____, boarded the Spanish frigate.

    2. _____[*-ing* phrase]_____, she crossed the finish line of the marathon after four agonizing hours.

    3. _____[*-ing* phrase]_____ and _____[another *-ing* phrase]_____, the orator on the soapbox drew only smiles from the passing crowd.

As part of a unit in which students are writing descriptive essays, they may take time out to complete this exercise. An exercise like this requires very little if any formal instruction about participles and how they are formed. Grammatical terminology is not necessary for its success; it will work just as well if the participles are called simply *-ing phrases* (although there is no reason not to provide the standard name for them). With a little practice, students catch on to the nature of participles, and they begin very quickly to supply their own examples.

An exercise such as this works best if it is treated as a game and made as entertaining as possible. In a discussion after students have written the exercise, the teacher can solicit a variety of their responses, with special praise going to the more clever and more colorful examples. The class can also be shown examples of participles in the work of professional writers. A follow-up exercise can ask students to add participles to sentences for which no blank spaces are provided, such as this one:

    The mother ape confronted the human intruder.

Questions can be asked to encourage creativity in this exercise and to open students' minds to stylistic possibilities: Can more than one participle be supplied? In what places? Can participles modify *the intruder* as well as *the mother ape*? A discussion of dangling participles can arise naturally from this exercise; the class can consider whether a problem exists with a sentence such as *The mother ape confronted the human intruder, shaking her hairy fist.*

For such exercises to have a lasting effect, students must have the immediate opportunity to apply what they have learned to their own writing. As a follow-up to the modeling exercise on participles, students can revise a descriptive passage they have previously written so that it includes several participial modifiers. Furthermore, since they are engaged in a stylistic experiment, they can attempt to include as many participles as possible and then analyze the result. At what point do the participles become intrusive? Which ones work and which ones don't? Can the passage be revised again so that it contains only a few effective participles?

The point of such exercises is not to encourage the proliferation of participles for their own sake but to introduce students to new possibilities for effective writing and to increase their awareness of style. Like all attempts to teach applied grammar, these exercises are effective because they involve students in actual writing. No amount of isolated instruction *about* participles can have an equivalent effect. In addition to active participles, many other constructions, including appositives, absolutes, gerunds, and relative clauses, can be introduced in similar ways.

It is important to see the difference between such exercises and traditional drills, which lack any direct connection with actual writing and frequently bore students besides. Exercises, for example, where students are asked to underline and label participles and other modifiers or verbals from a list of sentences or where they are told to find and correct dangling participles in a list of sentences or even where they are told simply to invent a few sentences containing participles may do more harm than good. Whatever information they provide is unlikely to be retained; students are more likely to be alienated than stimulated by such drills; and valuable time that could have been spent constructively has been wasted.

Modeling exercises are just one of many effective methods of developing a stylistic and grammatical range in student writing. Another is through *sentence combining*. Many grammatical constructions such as participles, gerunds, adverbial clauses, and relative clauses derive from embedded clauses (one S-clause embedded in another). Sentence-combining exercises cause students to broaden their syntactic repertoires by exploring various possibilities for embedding, as in the following example:

A Typical Sentence-Combining Exercise

Combine the following clauses in as many ways as possible:

> The dwarves approached the dragon's lair.
> The dwarves quaked with fear.
> The dwarves put on a brave front.

In the discussion that follows, students may propose combinations such as these:

> Quaking with fear but putting on a brave front, the dwarves approached the dragon's lair.

> Although they put on a brave front, the dwarves quaked with fear as they approached the dragon's lair.

> Having approached the dragon's lair, the dwarves put on a brave front to hide their quaking with fear.

> The dwarves who approached the dragon's lair quaked with fear but still put on a brave front.

Students can also be encouraged to vary or embellish the given clauses:

> Their bodies quaking inwardly with fear but outwardly showing only bravery, the intrepid dwarves approached their terrible goal, the lair of the dragon.

As variations are proposed, they can be written on the board, and the class can be encouraged to revise or add to them.

What is evident is the many different types of grammatical constructions used in these examples. The names of the constructions can be used in describing them, but sentence-combining works equally well without grammatical labeling. More important is discussion about the results: Which sentences work well? Do they have different effects? Which ones might we revise? In addition to single-sentence exercises, longer sentence-combining exercises are also effective. For example, students can be given a dozen or more clauses and asked to combine them into a paragraph or brief essay.

Sentence-combining exercises encourage students to extend their range by attempting new and diverse constructions, and the discussion afterward can bring the stylistic consequences of the various options into focus. It is important for students to have fun with these combinations. Creativity should be encouraged, even if it sometimes results in overwriting (as in the last example) or even in errors (errors are inevitable whenever students attempt to practice unfamiliar skills). Freedom to experiment and to take risks without fear of penalty is essential to the progress of language-learners at all levels. Modeled exercises and sentence-combining are two related types of exercises that can teach applied grammar. Variations can be adapted for different grade levels, and many other activities are equally valuable. As useful as they are, however, these exercises should be only supplements to a program of writing instruction, never its central focus. Reading and writing should continue to be the focus and principal activity of the language-arts curriculum.

Direct Instruction in Grammar

What then about direct instruction in grammar? There is no point in teaching grammar if students do not understand it or, worse, if they detest it. Two primary goals of grammar teaching are for students to gain insight into the workings of the English language and to gain a love for it as well. Grammar instruction that fails to accomplish these goals is worse than useless.

Unfortunately, grammar as it is often taught is so much stale drill and memorization, a subject which pleases a few and antagonizes many. Countless adults have unpleasant memories about school English largely because of grammar. (Like most others in my profession, whenever I am asked by new acquaintances what I do, I steel myself for their reaction to "English teacher": They suddenly become visibly wary and make some nervous joke about watching their grammar.)

It should not be so. There is no reason why grammar should not be made clear enough for students to understand nor any reason why it shouldn't be interesting and fun as well. How well grammar is taught depends on the wisdom and skill of the teacher.

Our teaching is unlikely to be perfect, however, or to succeed with every student, and beginning teachers should not be crushed by their lack of perfection. Still, they should set their sights high. If grammar were taught ideally in an ideal world, it would be quite different from the way it is often taught today. Textbooks would be up to date, based on modern discoveries about our language, not discredited traditions. Teachers would teach principles of syntax suitably adapted for each grade level. Information would be accurate and clear, students would be involved participants in the discovery of grammatical principles, and they would find the experience rewarding.

The world we live in, regrettably, is not ideal, but it does not have to be terrible either. Even with the constraints imposed upon teachers by mandates and textbooks over which they have no control, they can still make grammar instruction worthwhile if they adhere to some general guidelines:

1. **Teachers should involve students in discovering grammar.** The operational method of my college course in grammar is a search for the principles of our grammar, and the course's organization is from simpler to more complex concepts. We encounter data in the form of English sentences, and we attempt to discover the structure of these sentences and the way they have been formed. Grammar-as-discovery is the best teaching method in the schools as well as in college courses. Students should not simply be told about grammar; they should *do* grammar for themselves. Teachers can adapt similar methods of discovery to the abilities and needs of any grade level.

2. **Teachers should make it clear.** Analysis that is appropriate for college students would not always be clear to high-school-age or younger students. Teachers must keep grammatical analyses sufficiently simple so that they can be understood by their students. The study of different classes of infinitives (to take one example) is highly complex even for college students, but eighth graders are fully capable of recognizing infinitives and discovering insights into how they work. An eighth-grade teacher can ask a class to analyze a pair of sentences such as *Harry is eager to please* and *Harry is easy to please*. The class can make many discoveries: They will see that in the first sentence, Harry is doing the pleasing while in the second, someone else is pleasing him. A conclusion the class can draw is that infinitives have underlying subjects which do not appear in the spoken sentence.

3. **Teachers should make it fun.** The more that teachers involve students in making discoveries for themselves (as in the preceding example about infinitives), the more likely they are to accomplish their goals. The following sample activity involves noun phrases.

Can you rearrange the following groups of five words so that each makes sense as a phrase?

    a. players the basketball tall five

    b. many those recipes new dessert

    c. radio favorite two stations my

Students will all report the same answers (*the five tall basketball players* and so on). What conclusions can they then draw about how such phrases are ordered? Do the last words in each phrase (*players, recipes, stations*) have something in common? What about the words that come second (*five, many, too*)? As this lesson continues, the class can conclude that the words fall into five distinct categories, which we know as determiners (other than quantifiers), quantifiers, adjectives, noun modifiers, and nouns. They discover that when these words occur together in a phrase, they do so in that particular order. Students can also explore whether the basic order can ever be varied. Is the phrase *the tall five basketball players* ever possible? If so, what does it mean? (Perhaps "the *tall* five," as opposed to some shorter set of five basketball players?)

Such an exercise introduces the concepts of noun phrases and modifiers. It demonstrates to students that when we speak we follow certain principles that we are not consciously aware of and that it can be interesting to discover what they may be.

4. **Teachers should adapt and supplement the available materials.** The realities that teachers must deal with include some undeniable constraints on their teaching. Mandated textbooks may include some of the worst features of traditional grammar. Instruction may need to be directed so that students succeed on the grammar section of a particular achievement test. Parents and administrators may place demands for certain instructional goals and methods. It would be foolhardy for teachers to ignore such realities. Fortunately, even poor textbooks provide much valid and valuable information about English grammar, and the classifications and terminology they use are usually those accepted by most linguists. Good teachers can adapt those materials to worthwhile purposes, and they can provide their own supplementary exercises and discussions as well. They can also use many innovative and nontraditional strategies, but, if so, they will find it prudent to keep parents informed of their methods and reasons. For example, a teacher may have sound pedagogical reasons for not marking every spelling or grammatical error on a student's papers, but unless parents are informed of those reasons, they may complain that the teacher is slipshod or ignorant.

5. **Teachers should not lose sight of real goals.** The purpose of applied grammar study is to help students develop their language skills, and the purpose of direct instruction is to provide students with an understanding and appreciation of the English language. Training in advanced linguistics is not a goal of the schools. Primary and secondary students do not need a sophisticated command of theoretical grammar. Instead, they need to understand general principles about language and to be acquainted with the major grammatical constructions of our language. Diagrams, such as the tree diagrams used in transformational syntax, can be a useful tool because they make sentence-structure clear and because students usually enjoy drawing them, but they are not an end in themselves. It is also not important for students to understand all details of sentence derivations, particularly when those details are especially complicated. If through their instruction students learn to speak, read, and write with competence and confidence; if they gain an understanding and love of the English language; and if they develop a curious and inquiring attitude toward language—then their schooling will serve them well. They will be well prepared for using language in everyday life, and they will be prepared for whatever more advanced linguistic study they undertake in the future.

Index

Brackets [ ], in diagrams, 10–11